# 2

## The Corporate Transformation Of Health Care

# PERSPECTIVES & IMPLICATIONS

### J. Warren Salmon, Editor

**POLICY,
POLITICS,
HEALTH AND
MEDICINE**

Series

**Vicente Navarro, Series Editor**

D0146882

## Baywood Publishing Company, Inc.

### Amityville, N.Y. 11701

ISBN: 0-89503-104-3 (Paper)
ISBN: 0-89503-103-5 (Cloth)


**Library of Congress Cataloging-in Publication Data**

The corporate transformation of health care.
    (Policy, politics, health, and medicine series)
    Includes bibliographical references and index.
    Contents:   1.   Issues & directions – – 2.   Perspectives
& implications.
    1.   Medical corporations– –United States.   2.   Medical
policy– –United States.    I. Salmon, J. Warren (Jack
Warren). II. Series: Policy, politics, health, and
medicine series (Unnumbered). [DNLM: 1. Delivery of
Health Care– –trends. 2. Hospital Administration.
W1 P0211R W 84.1 C822]
RA410.53.C68 1990      362.1     90-16

# Acknowledgments

A number of contributions in this book have their roots in articles which originally appeared in the *International Journal of Health Services*. These have been edited and updated. A few other contributions are original to this volume. Special acknowledgment is given to the *Annals of Internal Medicine* for permission to reprint *The Corporate Compromise: A Marxist View of Health Maintenance Organizations and Prospective Payment*, (109:6, 15 September 1988, 494–501); to the *Milbank Quarterly* for permission to reprint *Reflections on Modern Doctoring*, (66:2, 1988, 76–91), *The Changing Character of the Medical Profession: A Theoritical Overview*, (66;2, 1988, 10–32), *Professional Dominance or Proletarianization?: Neither*, (66:2, 1988, 57–75), and *Canadian Medicine: Dominance or Proletarianization?* (66:2, 1988, 92–116). *The Futures of Physicians: Agency and Autonomy Reconsidered* (Theoretical Medicine 11, 1990, 261–274) is reprinted by permission of Klumar Academic Publishers.

# Preface

## Victor W. Sidel

The population served by the U.S. health care system has changed significantly over the past twenty years. Our people have aged, with a considerably higher percentage of the population over age sixty-five and an even sharper increase in the percentage of the population over age seventy-five. Our disease pattern has changed, with the emergence of AIDS and the resurgence of diseases that had been considered conquered or on the way to elimination, such as tuberculosis and measles. More and more people have been driven into poverty, including an increasingly greater number of children and their mothers; many poor or "near poor" people experienced homelessness, hunger and hopelessness, which in the absence of other services has put additional demands on the health care system.

The structure of our health care system has also changed, with changes occurring in each of its components: (*a*) "medical care"—treatment of the individual patient (or family) to provide comfort and hope, ease symptoms and when possible prolong satisfying and productive life or even "cure" the disease; (*b*) "preventive medicine"—guidance for the individual patient (or family) in promoting health and preventing disease; (*c*) "public health"—advocacy and action for health promotion and disease prevention in the community; and (*d*) "social well-being" (as used in the WHO definition of "health")—includes the most important factors in health promotion and disease prevention, such as amelioration of hunger, homelessness, unemployment, and poverty.

With regard to medical care services, the implementation of Medicare and Medicaid in the mid-1960s improved access to medical care for a large number of our people, but both programs were tragically flawed. Medical care, in part driven by unrestrained Medicare reimbursement, shifted toward greater dependence on complex technology and increasing numbers of specialists, with a corresponding decline in the availability of adequate primary care. Medicare, for people aged sixty-five and over, now covers less than 50 percent of the medical care costs of its beneficiaries and they pay a greater percentage of their income out-of-pocket than before the initiation of the Medicare program.

Medicaid, for the "medically indigent," is administered by the states with federal financial participation and varies widely in its coverage and its reimbursement levels from state to state. Many medical care providers find that Medicaid reimbursements are long delayed and reimbursements fail to cover their expenses. Medicaid, in short, has maintained a two-class system of medical care.

Preventive medicine services have been inadequately provided for either rich or poor, with neglect of immunization and of screening for diseases better discovered early than late. Community-based public health services and other human services, desperately underfunded, have deteriorated and have failed to meet urgent health and social needs. Middle-class people as well as the poor have been affected by the inadequacy of both personal and community services, but of course the poor have suffered most.

Some of the most dramatic changes in the medical care system over the past twenty years, as this book documents, were caused by the entrance of large profit-making corporations. These changes, like the shift toward often unneeded high technology services and the shift away from primary care, were frequently driven by the desire for profit and had little basis in the need of the population for effective, efficient, culturally responsive and compassionate services. Indeed there is evidence that these aspects of medical care deteriorated in many areas.

Among hospitals, the appearance of large for-profit chains—such as the Hospital Corporation of America, Humana, National Medical Enterprises, and American Medical International—shifted the balance from not-for-profit institutions to profit-making ones. For other services, such as local pharmacies, where there was already a predominance of small profit-making enterprises, the shift was toward the large corporate chains. The bottom line was increasingly viewed not only as the level of profit rather than the level of service, but the profit was usually destined for investor-owners who had little interest in and less control over corporate policies. Management was left in the hands of a cadre of managers whose imperative was to demand high salaries for themselves and for other administrators and high-level professionals while creating profit for their investors; the managers were often far removed geographically and socially from the institutions themselves and even further from the communities the institutions served.

Much of the current political discussion of health care reform in the United States—in its narrow concern with cost control and with coverage of costs for medical care for the currently uninsured or underinsured—has ignored the other elements in the health care system and has virtually ignored the dangers that corporate control poses both for medical care and for other aspects of health care. Efforts to improve the public's health must in my view be directed at all four components of health care: (*a*) ensuring equitable access to an effective, efficient, culturally responsive and compassionate *medical care* system constrained within appropriate limits; (*b*) encouraging use of medical care resources for *preventive medicine* by educating practitioners, targeting reimbursement and other methods;

(c) improving training, infrastructure, research and support for *public health* activities; and (d) increasing resources and services to improve *social well-being*. We must resist falling into the trap of viewing these components as directly competing with each other for resources. A nation that spends billions on militarism, on bank bailouts, on tobacco and alcohol, on prolongation of dying, and on medical duplication, overuse, misuse and insurance costs can well afford appropriately to support all four components of health care.

Additional resources will of course be needed and these will have to come from higher levels of sharply progressive taxation. The U.S. collects taxes at local, state and federal levels combined at a level of 30 percent of gross domestic product (GDP). The countries of Western Europe and Canada collect taxes at levels that range from 35 to 50 percent of GDP. In the U.S. the wealthiest 1 percent of the population owns approximately 36 percent of national wealth. There is no reason, except for resistance caused by the false propaganda that the U.S. is "over-taxed," that additional tax revenues could not be made available, particularly for support of public health services and for the strengthening of social well-being.

Corporate transformation has not only poisoned the medical care system; it has also made more difficult the appropriate emphasis on, and appropriate support of, the other elements of health care. This book, like the others in the series on Policy, Politics, Health and Medicine and like other articles in the *International Journal of Health Services*, from which most of these chapters were updated and edited, is an important weapon for use in the construction of a just health care system that will meet our needs. The analyses in this volume make clear the nature of the corporate poison and suggest the antidotes. Read the following chapters, discuss them with colleagues, patients, clients, and members of your community, and above all act to bring about the changes in health care that all of us urgently need!

# TABLE OF CONTENTS

# Introduction

## J. Warren Salmon

In 1964, when I began working in health care, it was not called an industry. U.S. health expenditures were less than $40 billion, a mere 5.9 percent of the gross national product (GNP) (1). The boundaries of this "nonsystem" were not conceived of much beyond doctors' offices and community hospitals (2, 3). The medical profession was believed to be dominant in shaping medical knowledge and its institutions (4, 5), most of which were nonprofit. Of course, there were educational institutions and a collection of manufacturers and suppliers of pharmaceuticals, technological equipment, and medical supplies. The connections between these interests came with the unparalleled advances in medical science after the founding of the National Institutes of Health (6). Medical research was only conducted at select teaching hospitals, which had yet to become part of "medical empires" (7). Medical school affiliations were only clinical, typically with municipal and/or Veterans Administration hospitals.

In the early 1960s there were no federal monies for nurses' training, health professions education, graduate public health fellowships, neighborhood health centers, community mental health centers, or hospital outpatient department construction (8). While Hill-Burton funds helped build hospitals across the country, the Regional Medical Programs and Comprehensive Health Planning Agencies did not exist. Blue Cross, the grand old friend of the hospital industry, signed checks based upon "cost-plus" reimbursement, which covered substantial "free care" offered to the poor, aged, and otherwise uninsured (9, 10). A plethora of private insurance companies had begun to pay even higher "charges," which, from my own observations in hospital finance, made the commercially insured patient much coveted by hospital administrations.

1

The MBA "Chief Executive Officer" and his minions had not yet arrived on the hospital scene. The single, small doctor-owned hospitals from the earlier part of the century had never secured much of a foothold. One, maybe two, administrators ran the nonprofit community hospital, whose structure was simplistically flat. Accounting, billing, and collections were performed manually. Philanthropic donations added equipment, and sometimes a new pavilion. The board of trustees came from the uppercrust of the community, with some members involved in supply businesses to the hospital. A rhetoric of professional altruism was drummed into medical students and student nurses alike. Many professionals, as well as poorly paid, non-unionized, nonprofessionals, self-sacrificed at religiously sponsored institutions in support of their charitable mission.

I do not wish to reminisce about the "good old days," often referred to as the "golden age of medicine." Hospitals paid phenomenally low wages then. Exploitation of physicians in training and of student nurses was commonplace. The hours and responsibilities for interns and residents bordered on a form of torture. Third-year student nurses were responsible for night shifts of 30 patients on medical/surgical wards at the hospital where I worked. Health care had perhaps a more extreme labor market segmentation. The male physician presiding over female nurses was merely one facet of hierarchical oppression, often supplemented by all white professionals over third-world nonprofessionals, stemming from prevailing class, race, and gender power relations in the larger society (11).

A huge segment of the population was measurably less healthy. There were limited public health activities, mostly confined, as now, to the public sector in certain communities. The existence and importance of adjunctive social services to the mainstream of medicine was not established in the minds of most professionals. Because of their class, race, location, and sometimes age, many Americans did not participate equally, or in some instances at all, in the health care system. The emergency room and outpatient clinics served as "community physician" for minority urban dwellers, while white folks had private physicians. The civil rights movement had only recently eased segregation in northern hospital wards. Such blatant inequities in the receipt of services propelled the subsequent Great Society programs.

My initiation as a health care worker came during the raging battle over Medicare. The American Medical Association (AMA) bellowed about impending government interference in the practice of medicine, not recognizing the impending corporate interference. Few analysts predicted a "health care crisis," which President Richard Nixon was to proclaim only five years later (12). With the passage of Medicare and Medicaid, health care expenditures jumped from $42 billion in 1965 to $75 billion in 1970, an increase from 6.1 percent of GNP to 7.6 percent, or a rise in per capita expenses from $182.00 to $313.00 (13). Many of the inequities went unaddressed, however.

It was during this historical period of rapid expansion that a new configuration of health care delivery arose, which has yet to cease. Today a key feature—indicating its transformed character—is the ever-increasing ownership by investor-owned enterprises of both the supply and delivery functions. The *Health Commerce Line* posts financial data on over 300 companies presently offering services and/or products for the health care industry (14). Unlike only 20 years or so ago, health care in the United States is now solidly a corporate endeavor (15).

The mortality and morbidity patterns in the U.S. population still represent phenomenal inequality in the distribution of health. Disease and death rates in the United States are influenced not just by environmental and personal attributes, but also by the health care system itself—the products and services offered, who becomes the "target market," on what terms the products and services are sold, etc. The system's organizational priorities, skewed highly by the profit motive, influence health outcomes over and beyond, and even despite, the individual's characteristics and behaviors (16).

The avalanche of for-profit change introduced an increasing complexity and diversity to the business of health care. A number of examples are illustrative.

By 1987—22 years post-Medicare—the four largest hospital chains—Hospital Corporation of American (HCA), Humana, National Medical Enterprises, and American Medical International—each exceeded the sales of most pharmaceutical manufacturing firms (i.e., in excess of $3 billion then). Priorly for-profit health care was virtually absent, and financial growth of this magnitude had been unknown in health care.

Twelve nursing home chains with total sales of $4.5 billion in 1990 now dominate the market(14); 80 percent of nursing home facilities in the country are proprietary. Beverly Enterprises, by far the largest, grew over the 1980s to a $2.1 billion multistate operation despite a host of well-publicized financial and quality problems. Large patient populations are now at risk due to a single organization's performance.

Similarly, a number of for-profit health maintenance organizations (HMOs) experienced difficulties serving their enrolled populations in the last decade; the bankrupt Maxicare chain is a prime example. Ten publicly owned entities make up a $6 billion market (14), besides other privately held for-profit HMOs and the numerous so-called "not-for-profit" HMOs.

A $42 billion Wal-Mart empire of 1800 stores nationwide replaced thousands of small-town independently owned pharmacies (17). Together, corporate-chain drug distributors have grabbed almost 70 percent of the U.S. prescription market according to the National Association of Chain Drug Stores (18). The most rapid growth in market share came from mail-order pharmacy, which in 1991 had 8.9 percent of market share, up from 3.7 percent in 1987 (19) according to the American Managed Care Pharmacy Association (20).

The forces that facilitated the advance in corporatization included: (*a*) preserving private sector control over the financing and delivery of care for the bulk of the population; (*b*) the abandonment of a national health policy regulated by the federal government; (*c*) the increased purchasing power of corporate employers in health care and their responses through mechanisms, such as self-insurance, to exert that power; (*d*) the shift in government acting as "prudent buyer" for poor and elderly beneficiaries to protect the budget; (*e*) networking providers for greater efficiency, and measures to improve productivity by corporate purchasers and payers; (*f*) the Reagan administration's and many state governments' encouraging "competition" against traditional providers; and (*g*) a variety of means to contain or stabilize cost increases, including shifting costs wherever possible from purchasers and payers to the beneficiary, employee, and patient. Such goals were met to a large extent.

## THE CORPORATIZATION OF THE DELIVERY SYSTEM

The following sections introduce the subject of the corporate transformation of health care. After giving a brief history and describing the dimensions to the for-profit invasion of the health sector, I link the changing business-purchaser directions to the now dominant mode of delivery in managed care, which holds vast implications for practicing professionals. A glance at developments in the larger economy provides some context for these directions.

This discussion both provides background to the subsequent chapters and reiterates and updates many of the most salient points expressed in *The Corporate Transformation of Health Care, Part I: Issues and Directions* (21). In that volume, which I also edited, the for-profit penetration in health care was examined and critiqued. It should be noted that the implications of profit-maximizing go well beyond the presence, size, and growth of investor-owned entities in both the delivery and supply functions in the health sector (22). Combined with competitive policies promulgated by the Reagan and Bush administrations to foster the "health care market," the dynamics of for-profit health care now require unceasing assessment (23, 24). The authors of the chapters in this volume offer compelling perspectives on the many implications.

The term "corporatization of medicine" has been used widely. Different authors have assigned varying meanings (25–29). Therefore, it may be useful to describe the features of this social process, as well as to delineate why it has become a worrisome trend in health care in the United States.

With massive federal subsidies after 1965, health care became an extremely profitable market (30). Despite episodic cost containment efforts by public and private payers over the past two decades, it remains strikingly lucrative.

From that earlier period in the 1960s, a medical industrial complex initially gained a grip over the financing and supply aspects of health care (31–35). Concentration and centralization of capital greatly increased in the commercial insurance end of the business, which began to edge out Blue Cross/Blue Shield plans. Similarly, corporations thrived (through present times) in the design, manufacture, sale, or supply of medical, dental, optical, hardware, or services;

pharmaceutical biotechnology, medical diagnostics, and biochemical research and development; the construction of facilities; real estate investment trusts for health facility holdings; the provision of legal, accounting, and consulting services; and other products to assist providers in caring for patients (36–38). This supply side of health care now includes multinational companies that produce chemicals, cosmetics, and computers. Through the 1960s, these firms collectively gained enormous economic power, despite the fact that the direct delivery of services remained chiefly in the hands of "not-for-profit" and public institutions, and individual and small-group medical practices (39).

In the late 1960s, for-profit firms encroached upon the actual delivery of services more aggressively (40, 41). The ascent of HCA and Humana occurred in local markets in Nashville, Tennessee, and Louisville, Kentucky, respectively. From their origins as small groups of nursing homes or proprietary hospitals, each grew rapidly, branching out regionally only to discover about a dozen "look-a-likes." A *"new* medical-industrial complex" (42–44) was thus being fashioned.

The Nixon administration had encouraged private investment in health care primarily through its HMO strategy (40, 45–47). Subsequently, the rise and growth of regional, and then national, for-profit chains among hospitals, nursing homes, kidney dialysis centers, and home health care firms became an epiphenomenon to the HMO movement (42, 48, 49).

In the 1970s, expenditures grew rapidly in all Organization of Economic Cooperation and Development nations, but what distinguishes those health care systems from ours in that the U.S. government wrought a destabilizing of the health care system. Medicare and Medicaid outflows went beyond all projected estimates; the previously disenfranchised elderly and poor became a financing balloon. Formerly "free care" patients were now sources of handsome provider profit. Medicare paid for new technologies and capital costs. Besides this infusion of direct federal monies, a corollary rise in employer health insurance premiums reflected the inflationary momentum. Government subsidy of health care came indirectly with fringe benefits paid to employees; no tax burden was levied on either employer or worker. A related fiscal complication resulted from the climbing use of tax-free revenue bonds by health care institutions, with termination of the federal Hill-Burton hospital construction funding; in particular, for-profit hospitals relied heavily upon this mechanism for building expansion almost exclusively into (then booming) Southern and Southwestern states.

Concomitant with expansionary policies, the direct federal enlargement of medical schools and their enrollments greatly increased the physician supply. The numbers of specialists soared, with the distribution of medical personnel hardly addressed. The few attempts to induce physicians to practice in medically unserved and underserved areas were not that effective relative to the pull toward the high-paying, high-tech specialties in metropolitan areas. The resultant sub-specialist oversupply propelled expenditures even higher, driven by hospital-based technology.

Other trends in insurance and payment for care included passage of the 1973 HMO law requiring employers to offer dual choice coverage to employees, and in the 1980s facilitation by the states for the preferred provider organization (PPO) mechanism. The self-insurance option under the federal ERISA legislation allowed employers to forego ties with indemnity insurance companies. All signified a death knell to much cross-subsidization within hospitals by the "overcharged wealthy" for care to the indigent.

Most critical in the 1970s, however, was the investor-owned entry into hospital operations and a rise to dominance of for-profit chains in the nursing home, psychiatric hospital, and home care lines of the "business." These for-profit enterprises were initially confined to low-regulation states, locating in middle-class suburbs that could support hospital beds and where private insurance reimbursement was higher. Following Nixon's heralding the benefits of for-profit health care, multi-institutional systems providing vertically integrated care allowed for significant concentration of ownership, even among the traditional "not-for-profit" segment of the hospital industry. The new health care marketplace attracted all kinds, from "fast-buck" operators (purely in for the short run) to investors seeking stable market power. The business press extolled many such stories of favorites of Wall Street; they became the envy of chief executive officers (CEOs) in much less lucrative industries.

Over the past 20 years the corporatization trend yielded a new array of services, particularly in the out-of-hospital area. Diversification has allowed for the growth of psychiatric services, retirement centers, physical rehabilitation, ambulatory and surgical centers, and durable medical equipment (50). Physicians and traditional community hospitals had not responded quickly to "rising consumer demands" for new technologies, nor to the outpatient benefit expansion in insurance after the 1982 TEFRA legislation. Inpatient hospital profits declined precipitously to aid the diversification. As a result, many for-profit chains tied up the market in a range of services, encompassing most notably surgical centers, diagnostic imaging, and durable medical equipment suppliers.

Diversified, multiservice, multiple-site for-profit facilities became established in almost every metropolitan area after the initial Sunbelt success. They were sustained by the well insured middle class who could, and would, pay additional out-of-pocket fees. In numerous locales, so-called "not-for-profits" (and even some public sector providers) mimicked their for-profit counterparts under competitive health policies. Many of the former amalgamated into systems, marketing to paying customers, as well as triaging to the public sector undesirable patients and lower-income populations who did not contribute to their bottom-line (51–53). The convergence became clearer as multihospital systems and hospital alliance behaviors became virtually indistinguishable from the for-profit chains. Relman (24, p. 854) states: "our voluntary not-for-profit hospitals have become much more entrepreneurial and have come to resemble their investor-owned competitors in many ways."

All of these combined to create a double-digit inflationary spiral in health care. Expenditures rose from $69 billion in 1970 (7.2 percent of GNP) to $249 billion in 1980 (9.4 percent of GNP) (54). However, it was during the first administration of Ronald Reagan that the largest spurt occurred. Total expenditures jumped to $423 billion by 1985, even with the implementation of diagnosis-related group (DRG) payments under Medicare, which slowed the rate of hospital increases. Unregulated physician Medicare expenditures greatly increased due to the shift to out-of-hospital services after 1982; home health care outlays more than doubled; and nursing home expenses rose from $20 billion in 1980 to $34 billion in 1985. All indicated greatly enhanced revenues to numerous parties in the new medical-industrial complex (55). For instance, for-profit hospital chains registered a 38 percent revenue rise in 1983 and 28.5 percent rise in 1984 (56).

The competitionists who strategized for the Reagan administration were able to make a convincing case for the efficiencies of the "competitive market," rather than federal regulation. The objective was to preserve and extend a privatized employment-based model of health and social welfare services for the nation. The idea of national health insurance was defeated in the 1970s. The failings of health planning had become rather obvious. The advertised surplus of physicians, the overbedding of hospitals in most metropolitan areas, the arcane reimbursement in paying either piecemeal for service or without economic incentive for efficiency—all were parlayed into an attack upon the public sector. By pointing the finger at problematic public policies and management, the pro-competition forces promised that their new economics would lead to containing costs. In relatively no time at all, the appetites of for-profits and "not-for-profits" alike proved this wrong.

Investors in health care (and their managers) have a clear central purpose: maximum return on their investment. To achieve this, they strive for greater market power. Larger health care firms have taken on highly complex forms that are constantly being rationalized to improve production. In addition, managers are forever trying to influence their external environment, as an individual firm and in concert with others through trade organizations. This includes direct involvement in the formulation and implementation of regulatory policies in states where operations occur and now, more importantly, at the federal level. Such public policy influence by pharmaceutical manufacturers has surely been evident and by a host of others in the "old" medical-industrial complex. A similar path has been followed by for-profit delivery forces. All corporate health firms heavily lobby state legislatures and federal agencies. For-profit health care firms have major dealings with commercial insurance companies, and the health provider accrediting groups too. Health-related corporate political action committees (PACs) provide substantial sums to elected representatives to foster favorable relations. The sphere of influence established by these new economic powers in health care is enlarging, with intensified efforts to forestall progressive health reform.

Taken as a whole, the growth of for-profit health corporations has been remarkable. Many of these firms did not exist 20 years ago, particularly those in the delivery of services. Those that did were a small fraction of their present size. Again, the extremely profitable health care market, subsidized by government and *not* held in proper check by payers for services, attracted large capital seeking lucrative investment outlets, as well as upstart entrepreneurs. While many new ventures recorded business failures or became acquisitions, more than a few firms found growth and profit trajectories worthy of making them case studies in the nation's business schools.

More recently, a merger mania is combining diverse firms for integrated product lines. The American Hospital Association reported a merger mania throughout the 1980s, with 400 U.S. hospitals consolidating into multi-institutional systems (57). In 1988 alone hospital mergers tripled over the previous year. Joint ventures, strategic alliances, and diversification schemes also proliferated. While the bulk of combinations among hospitals during the last decade were among "not-for-profit" facilities, large health capital has further concentrated the entire health care industry.

These dynamics among converging for-profit and "not-for-profit" providers extend from larger corporate mergers in the finance and supply functions (e.g., CIGNA acquiring Equicor), diversification (Baxter opening physician services networks), and strategic alliances (e.g., Merck with Johnson & Johnson for switching prescription drugs to over-the-counter medications). Chronicling such concentration takes up much space in business journals, revealing blurring lines between product and services categories. It is remarkable how changing ownership patterns have escaped more thorough analysis by policy makers and academics alike.

Profit margins in most health corporations have been envied, and often resented, by CEOs in other manufacturing and service industries (Table 1). These latter firms (and their employees through total compensation package reductions) must foot the bill for prolific health spending, while faced with international competition, sluggish consumer spending, and other recessionary woes.

## PURCHASER BENEFIT DIRECTIONS

While no other nation in the world witnessed as absolute or rapid a growth in health expenditures, no other nation has such a for-profit presence in its health sector. Nowhere else do health providers and suppliers enjoy such magnanimous returns on investment (58).

While health sector growth has zoomed since 1970, the U.S. economy has generally been recessionary, or has merely inched along quite unevenly. It must be remembered that most other industries have not even come close to the profit streams enjoyed by health care supply and delivery corporations (59).

The connection between health expenditure growth and corporate greed should be obvious. It brings to light the pressing contradiction within the corporate class between those who benefit from public and private health care spending and those from whom the payment is extracted.

Table 1

Major investor-owned health care corporations, 1991[a,b]

| Company | Sales, in $ billions | Profits, in $ billions | Margin, percentage | Business line |
|---------|------|------|------|------|
| Abbott Laboratories | 6.9 | 1.09 | 15.8 | Medical supplies |
| American Home Products | 7.1 | 1.36 | 19.4 | Medical supplies |
| Amgen | 0.7 | 0.98 | 14.3 | Pharmaceuticals |
| Baxter | 8.9 | 0.59 | 6.6 | Medical supplies |
| Becton Dickson | 2.2 | 0.18 | 8.3 | Medical supplies |
| Berger Brunswig | 4.9 | 0.05 | 1.1 | Wholesale pharmacy |
| Beverly Enterprises | 2.3 | 0.03 | 1.3 | Nursing homes |
| Bristol-Myers Squibb | 11.2 | 2.05 | 18.4 | Pharmaceuticals |
| Carter-Wallace | 0.6 | 0.05 | 6.8 | Pharmaceuticals |
| Community Psychiatric Centers | 0.4 | 0.05 | 11.5 | Psychiatric hospitals |
| Critical Care America | 0.2 | 0.01 | 5.7 | Emergency care |
| Eli Lilly | 5.7 | 1.31 | 23.0 | Pharmaceuticals |
| FHP International | 1.4 | 0.03 | 2.3 | Health maintenance organization |
| Forest Labs | 0.2 | 0.05 | 20.4 | Laboratory testing |
| Foundation Health | 1.0 | 0.04 | 3.5 | Health maintenance organization |
| Health Trust | 2.1 | 0.02 | 1.1 | Hospital |
| Humana | 6.1 | 0.36 | 5.8 | Hospital |
| Johnson & Johnson | 12.4 | 1.46 | 11.7 | Medical supplies |
| Longs Drug Stores | 2.4 | 0.05 | 2.3 | Retail pharmacy |
| Manor Care | 0.8 | 0.04 | 4.3 | Nursing homes |
| Marion Merrell Dow | 2.9 | 0.58 | 20.5 | Pharmaceuticals |
| Medco Containment | 1.6 | 0.84 | 5.5 | Mail order pharmacy |
| Medtronic | 1.1 | 0.15 | 13.7 | Pharmaceuticals |
| Merck | 8.6 | 2.12 | 24.7 | Pharmaceuticals |

Table 1 (Continued)

| Company | Sales, in $ billions | Profits, in $ billions | Margin, percentages | Business line |
|---|---|---|---|---|
| Mylan Laboratories | 0.1 | 0.04 | 31.7 | Laboratory testing |
| National Health Labs. | 0.6 | 0.10 | 17.2 | Laboratory testing |
| National Medical Enterprises | 3.9 | 0.29 | 7.4 | Hospital |
| Pacificare Health Systems | 1.3 | 0.03 | 2.2 | Health maintenance organization |
| Pfizer | 6.9 | 0.72 | 10.4 | Pharmaceuticals |
| Phone-Poulenc Rorer | 3.8 | 0.33 | 8.5 | Pharmaceuticals |
| Rite Aid | 3.7 | 0.12 | 3.2 | Retail pharmacy |
| St. Jude Medical | 0.2 | 0.08 | 40.0 | Hospital |
| Schering-Plough | 3.6 | 0.65 | 17.9 | Pharmaceuticals |
| Surgical Care Affiliates | 0.2 | 0.02 | 12.2 | Surgicenters |
| Syntex | 1.9 | 0.45 | 23.0 | Pharmaceuticals |
| United Health Care | 0.8 | 0.07 | 8.8 | Health maintenance organization |
| Upjohn | 3.4 | 0.54 | 15.7 | Pharmaceuticals |
| US Health Care | 1.7 | 0.15 | 8.8 | Health maintenance organization |
| US Surgical | 0.8 | 0.09 | 10.8 | Medical supplies |
| Walgreen's | 6.9 | 0.19 | 2.9 | Retail pharmacy |
| Warner Lambert | 5.1 | 0.14 | 2.8 | Pharmaceuticals |

[a] **Source::** *Fortune.*
[b]Not including subsidiaries of conglomerates or non-publicly held corporations.

When examining the most recent health policy changes during the Reagan and Bush administrations, one does not find a consistent program or projection. Rather a tension seems to exist between two potentially different directions for managing the health sector. One direction has been to stimulate market forces to encourage private investment in health care. The second is to work in concert with corporate purchasers to restrain the growth.

Employers and governments who purchase health services for employees and public beneficiaries now seek a complex imposition of controls. Besides the division within the corporate class, government represents its own, often confused interests. Lobbying and clout by health care industry interests within partisan politics at the federal level and among state governments often obscure the dynamics. Nevertheless, the public at large—as tax payers and consumers of services—find themselves increasingly questioning the real benefits from continued expansionary policies. Public sentiments are growing more akin to those of business purchasers, who have come to demand "value improvement" from more expensive medical care.

From the late 1970s on, employers began in earnest to find ways to reduce their health outlays (60). By the beginning of the next decade, a number of firms were in full gear to shift the burden of medical care cost to their workers. In the prevailing marketplace mentality, the objective was to have the consumer bear the financial burden, so as to achieve more prudent use of services. The numbers of consultants in benefits redesign multiplied, though their recommendations were rarely evaluated by academicians (61). But studies surely do not affect overall purchaser policies (62).

What prevailed in the anti-labor atmosphere perpetrated by business leaders during Reagan's reign led to a rather carefree attitude in lessening health plan provisions. Included were options for joining price cutting HMOs, increases in employee premium contributions, and implementation of utilization controls and claims reviews. These attempts at managed care were supposed to assess the appropriateness of care, but failed to contain costs (63, 64). The number of employers not requiring employee premium contributions dropped to near zero. Moreover, more than 50 percent of large corporations became self-insured, whereas in the 1970s only 10 percent of firms used self-insurance mechanisms (65). The employee percentage of payments zoomed by the middle of the 1970s, as did the use of major medical deductibles. Partly as a result of this shift, according to the AFL-CIO (American Federation of Labor-Congress of Industrial Organizations), more than half the workers who went on strike in 1990 did so over health benefit issues (66).

In the 1970s Sapolsky and colleagues (67) had reported that major employers were largely unconcerned with the increase in health care costs. These authors maintained that fringe benefits, once given, could not be withdrawn easily. Generous benefits over the previous two decades had grown due to worker demands, requirements of competitors, or fears that unions would organize the workforces. This perspective stood in opposition to exhortations by corporate planning bodies which, since Nixon's "health care crisis," sought remedy from burdening medical costs on their income statements and balance sheets (33). The 1980s prove this academic perspective wrong. Corporations engaged in widespread health benefit cuts in response to climbing costs passed on to them. More fundamentally, corporate leaders withdrew health benefits because the political economic climate allowed them to do so. Yet by 1991, a *Business and Health* poll still found rising concerns over insurance premium costs, workers' compensation, and communicating benefits and costs to employees (68).

Self-insured firms became more active in reducing their responsibility for retiree health benefit costs.

The Financial Accounting Standards Board is requiring firms by 1993, to show the costs of health benefits for present and future retirees on their balance sheets as an accumulating liability (69). The total cost is estimated to reach $227 billion. This ruling has provoked great scrutiny of potential outlays to retirees, and reductions in retiree benefits are forthcoming (70). Witness the Caterpillar Tractor takebacks in 1992 as one example.

Across 20 or so years, corporate interest in containing health care outlays clearly was awakened, not only due to the unprecedented cost rise in fringe benefits, but because of added retiree benefit costs, workers' compensation, occupational safety and health, and other health-related expenses. In a growth economy, such increases were always passed on to consumers; in a general profits squeeze, executives find such health expenses and workers' wage increases significantly denting their profit margins. The comparison bantered around is that business outlays for health care benefits equal the total recorded profits of U.S. corporations.

As mentioned above, there have been few assessments of these widespread employer adoptions of cost containment measures. Some concerns were voiced in the context of the Reagan tax proposals to end or limit the tax-free status of employer-paid premiums or to require employer-sponsored plans to include catastrophic illness coverage so as to ease consumer out-of-pocket expenditures. A provision was enacted to force employers to allow workers losing jobs to continue in the group health insurance plan, provided they pay premiums themselves. A number of firms ended their "peripheral" coverage for certain services such as vision and dental care (71, 72). Health insurance outlays as a percentage of gross pay more than doubled during the first part of the 1980s. In the debate over the desirability of federally induced reforms that might mandate particular fringe benefit policies, certain business groups began raising doubts about the value of medical care services given to employees.

From the last decade into the 1990s, corporate premiums for workers' health benefits have included some measure to make up for low payment to providers from state Medicaid programs, and for uncompensated care to those with little or no coverage at all. This cost-shifting, particularly due to small employers that provide no insurance and major corporations that do not provide insurance to the worker's family, should logically lead to some corrective intervention. Moreover, since unions and employees in general have been agitated about health benefits, purchaser demands for amelioration may become more directed.

A number of multinational firms in certain sectors of the economy have historically provided a high level of health benefits for their employees. Most such firms now prefer self-devised mechanisms to contain their outlays, but again, many of these have been found to be generally ineffective. Corporate recourse to self-insurance, the institution of substantial employee co-payments, and encouraging (or forcing) the use of managed care arrangements have only moderated cost increases at the margin. Bypassing insurance companies to purchase services directly from preselected providers (73) is under experiment, with steering to transplant centers becoming common (74).

Still paradoxical is that major corporations have *not* been more aggressive in engaging both the federal and state governments in overall system reform. Only a minimum number of executives (notably in the auto industry) argue for federally initiated steps. Their health cost increases, even when negotiated downward through self-insurance schemes and managed care arrangements, have been especially problematic during the recession. It is interesting to note that the U.S. Bi-Partisan Commission on Comprehensive Health Reform (the Pepper Commission) made a number of recommendations in the corporate purchaser interest, but in its immediate political environment, most received lukewarm reactions.

However, *Fortune* magazine found 24 percent of CEOs in 1991 favoring a "nationalized health care system, financed by taxpayers" (75). This represents a decidedly new view. Other accounts in the business press reflect frustrations by business executives in their individual firms' attempts to curb climbing costs through utilization management schemes (76). What may gain favor in the executive suite are proposals to end the tax-free nature of health benefits or to switch to fully employee-paid coverage to relieve firms bottom-line.

The National Leadership Commission for Health Care Reform, a blue-chip corporate and labor group (excluding health interests), seeks to require every employer to provide a set level of health benefits or pay a tax (similar to the Democratic Party proposal, "play or pay"). It also is proposing a comprehensive cost containment strategy. In commenting on the National Leadership Commission, Kuttner (77, p. 14) writes in *Business Week:*

> It is not yet clear that more than a handful of the 200 or so Business Roundtable CEOs, who tend to recoil from regulation in their own industries, are truly prepared to put aside ideological qualms and support a plainly socialistic [sic] health system-even one that saves them money. . . .Thus, we have another in a never-ending series of instructive contradictions of capitalism. Soaring health costs are cutting into corporate profits, and market-like approaches aren't restraining costs. Yet the villain of the piece is another set of corporations that misuse their entrepreneurial ingenuity to keep ratcheting up health costs. . . . It remains to be seen whether U.S. business can divine its true collective interest, let alone pursue it.

Given a general perplexity on better strategies, many CEOs seem more committed to cutting back provider revenues (i.e., physicians, hospitals, nursing homes) than directly taking on commercial insurance companies. Employer spending on health benefits (estimated to be near $4000 per worker in 1992) more than doubled from 1985 to 1991 (78). This figure has been projected to rise to over $15,000 by the end of the decade (79). While purchaser representatives have long complained about costs, organizational redundancies, and levels of inappropriate care, some local actions represent a wielding of their considerable influence. In Kansas City, Denver, Minneapolis, Rochester, St. Louis, Cleveland (80), and Memphis (81), corporate purchasers have banded together to address duplicative capital expansion, halt new technological purchases by hospitals, and set up "community information" monitoring. Coordinated by the National Business Coalition Forum on Health, such repositioning by purchasers has been aroused by the view of the economy's inability to support a trajectory of health care expenditures to $1.8 trillion, or 17 percent of GNP, by the year 2000. In 1991, the editors of *Business Week* (82) who often speak for manufacturers' interests, called for a national plan run by large organized health systems and purchasing cooperatives (what the Bush administration called health insurance networks) based on "managed competition." Their proposal speaks to universal coverage "while preserving the best of the market economy" (83, p. 158).

The direction seems to promote more accountability by health providers to purchasers (84). The widespread variations in medical practice (85, 86), rampant inappropriate care (87), and problems with quality (88) have been well noted by employee benefit managers. The major recent drive is assembling outcomes data. As one example, 24 employers and managed care organizations initiated a consortium to rigorously evaluate benefit programs in terms of outcomes of health care (89). Other cooperative employer endeavors include centralized data pooling and analysis related to medical interventions and mechanisms to feed back performance to payers, providers, and patients. The Washington Business Group on Health, and other regional and local business coalitions (such as the Midwest Business Group on Health), have specific monitoring projects, as in the meanwhile they advise member employers and lobby for public policy remedies in their interest (90). But their profile has been somewhat dormant compared to what may emerge in the new Administration's desire to intervene.

Studies contrasting HMOs under the prepayment mechanism versus fee-for-service medicine reveal differences in medical practice, in testing and diagnostic procedures, specialty referrals, hospitalization rates, use of allied health personnel, and more (91, 92). While profit-seeking remains common to both organizational forms, salaried HMO physicians are required by their managers to act to save on expenditures in order to reap their year-end bonuses. Fee-for-service practice does not reward parsimonious clinical decisions (93).

Similarly, the implementation of the Medicare DRGs payments changed hospital behaviors as bottom-line dictates took firmer command. Since DRG payments are higher for certain acute conditions, epidemiologic rates among the aged population seemed to alter as discharge diagnoses began to correspond to what the Health Care Financing Administration reimbursed (94). Similarly, studies of cesarean sections in California showed a 30 percent rate in for-profit hospitals, while the rate at a not-for-profit HMO was 19.4 percent (95). The medical care literature is replete with many examples of inappropriate care influenced by payment practices (96–99).

Such organizational influences have historically been significant; organizational characteristics are increasingly being found to affect the level of clinical decision making (100–102). As power has shifted from professional to managerial hands, greater implications are on the horizon even with prepayment policies in place (103–105).

## IMPLICATIONS OF MANAGED CARE

Managed care entities represent corporate purchaser hopes to control costs, in contrast to profit seeking in the delivery of services. While the growth of HMOs, PPOs, and other forms of managed care has been nowhere near early predictions, the shaping of this segment reveals the increasing corporate character of the industry. It is quickly becoming the dominant mode of delivery in the U.S.

HMOs peaked at 707 in 1987 (106); in 1991 there were 581 plans, the reduction reflecting acquisitions, mergers, or liquidations. A growing majority of HMOs have been in existence over six years, with nearly 30 percent dating back beyond ten years. These include prepaid group practices from the 1930s and 1940s (e.g., Kaiser-Permanente, Health Insurance Plan in New York, Group Health of Puget Sound, etc.) as well as a few remaining upstarts from Ellwood's advocacy of the HMO strategy for Richard Nixon (40).

The newest forms of open-ended options and point-of-service HMOs have seen the largest growth in recent years. The *Marion Merrell Dow Managed Care Digest* (106) reports:

> Employers have signaled that they are more comfortable signing up with an HMO and enrolling their nationwide work forces into HMOs when these hybrid plans are offered. Under an open-ended arrangement or point-of-service plan, individuals have greater freedom to choose providers. They can go to their own doctors or hospitals outside the HMO network at the time medical care is needed. Open-ended HMOs and point-of-service plans are nearly identical in definition and operation.

Historically, HMO enrollment only inched up each year, in 1991 resting at 16 percent of the U.S. population. It never achieved what Hughes calls (107) "exopthalmic growth" (i.e., eye-boggling). Ellwood was not the only person parlaying highly inflated forecasts; the business press touted them all the time. Wall Street lost interest in HMOs in 1986. Right about that time, there were fantastic declines in HMO stocks while the Dow Jones Industrials average was increasing. More than 80 percent of HMOs lost money in 1988–1989. The oversupply of firms led to a consolidation, which is continuing, though profit margins are generally not good for smaller HMOs and a few chains. The point should be made that the rate of recent enrollment increase is growing, with concentration among the 42 corporate chains. These multi-state entities alone control 74 percent of all HMOs. Over 33 million people were enrolled in corporate chain HMOs, representing more than four out of every five HMO members nationwide (106).

Besides Kaiser-Permanente, Blue Cross/Blue Shield Association, and the HMO Group (a network of smaller regional "not-for-profits"), CIGNA, PruCare, and Aetna Life and Casualty all have over a million enrollees nationwide.

Large commercial insurance companies dominate even more in PPOs. Forty-seven percent of the 824 PPOs are insurance company-owned (108). PPOs represent a growing force in health care since insurers, hospitals, medical foundations, and joint physician/hospital ventures initiated them during the 1980s. Groups of employers have also banded together forming PPOs to control costs. The number of PPO plans climbed 16 percent in 1990, with the number of corporate operators of those plans rising 17 percent.

Employers remain eager for the PPO concept (109); an estimated 38 million employees were eligible to use PPOs in 1990, representing a sharp annual increase of 26 percent. This would indicate almost 88 million people (with family members) being eligible for PPO use, though eligibility does not necessarily indicate a choice. Here again, concentration is at work. The largest 40 individual PPO plans cover over 10 million employees, representing 27 percent of the total.

Since their beginning, PPOs have evolved beyond general medical/surgical provider networks to encompass dental, vision, mental health/substance abuse, workers compensation, and pharmacy services. A hybrid form, known as the EPO (or exclusive provider organization), "locks in" enrollees to a preselected group of providers. This is the mechanism used by Allied Signal, which had CIGNA Insurance Company designate physicians and hospitals whose claims experience indicated utilization control and measures of quality.

The largest corporate chains of PPOs operate plans in different markets; these include Blue Cross/Blue Shield Association, U.S.A. Healthnet, Incorporated; Health Care COMPARE, Private Health Care Systems, Ltd.; Metropolitan Life; CCN, Inc.; Transport Life Insurance Company; Travelers Insurance; and Aetna Choice Health Plans. All have over a half million eligible employee enrollees, with Blue Cross/Blue Shield having almost 6 million. Compared to HMOs, PPOs for the most part reported profitable years from 1988 on, while the bulk of HMOs faced financial difficulties.

A more thorough assessment of managed care goes beyond the scope of this Introduction, but it is clear that the principles of cost containment implied in the operation of managed care entities are paving the way for an integration of finance, administration, and delivery of health care into large-scale systems. Over the 1980s, purchasers and payers (i.e., self-insured employers and insurance carriers) embraced fundamental managed care practices: preadmission certification, case management, utilization management, drug utilization review, and the like. Employers obtain uniform data on demographics and utilization from HMOs to aid their benefits negotiations (110). Also insurers and owners of HMOs have diversified their options to employers who are seeking to limit their increasing health outlays (111). Nevertheless, neither has yet delivered the results desired for cost containment (112, 113).

Emerging through managed care schemes are the beginnings of a move by corporate class interest toward new directions for the provision of services. Behind the business rhetoric for "quality, customer service, and value" lie anticipated stringent controls to stem rising expenditures. Yet, managed care may be years away from substantially paying off as expected (114). With health care costs projected to keep soaring at double digit rates, purchasers may be readying for an eventual federal bailout. Antagonisms between purchasers and insurers have, however, escalated. Several large insurers have closed out their health business completely, with many of the largest firms, (e.g., All-State, American General, Equitable, and TransAmerica) retreating from medical coverage by selling off or reducing their markets (115). A handful of giants remain (e.g., Aetna, CIGNA, John Hancock, Prudential, and Metropolitan Life), though none has been able to secure large profit margins by squeezing expenses, reducing overhead, or getting providers in line. The recent exit of the largest firms from the Health Insurance Association of America (HIAA), and its own policy reversal to endorse a "pay or play" scheme, indicates a new set of possibilities.

Over time, the private insurance industry (estimated at $210 billion in 1991) has tested consumer willingness to pay to the degree where the public and policy makers alike may balk. Insurers have invoked stringent underwriting standards for individuals and groups. The popular and business press both report multiple accounts of rejections of individuals and employee groups that are "at risk" for higher costs. Innumerable criticisms of the expulsion of "bad risks" have been levied; this forces employers to bounce from one insurer to another, a practice that contributes to the enormous administrative waste decried by Himmelstein and Woolhandler (116).

Despite extensive public relations by the HIAA, the insurance product remains prohibitively expensive, even for middle-income people. Indemnity policies average over $3,500 per year, even with limited coverage and extravagant co-payments. As patients pay increasing out-of-pocket sums, it is no wonder that the issue of "value" has come forth in public policy, which may force insurers to guarantee acceptance and renewal for all comers, besides community-rating for pricing.

Competition among private insurers has failed miserably in creating an environment in which providers strive for quality improvement and efficiencies. The experience of U.S. commercial health insurance since the 1950s provides convincing evidence in support of a single-payer, federally mandated national health plan (117, 118). The private insurance industry has expended significant effort in avoiding both insuring high-risk individuals and groups and paying out claims on the policies it has provided (119).

## THE CHANGING NATURE OF MEDICAL PRACTICE

The AMA's annual survey of physician income showed that in 1990 U.S. doctors pulled down an average of $164,300, a 4 percent increase over 1989.

Surgeons topped the charts with an average of $236,400 (57). The AMA notes that total physician income rose by only 6.3 percent in the 1980s, inflation-adjusted. While these surveys reveal only *reported* average real income, physicians may not be doing as well as the managers to whom they increasingly report. It is estimated that more than 50 percent of all practicing physicians were involved with managed care arrangements in 1990 (120), with a rapid increase soon expected.

McKinlay and Stoeckle (27) listed areas where the prerogatives of physicians have eroded over time: definition of entrance criteria to the profession; control over the scope and content of the medical school curriculum; control over the terms and content of their work; physician relationships to patients; the development of medical technologies; influence in organizational facilities; and the amount and rate of their remuneration. These authors presented data to suggest that a "process of proletarianization has begun. This means a divestiture of certain professional prerogatives, thereby subordinating the profession to broader requirements of production under advanced capitalism. While critics on the right and left have taken issue with their overall argument (29, 121–123), McKinlay and Stoeckle have been clear in saying that proletarianization is not a present reality, nor an outcome shortly to be achieved throughout the entirety of practicing physicians.

A more thorough assessment of corporatization, deprofessionalization, and proletarianization is awaited as my colleagues and I have called for (124). Any number of empirical questions remain to delineate the relative degree of loss in professional autonomy, decline in public esteem for the profession, and diminution in control over terms and conditions of medical work and over the content of medical work. Pending accumulating evidence and subsequent analysis, documentation of how the individual physician is becoming quickly and vastly different from his or her predecessor will describe the widespread nature of changes in medical practice.

It is not necessary here to detail assumptions in the professional dominance position; subsequent chapters in this volume do so in their critiques of Freidson (125–127). Nevertheless, an enriched debate over the profession's autonomy must take into account performance monitoring of physicians and the resultant standardization in medical practice to achieve goals for more cost-effective outcomes (128). It remains to be seen what organizations emerge as the most influential in defining practice standards. However, since managers control the collected cost, utilization, and clinical data, they will increasingly define the terms and conditions of physician employees' work (129).

## THE LARGER CONTEXT

While the shift to the corporate transformation of health care has been primarily due to internal forces, external pressures are playing a supporting role. These external pressures are linked to happenings in the larger economy. Briefly, let me sketch out a few contextual constraints to future health sector developments.

The spiraling public and private debt in the U.S. restricts possibilities for expansion in health and human services. This is especially so for social welfare programs heavily supported by government and, if right-wing political tendencies prevail, for the "unproductive" poor, elderly, and other economically marginalized segments of the population.

The 1980s' corporate raiding for greater acquisitions, leveraged buyouts, and overpurchasing of commercial property are the legacy of a weakening, recessionary economy. The credit crunch that resulted affected financial markets (130), particularly with the collapse of the so-called junk-bond market along with problems of repaying, or rolling over, the vast accumulated corporate debt.

In the 1990s, corporate and personal bankruptcies are at record levels; defaults on debts are higher than at any time since the 1970s; the credit standings of many nonfinancial companies face a rapid long-term decline; and downgrading of major corporations by the debt-rating agencies, such as Standard and Poor's, has been extensive. Many highly leveraged firms will have their corporate debt maturing in the early 1990s, including the coming due of many junk bonds. Fortunately, for many manufacturing firms, present lower interest rates should help them meet their debt obligations. But the sluggishness of consumer spending, the continued pretax profit slump, and the lack of upturn in the economy of 1991–1992 all coincide to force a true reckoning for their prolific borrowing.

This corporate debt obviously adds to the massive federal budget deficit ($331 billion in fiscal year 1993) and the many fiscal catastrophes pending for states across the nation. The federal debt of $2.6 trillion (as of December 1991) was built upon prolific military spending and other than public investment to stimulate improved long-term growth and lessen the burden on future generations. Aside from the savings and loan industry bailout, infrastructural needs in terms of mass transit, bridges, waste disposal, and environmental clean-up remain critical. The political push for a balanced budget amendment is being engineered to preclude greater social spending. Conservatives also seek to place mandatory spending caps on federal "entitlement programs," including Medicaid, unemployment compensation, and public assistance. Social security and Medicare—the two biggest programs-became the main targets of the Bush administration. Coupled with strident assaults by conservatives on domestic spending is an unwillingness by the public to pay higher taxes; yet people continue to demand more government services and support. Combined, this political and fiscal context may lead to serious restraints upon expansion of the health sector.

In addition, the ability of U.S. corporations to assure higher growth in the economy, expanding (higher paying) job opportunities, and rising incomes has come into doubt. The record length expansion of 1983–1990, which saw a transfer of wealth to the uppermost, provided for sluggish growth in productivity. The legacy of Reagan policies that "fostered" the private sector has obscured and postponed a needed examination of structural defects throughout the entire society. Actually, public spending was *not* cut; government interference was *not* reduced; the economic promises were *not* met (131). The federal deficit tripled under Reagan and continued to balloon under Bush. The concentration of corporate health entities, with huge appetites for profit and little accountability for performance under a new market ethic (132), exacerbates the inherent contradiction between purchasers and providers and has limited policy options for an easy way out.

In the four years of the Bush administration, the U.S. gross domestic product rose only 1.2 percent annually (133). *Fortune* (133, p. 40) magazine summed up the decade as:

> Since 1980 the income of the average American family, adjusted for inflation, has risen 11.4 percent to $33,722. ... Average income has risen mostly because it is being boosted up by the huge gains of those on the top fifth of the pile. The wealthy profited handsomely from the tax cuts of the early Reagan years. Mergers and acquisitions that put lots of ordinary people out of work made investment bankers—and plenty of CEOS—rich. Generous and tax-deductible corporate medical plans have helped doctors.

> Among families in the next rung down the income tower—those making $46,000 to $67,000—average after tax incomes have inched up 0.5 percent a year since 1980. ... In families whose main bread winner gets paid by the hour, two wages have become essential just to keep from falling further behind. ... Overall, weekly wages for private-sector workers who are not supervisors have fallen-in constant dollars—from $411 at the end of the Carter administration to $369 at latest count. ... Those who are at or near the bottom of the heap. . .may be doing slightly better than their incomes alone indicate. Low-or no-income women with children get quite alot of assistance in the form of food stamps, Medicaid, and rent support that doesn't show up in government reports, and a larger share of low-income Americans qualify for those programs these days. ... From 1980 to 1990 median family income, before taxes but adjusted for inflation, increased at a compounded annual rate of just 0.67 percent. That's not much better than the 0.54 percent rate of the 1970s. Nor is a return to the steady pace of the 1950s and 60s, when median family income rose at a 3 percent compound annual rate, anywhere in sight.

The economic torpor may stretch on through the foreseeable future (134). For sure, the demographic projection is not favorable for strong economic growth. In fact, the demography is depressing growth just as growth is most needed to cover the higher costs of health and human services and pensions for the aging. The increase in the poverty ranks (to nearly 36 million in 1991), especially for children (with accumulating health effects from unaddressed needs), also portends a pent-up demand for health services. These pressures are independent of the rising social epidemics, including AIDS, tuberculosis, and other infectious diseases. Moreover, increasing rates of chronic diseases are not being adequately addressed with preventive care or early interventions for at-risk groups. Managed care arrangements supposedly create incentives to do so, but they are not being extended, or are generally ineffective, beyond the healthier middle class.

The build-up of private and public debt poses a serious structural problem in the economy as both work their way out concurrently. The savings rate has fallen as baby boomers spend their nest eggs. The after-tax savings rate has been slipping appreciably through the current recession to less than 5 percent (135); this amounts to less than that of all other industrialized nations. For more than two decades, there has been a severe recession for lower income people in the U.S. In the face of declining disposable income in the 1990s, joblessness is a phenomenon not merely confined to the underclass, teenagers, and the otherwise unskilled. The ranks of discouraged workers include white collar employees, now permanently displaced even from middle managerial positions, and large numbers of formerly skilled and unionized workers. The huge layoffs from Wall Street firms, General Motors, and even IBM contributed to this. As the numbers of dropouts from the labor force grow, there is good reason to be pessimistic about employment possibilities for a huge segment of Americans, even given the service employment prospect. The dismal side of the scenario may deepen as public policy and corporate repositioning both fail to find suitable means to boost labor productivity and stimulate long-term growth.

Decisions by individual corporations, and even government, usually take place without regard to their external social impact. Numerous firms slashed staffs of college-educated personnel in painful restructuring attempts. In response to mounting deficits, state legislatures are streamlining their operations, and even public universities are dramatically downsizing with little concern about results for future labor force demands.

Displaced workers, of course, end up without health insurance coverage, contributing to the growing uninsured and underinsured who overwhelm financially strapped public and some community "not-for-profit" providers (51). All workers, coping with sustained strain on their finances, and ultimately on their living standards, find it difficult to assume growing consumer out-of-pocket expenditures for health care. This amounted to 37.4 percent of total health care spending in 1988 (136). Purchasers reduced their annual percentage from 29.2 to 28.8 percent in 1988, reflecting greater cost-sharing forced upon employees.

The 1990s introduced a growing instability in the world, which affects the U.S. domestic front (137). The Persian Gulf War, the breakup of the Soviet Union, and turmoil across Eastern Europe came with a recession across most nations and a slowdown in world trade. Global economic growth has been at its lowest level in nearly a decade, and there is growing, marked unevenness between selected northern hemisphere nations and the rest of the developing world. Anticipation of greater military conflicts in several regions is coupled with a rising tide of popular, ethnic and religious discontent. As the U.S. has sought to position itself as a world policeman for Bush's "New Economic Order," the price tag is one that our nation probably cannot endure. The domestic economy, uneasiness in the political parties, and mounting unaddressed social needs circumscribe the ability of the U.S. government to play out its past role in world affairs.

In the light of the shifting sands of international developments, the questions remain: will, or can, the U.S. embark on an industrial policy to nurture and promote technological advances in order to ward off European, Japanese, and other Pacific Rim competition? If so, how will this affect spending for health care? Given their debt and fiscal crises, can the federal and state governments do much to promote the growth of technologically advanced sectors of the economy in the face of pressing social and infrastructural demands? This bears greatly upon any health reform promulgated under a Clinton administration.

It remains to be seen how dramatic any changes in economic policy will be and what their impact may be on the health sector. As the new Democratic administration takes over, health reform proposals have yet to be articulated beyond support for "managed competition."

While the above contextual points may be speculative in nature, the future of U.S. health policy contains no easy answers. To the contrary, policy analysts have introduced a repeated parlance of only "hard choices." Ideologically, this may be to ease Americans into a new social and cultural climate for rationing services that may be politically unbearable. Nevertheless, such choices are made much harder by the ongoing consolidating corporate power vested in health care delivery and supply.

Still cloaked under calls for "privatization," or more recently "public-private partnerships," healthcare, like education, prisons, and other sectors formerly considered government responsibilities, will remain secure in the vice of forces of profit.

## THE VOLUME'S CONTRIBUTION

As a subject, the corporate transformation of health care in the United States has not been given sufficient scholarly attention. Critical assessments of the rapidly changing conditions within and without the health sector are long overdue.

The contributors to this volume lay an excellent foundation for future intellectual work on the wresting of control over the nation's health care delivery and its implications. Each of the selections imparts an interpretation to illuminate the dynamics within this unparalleled corporate involvement. Several of the chapters appeared previously in the "Special Section on the Corporatization of Medicine," which I have edited for the *International Journal of Health Services*. These pieces are edited and updated, while other relevant chapters are included in the collection to expand the overall discussion. My hope is that this volume promotes a policy reflection on the fundamental issues of control, social purpose, and direction of health care in the United States. Corporate self-interest, rightly understood, is so necessary at this time of public consideration for a national health program.

*Acknowledgments*  Special thanks to Maggie Garcia for her laborious assistance in the preparation of the manuscripts in this volume. I also appreciate the support and feedback of Agatha Gallo, Joe Feinglass, Will White, and Hind Hatoum on this Introduction.

## REFERENCES

1. Gibson, R. National health expenditures, 1979. *Health Care Financing Rev.* 2: 16, Summer 1980.
2. Wilson, R. The physician's changing hospital role. In *Medical Care*, edited by W. R. Scott and E. H. Volkart, pp. 408–420. Wiley and Sons, New York, 1966.
3. Freidson, E. *The Hospital in Modern Society.* Free Press, New York, 1973.
4. Freidson, E. *Patients' Views of Medical Practice.* Russell Sage Foundation, New York, 1961.
5. Freidson, E. Client control and medical practice. *Am. J. Sociol.* 65: 374–382, 1960.
6. Bowers, J. Z. (ed). *Advances in American Medicine: Essays at the Bicentennial.* Josiah-Macy, Jr. Foundation, New York, 1976.
7. Ehrenreich, J., and Ehrenreich, B. *The American Health Empire: Power, Profits and Politics.* Random House, New York, 1970.
8. Falk, I. S. Medical care in the U.S.A, 1932–1972: Problems, proposals, and programs from the Committee on the Costs of Medical Care to the Committee for National Health Insurance. *Milbank Mem. Fund Q.* 51: 1–40, Winter 1973.
9. Anderson, O. W. *Blue Cross Since 1929: Accountability and the Public Trust.* Ballinger, Cambridge, 1975.
10. Law, S. A. *Blue Cross: What Went Wrong?* Yale University Press, New Haven, 1974.
11. Navarro, V. *Medicine Under Capitalism,* Prodist, New York, 1976.
12. U.S. Dept. of Health Education and Welfare. *Toward a Comprehensive Health Policy for the 1970s: A White Paper.* U.S. Government Printing Office, Washington, D.C., 1971.
13. Wilson, F. A., and Neuhauser, D. *Health Services in the United States,* 2nd ed., pp. 124–125, Ballinger, Cambridge, 1982.
14. Scitec Services, Inc. *Health Commerce Line* 4(4), 1991.
15. Salmon, J. W. Introduction. In *The Corporate Transformation of Health Care, Part II: Issues and Directions,* edited by J. W. Salmon, pp. 5–12. Baywood Publishing Co., Amityville, 1990.
16. McKinlay, J. B. Bringing the System Back in: The Social Production of Equalities in Health. Keynote address at Health and Multi-cultural Societies conference. Public Health Association of Australia, University of Melbourne, Victoria, Australia, September 24–27, 1989.
17. Marsh, B. Merchants mobilize to battle Wal-Mart in a small county. *Wall Street J.* June 5, 1991, p. 1.
18. National Association of Chain Drug Stores. *Annual Report, 1991.* Alexandria, Va, 1992.
19. Miller, D. Mail order pharmacy. *Newsletter* 34(33): 6, Pharmaceutical Manufacturers Association, Washington, D.C., August 17, 1992.
20. American Managed Care Pharmacy Association. *Annual Report, 1991.* Arlington, Va, 1992.
21. Salmon, J. W. (ed.). *The Corporate Transformation of Health Care, Part I: Issues and Directions.* Baywood Publishing Co., Amityville, 1990.
22. Ginzberg, E. For profit medicine: A reassessment. *N. Engl. J. Med.* 319(12): 757–761, 1988.
23. Ginzberg, E. Health care and the market economy-a conflict of interest? *N. Engl. J. Med.* 326(1): 72–74, 1992.
24. Relman, A. S. Shattuck lecture—The health care industry: Where is it taking us? *N. Engl. J. Med.* 323(12): 854–859, 1991.

25. Salmon, J. W. Profit and health care: Trends in corporatization and proprietarization. *Int. J. Health Serv.* 15(3): 395–418, 1985.

26. McKinlay, J. B., and Arches, J. Towards the proletarianization of physicians. *Int. J. Health Serv.* 15(2): 161–195, 1985.

27. McKinlay, J. B., and Stoeckle, J. D. Corporatization and the social transformation of doctoring. In *The Corporate Transformation of Health Care, Part I: Issues and Directions*, edited by J. W. Salmon. Baywood Publishing Co., Amityville, 1990.

28. White, W. D. The "corporatization" of American hospitals: A 19th century industrial analogy? In *The Corporate Transformation of Health Care, Part II: Perspectives and Implications*, edited by J. W. Salmon. Baywood Publishing Co., Amityville, 1993.

29. Roemer, M. Proletarianization of physicians or organization of health services? *Int. J. Health Serv.* 16(3): 469–471, 1986.

30. McKinlay, J. B. Introduction. In *Issues in the Political Economy of Health Care*, edited by J. B. McKinlay, pp. 1–19. Tavistock, New York, 1984.

31. Salmon, J. W. Organizing medical care for profit. In *Issues in the Political Economy of Health Care*, edited by J. B. McKinlay, pp. 143–186. Tavistock, New York, 1984.

32. McKinlay, J. B. On the medical-industrial complex. *Monthly Rev.* 30(75), 1978.

33. Salmon, J. W. Monopoly capital and the reorganization of health care. *Rev. Radical Polit. Econ.* 9(12): 125–133, 1977.

34. Himmelstein, D. U., and Woolhandler, S. Medicine as industry: The health-care sector in the United States. *Monthly Rev.* 35(11): 13–25, 1984.

35. Meyers, H. The medical-industry complex. *Fortune* 81(1): 90–126, 1970.

36. Turshen, M. An analysis of the medical supply industries. *Int. J. Health Serv.* 6(2): 271–294, 1976.

37. Murray, M. J. The pharmaceutical industry: A study in corporate power. *Int. J. Health Serv.* 4(2): 625–640, 1974.

38. McCraine, N., and Murray, M. J. The pharmaceutical industry: A further study in corporate power. *Int. J. Health Serv.* 8(4): 573–588, 1978.

39. Starr, P. *The Social Transformation of American Medicine*. Basic Books, New York, 1982.

40. Salmon, J. W. The health maintenance organization strategy: A corporate takeover of health services delivery. *Int. J. Health Serv.* 5(4): 609–624, 1975.

41. Kennedy, L. The proprietarization of voluntary hospitals. *Bull. N.Y. Acad. Med.* 61: 81–89, 1985.

42. Relman, A. S. The new medical-industrial complex. *N. Engl. J. Med.* 303(17): 963–970, 1990.

43. Wohl, S. *The Medical Industrial Complex*. Harmony Books, New York, 1984.

44. Ermann, D., and Gabel, J. Multi-hospital systems: Issues and empirical findings. *Health Aff.* 3(1): 51–64, Spring 1984.

45. Nixon, R. Building a National Health Strategy. Special Message to Congress, Washington, D.C., February 18, 1971.

46. Ellwood, P. Health maintenance strategy. *Med. Care*, May-June 1971, p. 291.

47. Ellwood, P. Health maintenance organizations: Concept and strategy. *JAHA* 45(6): 53–55, 1971.

48. Light, D. W. Corporate medicine for profit. *Sci. Am.* 255: 38–54, 1986.

49. Institute of Medicine. *For-Profit Enterprise in Health Care*. National Academy Press, Washington, D.C., 1986.

50. Multi-unit providers survey, volume II. *Modern Healthcare*, June 2, 1989.

51. Whiteis, D., and Salmon, J. W. The proprietarization of health care and the underdevelopment of the public sector. *Int. J. Health Serv.* 17(1): 47–64, 1987.

52. Schiff, R. L., et al. Transfers to a public hospital: A prospective study of 467 patients. *N. Engl. J. Med.* 314(9): 552–559, 1986.
53. Renn, S. C., et al. The effects of ownership and systems affiliation on the economic performance of hospitals. *Inquiry* 22: 219–236, Fall 1985.
54. National Health Expenditure Trends, 1975-1989. *Health Care Financing Rev.,* Winter 1990.
55. Multi-unit providers survey, volume I. *Modern Healthcare,* May 2, 1989.
56. Dallek, G. Hospital care for profit. *Society,* July/August 1986.
57. *Medicine and Health* 46(26): 1–2, 1992.
58. Roemer, M.I. *National Health Systems of the World, Volume I: The Countries.* Oxford University Press, New York, 1991.
59. Autry, R., and Colodny, M. M. Hanging tough in a rough year. Special report on the Fortune 500. *Fortune* 121(9): 338–339, 1990.
60. Smith, L. A cure for what ails medical care. *Fortune,* July 1, 1992, pp. 44–56.
61. Morrisey, M. A., Gibson, G., and Asby, C. S. Hospitals and health maintenance organizations: An analysis of the Minneapolis-St. Paul Experience. *Health Care Financing Rev.* 4(3): 59–69, 1983.
62. Jensen, G. Feldman, R. and Dowd, B. Corporate benefit policies and health insurance costs. *J. Health Econ.* 3(3): 275–286, 1984.
63. Feldstein, P. J., Wickizer, T. M. and Wheeler, J. R. C. Private cost containment: The effect of utilization review programs on health care use and expenditures. *N. Engl. J. Med.* 318: 1310–1314, 1988.
64. Bacon, K. H. Firms haven't cut health costs by using prior-review programs, report finds. *Wall Street J.,* October 19, 1989, p. B4.
65. Hewitt Associates. *Company Practices in Health Care Cost Management,* Lincolnshire, Ill., 1984.
66. Department of Employee Benefits. *The Permanent Replacement of Workers Striking over Health Care Benefits in 1990.* American Federation of Labor–Congress of Industrial Organizations, June 1991.
67. Sapolsky. H., et al. Corporate attitudes toward health care costs. *Milbank Mem. Fund Q./Health and Society* 59, 1981.
68. The 1991 national executive poll on health care costs and benefits. *Business and Health,* September 1991, p. 61–71.
69. Cohen, L. Retiree health costs to hit books in 1993. *Chicago Tribune,* December 20, 1990, p. 3–1.
70. Schuett, D. FASB retiree health accounting. Hewitt Associates, Lincolnshire, Ill., January 30, 1992.
71. Phelps, C. E. *Health Care Costs: The Consequences of Increased Costing Sharing.* Rand Corporation, Santa Monica, 1982.
72. Wilensky, G., Farley, P. and Taylor, A. Variations in health insurance coverage: Benefits vs. premiums. *Milbank Mem. Fund Q./Health and Society* 62(1): 53–81, 1984.
73. Winslow, R. Firms perform own bypass operations purchasing healthcare from the source. *Wall Street J.,* August 19, 1991, p. B1.
74. Colburn, D. Steering patients to selected transplant centers. *Washington Post,* July 2, 1991, p. B1.
75. Sheeline, W. E. Taking on public enemy no. 1. *Fortune,* July 1, 1991, pp. 58–59.
76. Dentzer, S. Excessive claims. *Best of Business Q.,* Winter 1990–91, pp. 68–73.
77. Kuttner, R. Health care: Why corporate America is paralyzed. *Business Week,* April 8, 1991, p. 14.
78. *Medicine and Health* 46(5): 3, 1992.

79. Hendroff, R. Yes, companies can cut health costs. *Fortune,* July 1, 1991, pp. 52–56.
80. Meyer, H. Cleveland starts hospital quality project. *Am. Med. News,* September 14, 1990, pp. 6–7.
81. Winslow, R. How local businesses got together to cut Memphis health costs. *Wall Street J.,* February 4, 1992, p. 1.
82. Garland, S. B. A prescription for reform. *Business Week,* October 7, 1991, pp. 58–66.
83. We're for a universal care system. *Business Week,* October 7, 1991, p. 158.
84. Donkin, R. Medicine's search for "what works": What it means to employers. *Business and Health,* May 1989, pp. 18–25.
85. Wennberg, J. E. The paradox of appropriate care. *N. Engl. J. Med.* 314(5): 310–311, 1986.
86. Eddy, D.M. Variations in physicians practice: The role of uncertainty. *Health Aff.* 3(2): 74–89, 1984.
87. Brook, R. H., and Lohr, K. N. Will we need to ration effective health care? *Issues Sci. Technol.* 3: 68–77, 1986.
88. Berwicks, D. Continuous improvement as an ideal in health care. *N. Engl. J. Med.* 320(1): 53–56, 1989.
89. Consortium initiates outcomes management project. *Health Commerce Line* 4(4): 21, 1991.
90. Stein, J. New goals for business coalitions. *Business and Health,* June 1985, pp. 42–45.
91. Luft, H. S. *Health Maintenance Organizations: Dimensions of Performance.* John Wiley, New York, 1981.
92. Marning, W. G., et al. A controlled trial of the effect of a prepaid group practice on use of services. *N. Engl. J. Med.* 310(23): 1505–1510, 1984.
93. Luft, H. S. How do health maintenance organizations achieve their "savings"? Rhetoric and evidence. *N. Engl. J. Med.* 298(24): 1336–1343, 1978.
94. Brown, E. R. DRGs and the rationing of hospital care. In *Hospital Ethics: Guide for Ethical Thinking and Decision Making,* edited by V. G. Anderson and G. R. Anderson, Aspen Publications, Germantown, Md, pp. 69–90.
95. Schlesinger, M., Blumenthal, D., and Schlesinger, E. The economic performance of investor-owned and non-profit health maintenance organizations. *Med. Care* 24: 615–627, 1986.
96. Pattison, R., and Katz, H. Investor-owned and not-for-profit hospitals: A comparison based on California data. *N. Engl. J. Med.* 309: 347–353, 1983.
97. Watt, J. M., et al. The comparative economic performance of investor-owned chain and not-for-profit hospitals. *N. Engl. J. Med.* 314(2): 89–96, 1986.
98. Robinson, J. C., and Luft, H. S. Competition and the cost of hospital care, 1972 to 1982. *JAMA* 257: 3241–3245, 1987.
99. Chassin, M. R. Does inappropriate use explain geographic variations in the use of health care services? *JAMA* 258: 2533–2537, 1987.
100. Eisenberg, J. M. How will changes in physician payment by Medicare influence laboratory testing? *JAMA* 258: 803–808, 1987.
101. Greenspan, A. M. Incidence of unwarranted implantation of permanent cardiac pacemakers in a large medical population. *N. Engl. J. Med.* 318: 159–163, 1988.
102. Matchar, D. B., and Pauker, S. G. Endarterectomy and carotid artery disease: A decision analysis. *JAMA* 258: 793–798, 1987.
103. Oppenheimer, M. The proletarianization of the professional. *Sociol. Rev. Monograph* 20: 213–217, 1973.
104. Haug, M. The erosion of professional authority: A cross-cultural inquiry in the case of the physician. *Milbank Mem. Fund Q.* 54: 83–106, 1976.

105. Larson, M. S. Proletarianization and educated labor. *Theory and Soc.* 9: 131–175, 1980.
106. Marion Merrell Dow, Inc. *Managed Care Digest HMO Edition, 1992.* Kansas City, 1992.
107. Hughes, E. F. X. Managed Health Care. Business Week Midwest Managed Care Congress, Chicago, September 5, 1991.
108. Marion Merrell Dow, Inc. *Managed Care Digest PPO Edition, 1991.* Kansas City, 1991.
109. Kralewski, J. E., et al. Employer perspectives on the preferred provider organization concept. *Hospital and Health Services Administration,* 1984, pp. 123–139.
110. Gold, M., Tucker, A., and Palsbo, S. The comparative database for managed care systems: An initiative to develop uniformity and consensus on data for a maturing industry in an uncertain environment. *J. Ambulatory Care Management* 12: 38–47, 1989.
111. Gold, M., and Hodges, D. Benefits, premiums, and market structure in 1989. *HMO Industry Profile,* Group Health Association of America, Washington, D.C., 1990.
112. Managed care not delivering big savings, study finds. *Am. Med. News,* February 3, 1992, p. 5.
113. A. Foster Higgins. Managed Care Plans, Report 1. *Health Care Benefits Survey, 1989.* Princeton, N.J., 1989.
114. Gold, M. Health maintenance organizations: Structure, performance and current issues for employees health benefits design. *J. Occup. Med.* 33(3): 288–296, March 1991.
115. Smart, T., et al. Needed: A prescription for ailing insurers. *Business Week,* August 24, 1992, p. 67.
116. Himmelstein, D. U., and Woolhandler, S. Cost without benefit: Administrative waste in U.S. health care. *N. Engl. J. Med.* 314: 441–445, 1986.
117. Himmelstein, D. U., and Woolhandler, S. Socialized medicine: A solution to the cost crisis in health care in the United States. *Int. J. Health Serv.* 16: 339–354, 1986.
118. Himmelstein, D. U., Woolhandler, S., and the Writing Committee of the Working Group on Program Design. A national health program for the United States: A physicians' proposal. *N. Engl. J. Med.* 320: 1102–1108, 1989.
119. Light, D. Excluding more, covering less. *Health PAC Bull.* 22(1): 7–13, Spring 1992.
120. Norman, J. The flowering of managed care. *Med. Econ.* 67: 89–105, 1990.
121. McKinlay, J. B., and Arches, J. Historical changes in doctoring: A reply to Milton Roemer. *Int. J. Health Serv.* 16(3): 473–477, 1986.
122. Chernomas, R. An economic basis for the proletarianization of physicians. *Int. J. Health Serv.* 16: 669–674, 1986.
123. Mechanic, D. Sources of counter vailing power in medicine. *J. Health Polit. Policy Law* 16(3): 485–498, 1991.
124. Salmon, J. W., White, W. D., and Feinglass, J. The futures of physicians: Agency and autonomy reconsidered. In *The Corporate Transformation of Health Care, Part II: Perspectives and Implications,* edited by J. W. Salmon. Baywood Publishing Co., Amityville, 1993.
125. Light, D., and Levine, S. The changing character of the medical profession: A theoretical overview. In *The Corporate Transformation of Health Care, Part II: Perspectives and Implications,* edited by J. W. Salmon. Baywood Publishing Co., Amityville, 1993.
126. Coburn, D. Canadian medicine: Dominance or proletarianization? In *The Corporate Transformation of Health Care, Part II: Perspectives and Implications,* edited by J. W. Salmon. Baywood Publishing Co., Amityville, 1993.

127. Navarro, V. Professional dominance or proletarianization. Neither! In *The Corporate Transformation of Health Care, Part II: Perspectives and Implications,* edited by J. W. Salmon. Baywood Publishing Co., Amityville, 1993.

128. White, W. D., Salmon, J. W. and Feinglass, J. The changing doctor/patient relationships and performance monitoring: An agency perspective. In *The Corporate Transformation of Health Care, Part II: Perspectives and Implications,* edited by J. W. Salmon. Baywood Publishing Co., Amityville, 1993.

129. Feinglass, J. and Salmon, J. W. The use of medical management information systems to increase the clinical productivity of physicians. In *The Corporate Transformation of Health Care, Part II: Perspectives and Implications,* edited by J. W. Salmon, Baywood Publishing Co., Amityville, 1993.

130. Hector, G. How junk regained its shine. *Fortune,* July 15, 1991, pp. 98–100.

131. Rothchild, E. The real Reagan revolution. *N. Y. Rev. Books,* June 30, 1988, pp. 3–5.

132. Relman, A. S. What market values are doing to medicine. *Atlantic Monthly* 269(3): 99–106, March 1992.

133. Smith, L. Are you better off? *Fortune* 124(4): 38–48, 1992.

134. Farrell, C., et al. Industrial policy. *Business Week,* April 6, 1992, pp. 70–76.

135. Malabre, A. L. U.S. living standards are slipping and were even before recession. *Wall Street J.,* June 17, 1991, p. 1.

136. Stout, H. Health costs. *Wall Street J.,* April 12, 1991, pp. B1.

137. Thurow, L. *Head-to-head: The Coming Economic Battle Among Japan, Europe and America.* Morrow, New York, 1992.

# PART 1

# Background and Current Issues

In the past, medical care services were not amenable to mass production techniques; physicians and voluntary hospitals both resisted newcomers, including prepaid group practices, industrial medicine, and doctor-owned proprietary hospitals. From the turn of the century, the workshop of the physician increasingly became the non-profit community hospital. Its internal bifurcation of control between physicians and administrators seems to account for part of the historical lag in corporatization.

Today the character of health care has surely changed. Hospitals are no longer the only dominant player, and they themselves are widely differentiated by size, ownership, chain membership, teaching affiliation, and technological capacity. Moreover, conditions in the larger economy and the social function of the health sector are much different than prior to Medicare and Medicaid.

While complex forces lie behind the present corporatization trend in medicine, its momentum can be attributed to market reforms promoted by the Nixon through Reagan-Bush administrations. Market-oriented policies were in response to changes within and without the health sector. Such policies attracted a whole host of new business entities to health care for lucrative returns. This propelled the corporate transformation of the sector (1).

The adoption of the corporate ideology, as well as implementation of an array of managerial techniques to increase profitability in the health care enterprise, has enormously increased managerial power in ways never accomplished before. Spurred on by federal and corporate purchaser actions, organizational structures, the nature of the "product" (i.e., the services rendered), and the production process itself have been turned upside down by the new "medical marketplace." Such influences on decision making in health care institutions have not only altered managers' roles, but now profoundly affect care-giver behaviors as well.

Today, the consolidation among national and multi-national forms of horizontally and vertically integrated health firms has advanced beyond the comprehension of most professionals, and remains unseen by the American public. These new economic powers in the health care industry emerged within two short decades, with their centralized management hierarchies reaching into all areas of regional to nationwide firms. Trends for mass marketing of name-brand services through direct provider contracting with Medicare or large employer groups are on the rise. Large economies-of-scale were previously not that significant in health care, but now administrative coordination through organizational systems is helping to reap lucrative returns. This is made possible by sophisticated marketing. Economies-of-scale are even more evident with information systems monitoring that allows for extraction of cost savings based upon professional decisions. The latter can be implemented in the name of total quality management, or mere administrative norming of standardized clinical interventions.

In the first chapter of Part 1, White delineates attempts from the 1920s onward to introduce techniques from the manufacturing sector to advance hospital performance. He illustrates how the major processes toward rationalization of the hospital in the early part of this century affected the production of hospital services. But through that time and up until recently, health care still did not fully become a "business" insofar as physicians retained their professional control. White contrasts the slow historical shaping of health care institutions with what had *not* previously occurred.

The new emphasis on profit maximization directly affects consumers, whether they are considered patients or, in the more common parlance of corporate medicine, customers of product lines. Some results clearly have been beneficial to patients—when service goals are *not* compromised with efficiencies, and real quality of care improves and greater patient satisfaction results. Nevertheless, White raises serious concerns about the implications for physicians, nurses, pharmacists, and other professionals, now increasingly having to practice in these command bureaucratic structures.

In the chapter, "Walk-in Chains: The Proprietarization of Ambulatory Care," Berliner and Burlage examine this segment of the health care industry as an investment outlet for venture capital. Ambulatory surgery centers became a means for physician groups to capture hospital funds. Conflicts of interest over physician self-referrals for diagnostic and treatment interventions have distorted care patterns, besides driving up costs for inappropriate care and raising ethical concerns as well. Following implementation of Medicare's prospective payment based on Diagnosis-Related Groups, significant growth in unregulated ambulatory services ballooned physician office-based revenues. Early on, many upstart local firms secured venture capital, which allowed for market penetration into expanded areas of service, eventually leading to the launching of stock offerings. Corporate entities in the ambulatory care business attracted the avid interest of Wall Street brokers, though it has waxed and waned over the last eight years with a 1990s comeback in certain stocks of the largest firms.

The giant corporate health firms have also staked out the ambulatory arena for diversification beyond the hospital, including services provided in the home setting. In a little more than a decade, their efforts to establish new markets for more predictable reimbursement have not been as successful in terms of profit streams as durable medical equipment firms were in the mid 1980s. It should be noted that the ambulatory arena is generally exempt from federal and state regulation.

After reviewing these developments, Berliner and Burlage update their analysis from a previous publication (2). More recently, there has been a move beyond pure physician ownership to larger corporate health entities promoting multiple ambulatory activities in more integrated forms. HMO, PPO, and other managed care entities will likely spur these forward.

Federal health policy under the Reagan administration and a flurry of fast-buck operator diversification led to corporate involvements in health promotion. Milio examines how forces of the marketplace took on the rhetoric of prevention and health promotion to design new products for paying customers anxious about their health. While government-operated public health departments stagnated across the 1970s and 1980s, new upstart firms began to market wellness and health education programming to employers for their workers, and to anyone else willing to pay for many unproven means and methods to enhance health. Thus, health promotion literally became "commodified, packaged, brand-labeled, and sold or franchised through advertising techniques" by hospital corporations, insurance firms, and employers alike. Milio dissects such developments, addressing downsides and consequences. She concludes her critique of the commercial character of health promotion with a plea to return to policies and programs to safeguard social and environmental conditions, which she sees more relevant to health in the whole population.

In the final chapter of Part 1, Himmelstein and Woolhandler provide a critical perspective on the U.S. health care system, within which they place private capital accumulation as primary. In their view, capitalist development in the health sector existed earlier, but over the last 30 years it has seen enormous growth, now more evident with corporate entities dominant in the hospital, HMO, and nursing home segments of the industry. Their historical perspective is essential to understanding the growing conflicts between profit-seeking by health care firms, and payers funding health benefits for employees and public beneficiaries. Himmelstein and Woolhandler conclude with an assessment of this division within the corporate class by examining HMOs and prospective payment as cost containment strategies that have propelled an enormous expansion of the administrative apparatus over health care. As in other writings (3–5), they maintain that the vast sum spent on health care is sufficient to provide quality service to all Americans. However, the imperatives of corporate profitability, now so imbedded in American health care, foster massive irrationality and administrative waste.

## REFERENCES

1. Salmon, J. W. (ed.). *The Corporate Transformation of Health Care, Part I: Issues and Directions*. Baywood Publishing Co., Amityville, 1990.
2. Berliner, H. S., and Burlage, R. K. The walk-in chains: The proprietarization of ambulatory care. *Int. J. Health Serv.* 17: 585–594, 1987.
3. Himmelstein, D. U. and Woolhandler, S. Cost without benefit: Administrative waste in US health care. *N. Engl. J. Med.* 314: 441–445, 1986.
4. Himmelstein, D. U., and Woolhandler, S. Socialized medicine: A solution to the cost crisis in health care in the United States. *Int. J. Health Serv.* 16: 339–354, 1986.
5. Himmelstein, D. U., Woolhandler, S., and Wolfe, S. M. The vanishing health care safety net: New data on uninsured Americans. *Int. J. Health Serv.* 22: 381–396, 1992.

# CHAPTER 1

# The "Corporatization" of U.S. Hospitals: What Can We Learn from the Nineteenth Century Industrial Experience?

## William D. White

In recent discussions of the "corporatization" of the health care industry, significant parallels have been asserted between current organizational trends in the industry and trends in U.S. manufacturing during the late 19th and early 20th centuries (1). Economic concentration is on the rise. Just as local cottage industries rapidly became dominated by large national firms ("big business") in products ranging from shoes to iron and steel, so locally controlled and financed hospitals are being replaced by huge horizontally integrated, multihospital regional, national and multinational systems. And just as the level of vertical integration increased in the late 19th century in industries ranging from oil refining to cigarette manufacturing as they became involved in securing their own raw materials and marketing their products, similar patterns are emerging in the hospital industry. In the course of this process, centralized management and mass marketing are developing as important organizational strategies for health care providers much as they did at the turn of the century for manufacturing firms. Moreover, while the majority of hospitals remain nonprofit institutions, there has been growing emphasis on profitability and "the bottom line" in decision making. Finally, there has been a shift away from self-employment towards employee status for physicians.

Citing parallels between the changing role of physicians and the "proletarianization" of craft workers in the 19th century, McKinlay and Stoeckle (2, p. 203) argue "that the industrial revolution has fully caught up with medicine." In this context, it is tempting to view health care as a johnny-come-lately to modern corporate organization and to see much of the current turmoil in the industry as the product, for better or worse, of a much delayed rationalization of a backward traditional sector. But the forces behind the current trend toward "corporatization" are clearly more complex. The notion that health care is a "business" and that decision making in the industry should conform to market oriented criteria is not new; nor are attempts to increase efficiency through the application of corporate managerial techniques. Health care underwent a major process of rationalization in the early part of the century, and the modern structure of the industry basically has its origins in this period.

This raises a number of obvious questions. Why weren't earlier efforts in the 1920s and 1930s to treat health care as a "business" successful in fully rationalizing the industry along corporate lines? Was the issue one of internal resistance, particularly from the medical profession? Or was it rather primarily difficulties in adopting managerial techniques and organizational structures geared to mass production to medical services? Beyond this, what is it about current conditions in the industry that is leading to a further process of rationalization at this point in time? Finally, is there anything to be learned about the future of health care from looking at past experiences in industry?

A useful starting point for examining these questions is to define what is meant by "corporatization" not only in the context of health care, but also of manufacturing. The term has not been specifically used in discussions of the rise of large for-profit firms in the manufacturing sector. But what in effect constitutes the "corporatization" of U.S. manufacturing at the turn of the century has been characterized in standard textbook discussions by three major features (3, 4). The first is a centralization and rationalization of production through the application of standardized mass production techniques epitomized by Henry Ford's assembly line for Model Ts. The second is the creation of managerial hierarchies designed to coordinate the activities not only of large individual plants, but also of horizontally and vertically integrated multiunit enterprises engaged in the distribution as well as the production of final goods, and the acquisition of raw materials (5). The third is a reorganization and standardization of work and training involving both the "deskilling" of traditional craft jobs and the creation of a new "professional/managerial" elite trained in standardized professional programs outside the workplace (6, 7).

Recent discussions of the "corporatization" of health care have focused on the penetration of large for-profit firms into an industry previously dominated by autonomous practitioners and nonprofit institutions (1, 8, 9). More generally, concerns have been expressed about the growing adoption of corporate managerial techniques and increasing emphasis on profitability and the "bottom line" by the nonprofit sector of the industry, accompanied by growing internal controls over physicians and the rapid formation of nonprofit multihospital systems (1, 2).

The latter, more general view risks confusing "corporatization" with broad efforts to rationalize the health care sector linked only casually with issues of for-profit orientation. On the other hand, focusing solely on the penetration of large for-profit firms risks overlooking two important aspects of "rationalization" efforts in the nonprofit sector. The first is that utilizing managerial techniques imported from the corporate sector may have subtle (and not so subtle) effects on decision making. Corporate techniques are designed for purposes of profit maximization. In nonprofit organizations, the use of these techniques may bias decision making toward financial goals at the expense of service objectives. A second and more important aspect of "corporatization" regarding nonprofit firms is that market pressures may force them to adopt profit-oriented strategies as a matter of financial survival in the wake of the combined effects not only of the entry of for-profit firms, but also of so-called "procompetitive" regulatory strategies. This chapter draws on the economic literature on industrial organization to compare and contrast trends in the modern hospital industry and late 19th century manufacturing with respect to plant and market size and vertical and horizontal integration.

## THE MANUFACTURING EXPERIENCE

The "corporatization" of U.S. manufacturing began on a large scale following the Civil War. It was largely complete by World War I. At an industry level, it was marked by sharp increases in market and plant size, growing horizontal and vertical integration, and increasing economic concentration. However, experiences varied considerably between industries, especially with respect to the level of horizontal and vertical integration and economic concentration. Economic models suggest not only why firms in some industries succeeded in integrating, but also why efforts at consolidation in others failed.

### The Rise of "Big Business"

Until the 1870s, U.S. manufacturing was characterized largely by small firms serving local markets. By the 1890s, "big business" had become a central feature of American life. In one industry after another huge factories employing hundreds, or even thousands, of workers and unprecedented amounts of capital replaced craftsmen working alone or in small shops. Until the 1870s, most goods had been produced for local or regional markets, usually on a customized basis. Now mass production became the norm as firms sought to realize economies of scale from large production runs of standardized goods churned out en masse to be sold nationwide. In the process, production became concentrated in the hands of large national firms in industries ranging from flour to shoes and steel to beef. In 1905, two thirds of all manufacturing capital was controlled by 328 firms. And at least one of these top 300 plus firms was represented in four fifths of all manufacturing industries (3).

The emergence of new corporate giants was accompanied by the growth of hierarchical systems of control designed to deal with the complex coordination problems created by large-scale mass production. Managerial functions became increasingly specialized. Activities such as purchasing and personnel were separated from day to day production activities. At the same time, new methods of centralized control were established. Cost accounting techniques, originally developed by the railways, became a standard method not only of monitoring expenses, but also of tracking the flow of goods through the production process and establishing centralized control over production activities on the shop floor. Meanwhile, capital budgeting and the systematic depreciation of plant and equipment were introduced as a means of routinizing and centralizing long term planning and coordinating investment decisions.

The rise of large corporate bureaucracies was accompanied by a fundamental reorganization of work under the banner of "scientific management." As production processes became increasingly standardized, many traditional craft jobs were "deskilled" and apprenticeship systems were replaced by centrally controlled on-the-job training. The division of labor increased, and work was broken down into discrete, routinized tasks, leaving little room for discretionary judgment by workers, who were expected to follow fixed protocols. Simultaneously, a new "professional-managerial" elite (7) was created to carry out decision making functions. Trained outside the workplace in newly standardized professional programs in colleges and universities, groups such as engineers and, later, business school graduates were prepared to perform complex managerial and technical tasks, coming to form the "technostructure" of modern corporations (10).

In the economic literature on industrial organization, the process of "corporatizing" manufacturing is usually divided into two phases. The first, between 1870 and 1890, is marked by a rapid growth in plant and market size. The second, between 1890 and 1905, is marked by a period of industrial consolidation culminating in the great "Merger Wave" of 1898 to 1903.

Beginning in the 1870s, individual firms began to significantly increase the scale of their plants and enter national markets, first in consumer goods industries such as sugar, flour, meat, and shoes, and later in heavy manufacturing industries such as iron and steel. Focusing on major manufacturing industries, O'Brien (11, p. 646) estimates that average establishment size doubled between 1869 and 1889 from about 11 workers per establishment to 22. By the 1880s, firms in many industries were expanding not only by increasing plant size, but also by integrating vertically forward into the distribution of final goods and backward into the purchasing (and sometimes production) of raw materials. For example, Standard Oil acquired oil fields and moved into the transportation and distribution of final products such as kerosene, and meat packers such as Swift &

Co. began distributing their products nationwide using refrigerated railway cars (3, 5). Increased firm size did not, however, always lead to greater market power for firms or an increase in the level of economic concentration. Many firms that had previously dominated local markets now found themselves facing sharp competition at the national level.

In the 1890s, the process of "corporatization" entered a second phase. A wave of horizontal mergers and acquisitions swept the manufacturing sector, the likes of which had never been seen before. Merger activity became particularly intense between 1897 and 1903 when there were over 2,800 mergers and acquisitions involving major firms, with some 1,200 mergers in the peak year of 1899 alone (12). Virtually all of these mergers involved consolidations of firms already in the same industries. Their effect was to sharply increase economic concentration. Of 93 industrial consolidations between 1895 and 1905 examined by Lamoreaux (13, pp. 1–5), 72 controlled at least 40 percent of their industries and 42 controlled at least 70 percent.

Not all industries were equally affected by the merger movement. The level of economic concentration remained relatively low in some, such as clothing and furniture. And not all consolidation attempts were successful in the long run. In his classic 1935 study, Livermore (14, p. 75) estimates that about a third of the major mergers occurring between 1888 and 1905 failed financially within ten years of formation and another 6 percent after ten years. He classifies only about half as clear financial successes. Nevertheless, the merger movement resulted in a permanent increase in the average level of economic concentration across manufacturing industries, and Livermore's list of successes includes many of the largest U.S. corporations today.

Another wave of merger activity occurred in the 1920s that also increased economic concentration in individual manufacturing industries. Between the 1930s and the 1970s, however, the level of concentration in individual industries remained relatively constant. While there was intense merger activity in the 1960s and 1970s, it involved mainly conglomerate mergers between firms in different industries. These conglomerate mergers increased the overall level of economic concentration in the manufacturing sector as a whole, but level of concentration within individual industries was largely unaffected (12). The impact of the merger boom of the 1980s remains to be seen.

## Why Did Big Businesses Get So Big?

Modern corporations are often cited as the epitome of market institutions. Yet paradoxically, as many students of the theory of the firm have noted, their central organizational characteristic is the creation of large hierarchical command and control systems for the nonmarket allocation of resources (15–17). To succeed in a market environment, this implies that firms must be realizing gains that markets cannot. At the individual plant level, explanations of the growth of large plants have focused on interactions between internal economies of scale and market conditions. Four major sources of gains have been identified in the economic literature to explain the existence of large horizontally and vertically integrated firms: (*a*) monopoly rents associated with increased control over markets; (*b*) financial considerations; (*c*) managerial economies resulting from more efficient coordination of economic activities within multiunit operations than could be achieved by markets, for example in areas such as product distribution and bulk purchasing; and (*d*) regulatory considerations (5, 18).

### Plant Size, Technology, and Market Expansion

Discussions in the economic literature of the first phase of the "corporatization" of manufacturing, the growth of large single-plant national firms, focus on the role of interactions between economies of scale within individual plants, new technologies, and expanding markets. In the 1870s and 1880s, declining transportation costs and growing urbanization combined to rapidly increase the size of markets for many goods. Growth in market size allowed firms to implement mass manufacturing techniques and sharply cut costs. Lower costs in turn stimulated the demand for goods, encouraging further expansion and fueling the growth of urban manufacturing centers. Falling railway rates and the introduction of the refrigerator car, accompanied by a rapid centralization of meat packing in Chicago, are a standard example (3).

### The Merger Movement: Motives and Impact

The rise of multiplant firms and the second phase of the "corporatization" of manufacturing, the merger movement, pose a new set of issues. For vertical and/or horizontal integration to benefit firms, gains must be achieved from some source other than simply economies of scale within individual plants. Moreover, for mergers to succeed in the long run, gains must be ongoing. Note, however, that it is possible different sources of gains may be important at different points in time; mergers may occur for one reason, but owe their survival in the long run to others. Both the question of why mergers occurred in manufacturing and the question of what determined their subsequent success or failure are of interest from the perspective of the present analysis. First consider factors motivating mergers.

*Market Power.* The potential for extracting monopoly profits through horizontal combinations was well recognized in the 19th century. So was the possibility of extending monopoly in one market into another through vertical integration (5). Price-fixing agreements were one popular way of attempting to realize these gains and to eliminate "wasteful" competition. But they were often difficult to enforce, and after 1890, the passage of the Sherman Anti-trust Act rendered them illegal. Mergers offered a legal option in the wake of the Act, while merging firms eliminated problems of cheating (13).

Lamoreaux (13) argues that the great merger wave at the end of the century in manufacturing was motivated primarily by efforts to control competition in response to a combination of short-run phenomena. Specifically, a rapid expansion of capacity in mass manufacturing industries in the late 1880s and early 1890s, followed by a severe business downturn beginning in 1893, created an extremely competitive environment that made consolidations especially attractive. She argues that, had not this particular conjunction of events occurred, the great merger boom might not have occurred either.

Whether consolidations realized hoped-for monopoly rents is another issue. There was a widespread hue and cry over mergers, but commentators ranging from Chandler (5) to Kolko (18) have questioned their effectiveness. Not infrequently, just as control was being consolidated over existing firms, new competitors appeared. This suggests that gains from simply consolidating market power may have been transitory. But this does not mean that short-run gains were necessarily trivial. In any case, for firms achieving market dominance for other reasons, anticompetitive practices stood to reap added returns. Overall, estimates by North and associates (19) suggest that monopoly profits may have been as high as 28 percent of total corporate profits in the period 1900 to 1909 following the height of the merger boom.

*Access to Capital Markets.* Two types of financial considerations potentially leading to mergers have been discussed in the literature: preferential access to capital markets and risk pooling. Davis (20) argues that in an era when equity markets were just developing for manufacturing shares, some firms enjoyed lower capital costs because of their connections with the financial establishment. These lower capital costs gave them a competitive advantage and created a financial incentive for mergers. Chandler (5) notes, however, that if preferential access to capital was a major factor in mergers, increases in economic concentration in industries and access to capital markets should be correlated. In practice, he finds no evidence that capital sources were available to firms in industries where concentration was increasing rapidly at the turn of the century (such as oil, sugar, cigarettes, or sewing machines) that were not available to industries where concentration did not increase rapidly (such as textiles, clothing, or furniture).

A second possible financial motive for horizontal integration was reductions in financial risks through risk pooling. One major source of risk for firms is fluctuations in demand, for example as a result of business cycles. To the extent that industries involved national firms producing uniform products, horizontal integration offered limited opportunities for reducing this type of risk, since changes in demand were likely to be similar across firms. However, some gains may have existed in industries where firms served primarily local or regional markets.

Beyond this, risk pooling offers a possible explanation of the emergence of multi-industry conglomerates after World War II as a means of allowing firms to spread investments across several industries and diversify their investment portfolio.

*Managerial Economies.* Economies of scale in support activities, such as bulk purchasing and the distribution of final products, have been cited as an important motivation for mergers in manufacturing, especially around the turn of the century when national branding and advertising emerged as important marketing strategies. Simply because economies of scale exist in purchasing or advertising does not, however, imply that firms necessarily should integrate horizontally to take advantage of them. Even if large economies of scale exist in purchasing and distribution, specialized independent firms may still be able to carry out these activities more efficiently. Thus, in many industries independent wholesalers perform the function of bulk purchasing. And many goods are distributed through independent national retailers such as Sears. These retailers may not only advertise and stand behind products produced by others, but may place their own brand names on them. For gains to occur from vertical integration, there must be a failure by existing external markets to respond to the needs of producers. That is, the potential must exist for a vertically integrated firm to outperform markets in coordinating activities. For example, Chandler (5) cites distribution problems as a motive for vertical integration in industries involving mass production of standardized but complex machinery for sale to consumers, such as sewing machines.

*Government Regulation.* Despite the strident rhetoric of turn-of-the-century "trust busters," direct government intervention seems to have played a relatively modest role in discouraging concentration in manufacturing. Indeed, Kolko (18) and others have suggested that some legislation in the Progressive era may have encouraged concentration. Thus in meat packing, consumer protection efforts may have reduced competition by making conditions more difficult for small, marginal producers. In any case, by far the most important role of public policy appears to be indirect, through the creation of stable national markets favorable to the development of "big business." It is sufficient to note here that had states been permitted to erect trade barriers and to pursue independent commercial and monetary policies, as they sought to do following the Revolutionary War, the scope for corporate expansion would have been sharply reduced.

### Who Survived? The Long-Run Viability of Mergers

As discussed, increases in the level of economic concentration varied across industries at the turn of the century. Many of the firms created by mergers during this period failed financially. Comparing successes and failures, Chandler (5) concludes that neither market power nor financial considerations were adequate to ensure the long-term viability of horizontal mergers. Nor do economies of scale from marketing or bulk purchasing alone appear to have been sufficient. Rather, large-scale mass production and vertical integration seem to have complemented each other in successful horizontally integrated firms.

Specifically, Chandler (5) argues that in industries such as cigarette manufacturing in which consolidations were successful in the long run, problems developed early on with existing distribution networks and raw material suppliers which limited firms' abilities to fully realize economies of scale in production at the level of individual plants. This led them to integrate forward into product distribution and backward into purchasing. Economies of scale from vertical integration in turn provided a basis for horizontal integration in production, leading to an increasing level of economic concentration. Horizontal integration itself seems to have played little role in sparking increases in plant size, however. Mergers may have added to the total size of successful firms, but O'Brien (11) argues that there was no significant change in average plant size in manufacturing in the wake of the great merger boom. Indeed, where increases in plant size did occur in individual industries, they appear uncorrelated to the level of economic concentration in these industries.

## THE RISE OF THE MODERN HEALTH CARE INDUSTRY

The modern structure of the health care industry has its origins in the early decades of the century. Efforts to put the industry on a "business" footing and to use corporate managerial techniques such as cost accounting to increase efficiency were an important factor in its development. Any analysis of the current "coporatization" of health care needs to take into account this earlier effort at rationalization. The rise of medicine, and particularly the modern hospital, has been chronicled elsewhere (21–24). But it is useful to briefly recap this history from an industrial organization perspective in order to provide some background for discussing recent developments.

### The Rise of the Modern Hospital

In the mid-19th century, medicine was truly a cottage industry. Little in the way of capital or support personnel was required, while training was highly variable. Most care was provided by physicians in solo practice on a for-profit, fee-for-service basis in their offices or in patients' homes. There was no health insurance. Patients paid for care directly out of pocket and bore most of the financial risks associated with illness, although many physicians provided charitable care as part of their private practices, and a sliding fee scale was common (21).

Until the end of the century, the role of hospitals in delivering medical care was very limited. As late as 1870, there were less than 200 hospitals in the entire country (25). Funded by private philanthropy and the public purse, their primary function was charitable and didactic. There was little technological reason for them to exist. Indeed, going to a hospital entailed a health risk and there was virtually no market for their services among paying patients. Anyone who could avoid them generally did; except for an occasional traveler, their primary clientele was the poor (21, 22).

Beginning around 1890, technological, social, and economic forces combined to dramatically transform the organization of health care delivery. Several features of this process have close parallels in manufacturing. One is the rapid centralization of production in large-scale plants (hospitals). Another is efforts at the standardization of inputs. The growth of hospitals fits the basic technology/market expansion model. New surgical and, later, new diagnostic techniques required growing amounts of capital and support staff. Economies of scale from centralizing facilities enabled hospitals to begin offering paying patients higher quality services at lower cost than they could obtain at home or in physicians' offices, at first for surgical services and then for medical services as well. These changes on the supply side created a rapidly expanding market for hospital services among paying patients. Changes on the demand side of the market reinforced this trend. Increasingly, hospitals became the accepted location for care. Spurred on by rising incomes and growing urbanization, a hospital building boom followed.

By 1928, there were over 4,000 general short-term hospitals in the United States with an average bed size of 78 beds (26). And in the process of growth, hospitals began to entail increasingly large capital investments in plant and equipment and to employ growing numbers of highly specialized nursing and technical personnel. However, in contrast to manufacturing, these new centralized hospital production facilities were almost exclusively local and regional in orientation. In smaller communities, market size placed significant limits on hospital size. But market size alone was not the only limiting factor. Even in large urban areas, community hospitals whose primary mission was caring for paying patients tended not to be more than several hundred beds, suggesting limits on internal economies of scale. (Teaching hospitals and public hospitals acting as vendors of last resort in urban areas were often much larger, but their missions were different, serving primarily didactic and charitable functions.)

Centralization of production in hospitals was accompanied by massive efforts at standardization in the industry for both personnel and facilities. Reforms in medical education following the Flexner Report in 1910 were the most visible manifestation (27). But contemporaneously a similar process was also taking place in medical specialties and in nursing (28–30). Standardized programs for technical support personnel and hospital administrators were soon to follow. In 1919 a standardization program was also established for hospital facilities by the American College of Surgeons. This program, later taken over by the Joint Commission on Accreditation of Hospitals, not only set minimum standards for facilities and staffing, but represented part of a more general effort to rationalize the organization of hospitals (21).

During the 1920s and 1930s, the pages of journals such as *Modern Hospital* were filled with discussions advocating the use of corporate cost-accounting and capital-budgeting techniques and the systematization of personnel practices in order to achieve greater administrative control over hospital operations (see, for example, 31, 32). Similar sentiments appear in the reports of the Committee on the Costs of Medical Care (21). In this spirit, Rufus Rorem, who was a Certified Public Accountant on the Committee's staff, wrote in 1932: "Hospitals are in many respects typical of all business enterprise. Procedures of scientific management in a hospital are much the same as those in a hotel or other place of business" (33, p. 19).

Turning from similarities to differences between health care and manufacturing, several features stand out immediately. The most obvious difference is the absence of the use of mass production techniques. There was no successful routinization of the production process in health care. Standardized treatment protocols did not emerge. Instead, medical services continued to be produced on a customized, individual basis. A second striking difference was the rapid penetration of the for-profit, fee-for-service sector of the industry by nonprofit institutions through the establishment of nonprofit hospitals to serve paying patients.

In the early stages of the hospital boom, for-profit hospitals emerged as a dynamic force in the industry. Many of the new hospitals established around 1900 were proprietary. Especially in communities where there was no hospital, physicians often opened their own (34, 35). However, there appears to have been a consensus among both physicians and the general public that nonprofit hospitals were preferred where markets (or the public purse) were sufficiently large to support them (25, 34, 35). By 1935, not only were 90 percent of all hospital beds in nonprofit institutions, but nonprofit institutions accounted for 94 percent of hospital capital (25).

A third distinctive feature was the emergence of a decentralized, bifurcated system of control in hospitals. In contrast to administrators in the type of monolithic, hierarchical systems of control typical of manufacturing firms, hospital administrators occupied a weak position. Despite hospitals' role as centralized facilities, clinical decisions were left in the hands of autonomous physicians, loosely organized as a "staff," but economically largely independent. Physicians, not hospital administrators, made the decisions about what services to produce and how. In for-profit and nonprofit institutions alike, administrators were largely relegated to the task of coordinating support services. And even in their own realm, they faced challenges not only from physicians, but also from hospital trustees and employees such as nurses.

A final development in health care setting it apart from manufacturing was the growth of private insurance for hospital care beginning with Blue Cross plans in the late 1930s and the 1940s, followed by the rise of commercial insurance plans in the 1950s. These plans had the effect of driving a "wedge" between buyers and sellers of care. Increasingly, those who received care no longer paid for it directly, with far-reaching implications. The initial effect of these plans, however, was primarily to reinforce the basic fee-for-service, physician coordinated mode of production in the industry (36–37).

### The Hospital as a "Blocked" Institution

Focusing on the bifurcated system of control in hospitals and contrasting it with centralized, hierarchical systems of control in manufacturing, Starr (21, p. 179) refers to the hospital as a "blocked" institution. A central question is what caused this "blockage." One interpretation is that institutional inertia, combined with physician resistance, directly blocked the introduction of centralized systems of control. An alternative explanation is that this aspect of the "corporatization" of manufacturing was "blocked" because corporate administrative structures were not well adapted to the production of medical services from an efficiency perspective.

The aggressive standardization of medical education and health facilities, as well as the rapid transformation of hospitals from custodial institutions into the central workplaces of the industry, argue against the notion of institutional inertia as a sole explanation. Moreover, most hospitals themselves were newly created institutions. There is no question that physicians and other professional groups wielded extensive power in the industry on the eve of modernization. But so did many other craft groups in manufacturing prior to restructuring, suggesting that more was involved than simply professional power or historical accident.

This turns attention back to the first distinctive feature of health care in relation to manufacturing noted above—the absence of standardized mass production. The acme of the new corporate hierarchies emerging in manufacturing was administering the rapid performance of repetitive, highly routinized tasks; the longer the production run, the better. In contrast, medical services were and remain extremely heterogeneous with major implications for the organization of both the production and distribution of health care.

Even for patients with similar diagnoses, an effective treatment for one may be inappropriate for another, making it difficult to routinize production. In addition, heterogeneity creates serious informational problems for consumers. This makes it attractive to employ physicians as agents. But as dicussed elsewhere in this volume (38), informational problems also create opportunities for abuses of the doctor-patient relationship.

The combination of input standardization, autonomous fee-for-service physicians, and nonprofit hospitals which emerged after 1900 may be seen as an effort to rationalize production in a market oriented system in the face of agency problems in health care. As discussed elsewhere (38), employing physicians as autonomous agents created incentives for the physician to be sensitive to patient preferences because repeat purchases were critical to building a medical practice. Had physicians been, for example, employees of prepaid group practices, as advocated by the Committee on the Cost of Medical Care (21), utilizing information about patient satisfaction would have been more difficult. At the same time, the extreme heterogeneity of medical services limited opportunities for providers to internally apply quality control techniques from industry, especially in the face of high information-processing costs.

Keeping physicians autonomous also kept doctors from having a direct interest in the sale of hospital services. Conversely, physician autonomy limited hospitals' ability to interfere with care to promote their own interests. Nonprofit status and checks by professionals and hospital trustees on hospital administrators presumably made hospitals more service and quality oriented than they would have been as for-profit institutions. In addition, it provided a financial and institutional framework for extending to inpatient care the traditional pattern in outpatient care of subsidizing charity care out of fees from paying patients.

It is important not to be overly deterministic in viewing the evolution of this system (39). In some hospitals, physicians in areas like radiology and pathology were employed on a full time basis. And other countries evolved significantly different systems. But the pattern of reorganization in the industry in the early decades of this century is consistent with a general process of rationalization. The structure that emerged may be viewed as an accommodation, albeit not necessarily an ideal one even on its own terms, of mass manufacturing techniques to problems with heterogeneity and monitoring performance in the context of a market oriented system. Had the underlying institutional framework been different, (e.g. a national health insurance system), so might the outcome of this process.

### The Restructuring of Health Care Finance

By World War I, cost increases associated with new technologies and increased use of hospitals were placing severe strains on the traditional system of financing health care through direct patient payments. In response, a variety of innovative payment schemes were put forward (40), the proposal by the Committee on the Costs of Medical Care for prepaid group practices being one of the most publicized (21). Had such a plan been adopted, this would have significantly altered the organization of health care delivery.

However, not only were proposals such as that of the Committee never implemented, but private health insurance did not become widely available until after World War II, when Blue Cross and private commercial insurance were secured as fringe benefits in the workplace. Public provisions for assuring financial access to care for those outside the workplace, such as the elderly and the poor, were not enacted until the introduction of Medicare and Medicaid in 1965. And in both the private and public sector, when third-party payment was introduced, a retrospective, cost based system of reimbursement was the norm. The result was to reinforce the existing system of fee-for-service oriented health care delivery while buoying the demand for services, basically placing third-party payors in the position of passive conduits for funneling funds to providers.

One important factor in explaining long delays in introducing health insurance and the type of reimbursement structure that ultimately developed was the resistance of organized medicine. The American Medical Association vigorously opposed prepayment plans, while viewing indemnity insurance as a necessary evil (21). Medicine's success in achieving financial accommodation to the newly emerged status quo in health care delivery cannot, however, be attributed to its own efforts alone. The economic crisis of the Great Depression played a role in derailing proposals of the Committee on the Costs of Medical Care, whose final report was issued in 1932 (41).

At least three factors help to explain the accommodation between payors and providers in the postwar period. One was the high level of economic prosperity after World War II, making it relatively easy for corporate (and later public) payors to absorb rising costs. A second factor was agency concerns (already discussed) about the effects of embedding physicians in hierarchical organizations, for example prepaid group practices. Finally, there was a general perception that more medical care was better in the wake of scientific advances earlier in the century, reflected not only in generous benefits for those with private insurance, but also in public subsidies for medical research and hospital construction.

*The Post-Medicare Era*

Most of the developments associated with the "corporatization" of health care—the penetration of for-profit firms into the nonprofit sector of the industry, the reorganization of nonprofit institutions along corporate lines, and challenges to physician authority— date from the period following the introduction of Medicare and Medicaid in 1965. Medicare and Medicaid represented a major watershed in several respects. For the first time the federal government attempted to provide significant groups of the population outside the existing private insurance system with financial access to care. At the same time, these programs ushered in a period of unprecedented growth in government regulation and third-party involvement.

Initially, few strings were attached to Medicare or Medicaid payments, and in response to increased effective demand, the health industry entered a period of rapid expansion. Overall the percentage of gross national product spent on health care went from 5.9 percent in 1965 to 7.3 percent in 1970 (42, p. 74). During the same period, while the total number of hospitals remained fairly constant, the number of hospital beds in short-term nonfederal hospitals rose by 30 percent, while employment in hospitals nearly doubled (43, p. 98).

In the face of rapidly rising costs, the early 1970s saw a shift in emphasis by third-party payors from assuring access to controlling costs. Since 1970, containment efforts have passed through two major phases. They now appear to be entering a third. In the 1970s, initiatives came mainly from the public sector. Policy makers sought to control costs primarily through retrospective rate setting based on individual hospitals' actual cost experiences. But they also experimented with a range of other types of regulation. Certificate of need (CON) legislation sought to limit the construction of "unneeded" facilities and equipment acquisition. Health maintenance organizations (HMOs) were promoted as a less costly alternative to traditional fee-for-service care. Limited efforts were made to establish regional planning agencies, while PSROs (professional standards review organizations) were established to monitor the quality and efficacy of performance.

None of these strategies was very successful. Rate setting had only a limited impact on cost increases (44). Evidence on CON programs suggests that they had little effect on the overall level of investment (44, 45), while the growth of HMOs was slow. Nor does the impact of planning agencies and PSROs appear to have been significant (44). By 1980, total expenditures on health care had increased to 9.1 percent, while the number of hospital beds grew by 17 percent between 1970 and 1980 and number of hospital personnel by 50 percent (46, p. 149). At the same time, important changes occurred within the hospital industry. There was a 60 percent increase in the number of for-profit hospital beds (43, p. 98). And for the first time, large corporate hospital systems such as Hospital Corporation of America, Humana, and American Medical International emerged as important players in the industry, while nonprofit systems expanded their role as well.

The early 1980s saw a shift in policy toward so-called "competitive" cost-containment strategies and growing involvement by private third-party payors in efforts to limit health care expenditures. In both the public and private sectors, the central thrust of "competitive" strategies has been to shift financial risk to patients and providers. For patients, cost sharing has been increased, directly increasing their level of financial exposure. For providers, "risk based" systems of payment have been introduced which no longer allow them to simply pass along cost increases to payors, where the underlying notion has been to harness market incentives to increase efficiency.

In the public sector, the centerpiece of regulatory efforts has been the Medicare Prospective Payment System (PPS), introduced in 1983. Under the Medicare PPS, hospitals are at financial risk not only if their underlying costs of producing services are high, but also if there are random within-DRG variations in the treatment needs of patients (47). In the private sector, HMOs have proliferated, while under indemnity plans, patient cost sharing has increased sharply (48). In addition, there have been growing efforts by large private (and public) payors to use their market power to negotiate favorable rates from providers through PPOs (49).

Ideally, "competitive" strategies are supposed to stimulate efficiency and lower costs. The extent to which they have done so is unclear. Since 1983, hospital admissions and lengths of stay have dropped, creating considerable overcapacity in hospital beds. [Average occupancy rates fell from around to 75 percent in 1980 to 65 percent in 1985 (46, p. 141)]. But total health care expenditures have continued to rise, now approaching 11 percent of gross national product as use of outpatient services such as ambulatory surgery has grown and cost per hospital day has gone up (50).

Although the impact on the total costs of care is unclear, what does seem clear is that competitive strategies, coupled with overcapacity, have had a major impact on economic conditions in the industry and the way providers do business. Increasingly, hospitals have found themselves under intense financial pressure. While some types of hospitals, such as large urban and teaching hospitals, have made profits on Medicare patients under prospective payment, others, such as small urban and rural community hospitals, have not (51). Many hospitals have been hurt by cost containment by state Medicaid programs. And in any case, pressures for lower rates by Medicare, Medicaid, and private insurers have disrupted traditional systems of cross-subsidies for indigent care at a time when the number of patients with little or no health insurance has been growing, up from an estimated 12.5 percent of the U.S. population in 1980 to 15.3 percent in 1986 (46, p. 168).

Financial pressures are reflected in a wide range of ways. The number of hospital closures is up: 71 in 1986 compared with an average of 36 per year between 1980 and 1985 (52, p. xix). Many hospitals have cut staff and beds, while the growth of multihospital systems has accelerated. More generally, financial pressures have served to legitimize profit-oriented decision making by administrators (see, for example, 53). This has had important implications not only for policy decisions about what kind of services hospitals provide for whom and how, but also for the balance of power within these institutions. As the prominence of the "bottom line" has increased, so has the prominence of administrators.

Complementing "competitive" strategies in recent years has been a movement toward what may loosely be defined as "managed care." The essence of managed care is the use of standardized data from medical records to perform reviews of hospital and physician performance. In the public sector, this has been exemplified by the activities of professional review organizations (PROs) mandated by the federal government, whose role may soon expand significantly (54). In the private sector, a wide range of experiments are under way by third-party payors, and providers are developing internal systems of control to monitor physicians (55, 56).

One factor involved in the growth of managed care appears to be a shift in attitude toward quality/cost trade-offs. The notion "more is better" is no longer being unquestioningly accepted, and costs and benefits are being reassessed. Contributing to this shift has been the emergence of large public and private third-party payors as major players in the industry, shifting the locus of decision making away from individual patients. A third factor is that at the provider level, by design, risk-based payment has increasingly shifted the financial consequences of physician decisions to hospitals, creating powerful incentives for them to develop systems to control these decisions. Simultaneously, there has been a decline in the costs of operating large centralized monitoring systems. Not only have information processing costs fallen owing to advances in computer technology, but the availability of large-scale data bases for comparative purposes has been rapidly increasing.

## "CORPORATIZATION" AND THE HOSPITAL INDUSTRY

Nothing has happened to date in the hospital industry comparable to the emergence of large manufacturing plants serving national markets in the 1870s and 1880s. Recently, some private insurers have sought to set up preferred provider arrangements requiring patients nationwide to go to specific hospitals (57). However, this has been limited to costly, highly technical procedures with low volumes, such as organ transplants. Individual hospitals remain very small in relation to the total volume of service rendered in the country as a whole, and they continue to serve primarily local and regional markets, as has been demonstrated by a series of recent studies on hospital market structure (58–60). Average hospital size increased from 78 beds in 1929 (25) to 173 beds in 1985 (46). But especially recently, increases in average size have been due more to declines in the number of smaller hospitals than to the expansion of larger ones. Even in large metropolitan markets, the size of community institutions has remained relatively modest. Cost studies in the 1970s suggest an optimal size for community hospitals of around 300 beds, and there is no evidence of economies of scale within hospitals that have significantly altered this situation (44, 61).

The central change in the industry associated with "corporatization" from an industrial organization perspective has been a rapid increase in the level of horizontal and vertical integration. Although the level of economic concentration in the hospital industry is still low by manufacturing standards, the trend toward multihospital systems and growing vertical linkages marks a major departure from the highly atomistic structure of the past. Because experiences have been different for for-profit and nonprofit hospitals, it is worth examining trends by ownership as well as for hospitals as a group before turning to possible explanations of these trends.

### Horizontal Integration

The main force for horizontal integration in health care has been the formation of multihospital systems through mergers and acquisitions and leasing of facilities. But management contracts have also played a role and in 1986, 14 percent of all system beds were controlled through contractual arrangements (52). The existence of multiunit hospital systems is not new in the industry. Public systems have had a long history in some cities, for example New York, and in

California, Kaiser Permanente was forced to build its own hospitals in the 1940s and 1950s because of exclusion from local institutions. However, multihospital systems attracted relatively little attention until the late 1960s, when for-profit hospital systems rapidly began to acquire independent for-profit hospitals. By 1973 they controlled nearly half of all for-profit beds (62), while in 1985 their share was more than 70 percent (63, 64).

Data on the total number of hospitals in multiunit systems are not available until the mid-1970s and unfortunately include psychiatric and rehabilitation hospitals as well as general hospitals. Ermann and Gabel (65) estimate that in 1975 there was a total of 202 multihospital systems controlling 293,000 beds and 1,405 hospitals. They estimate that this included about a quarter of the community hospitals in the country. Between 1975 and 1983, according to Friedman (66), the number of systems grew at around 3 percent a year, the number of system hospitals at 5.5 percent, and the number of beds at 3 percent. Between 1983 and 1986, he estimates that growth rates accelerated, with the number of systems growing at a rate of 3.7 percent a year, the number of system hospitals at 7 percent, and the number of system beds at 4.4 percent. By 1986, the total number of systems was 278, the number of system hospitals was 2,514, and over 429,000 beds were either owned or leased (52). Friedman (66) estimates that this included about one third of all community hospitals in the country.

In 1986, 47 percent of all hospitals and 35 percent of all beds owned or managed by systems were controlled by for-profit systems. Nonprofit systems controlled just over half of all system hospitals and 65 percent of all system beds. Breaking down the overall pattern of growth by type of ownership, the number of nonprofit multihospital systems increased from 121 in 1978 to 224 in 1986 (52, 65). The number of for-profit systems remained relatively stable between 1978 and 1982 at around 30 (65). By 1986, however, it had increased to 54 (52).

While the growth of the number of nonprofit systems was much higher than that of for-profit systems between 1978 and 1982, the latter group had a higher rate of growth in terms of the total number of beds they controlled over this period: 4.8 percent versus 3.5 percent (66). Not only has the number of for-profit systems grown rapidly since the early 1980s, but between 1984 and 1986, for-profit systems accounted for over 70 percent of the growth in total system hospitals and beds, adding nearly 38,000 beds, while nonprofit systems added slightly under 14,000 beds (52, 63).

Comparing the relative size of systems, recently the average size of nonprofit systems has been growing, while the average size of for-profit systems has been falling. Between 1982 and 1986, the average size of nonprofit systems almost doubled, going from five hospitals to nine. Meanwhile, the average size of for-profit systems fell from 28 hospitals in 1982 to 22 in 1986 (52, 64).

These trends reflect several factors. Historically, while some nonprofit systems have been quite large, the level of economic concentration has been low among nonprofit systems. In 1986, the top five nonprofit systems ranked by revenue controlled about 13 percent of all nonprofit system hospitals and 17 percent of all nonprofit system beds (52, 67). In contrast, a few very large multihospital systems have dominated the for-profit segment of the industry. In 1986, the top five for-profit systems ranked by beds (67) controlled 57 percent of for-profit system hospitals and 71 percent of for-profit system beds (52, 68). However, while still very large, the role of big for-profit systems has been declining in recent years. Their rate of growth in terms of both beds and hospitals was only about 2 percent between 1983 and 1986 (66). And in 1987, the largest for-profit multiunit system, Hospital Corporation of America, spun off about a quarter of its hospitals, while the number of beds in the United States controlled by Humana, the second biggest for-profit system, rose by less than 1 percent (68). In contrast to the pattern in the past, most of the recent increase in for-profit systems has occurred through the growth of small local and regional for-profit systems, many of them quite new.

Turning to the effects of horizontal integration on economic concentration in the industry, it is not clear that the largest firms have had the greatest impact on concentration. Further research is needed. But given that most hospital markets remain local or regional in character, in many cases local and regional systems may have achieved a higher level of market control in specific areas than the big national and international for-profit systems, whose holdings tend to be more geographically dispersed.

*Vertical Integration*

Two main forms of vertical integration have occurred in health care. One has been mergers between community and tertiary hospitals. Especially in the case of for-profits, multihospital systems have been predominately composed of community institutions. But even in the for-profit sector, some linkages have been established with teaching hospitals (69, 70).

A second form of vertical integration is a movement into the areas of insurance and ambulatory care. Examples are linkages between hospitals and HMOs and indemnity insurance plans, and the establishment of free-standing ambulatory care centers. As Friedman (66) notes, these efforts have had two aspects. One has been attempts through mergers, acquisitions, and joint ventures by large for-profit hospital systems to integrate forward into insurance activities and ambulatory care on a national scale. The other has been much more modest attempts by individual hospitals and nonprofit hospital systems to move into these areas at a local and regional level. Efforts by large for-profits on a national scale have so far proved disappointing, and in a number of cases firms have pulled back. The decisions by Humana to liquidate its ambulatory MedFirst centers and by American Medical International to end its group health insurance activities are examples (67). On the other hand, overall the total number of hospitals having formal affiliations with HMOs more than doubled between 1980 and 1985 (66), while large for-profit systems have moved into specialty areas such as psychiatric and rehabilitation care (67, 68, 71). This suggests that despite some well-publicized failures by large for-profit systems at the national level, the general trend continues to be toward greater vertical integration, albeit on a smaller scale.

### Motivations for System Affiliation

The previous discussion of experiences in manufacturing suggests four major reasons for the creation of multiunit enterprises: monopoly power, financial considerations, managerial economies, and regulatory factors. In each case, in evaluating the long-run potential impact of mergers, the manufacturing experience suggests that it is important to distinguish between short-run transitory gains and those that may be ongoing.

Sorting out the relative importance of factors encouraging the growth of multihospital systems is difficult, especially as most systems are quite recent in origin. It is, however, at least possible to identify some of the major reasons why they have been created and the nature of the gains involved. Looking first at the issue of monopoly power, for the period leading up to 1983, Alexander and co-workers (72) find that increasing local market power was perceived by system administrators as an important motivation for acquisitions and mergers, especially in markets where overcapacity existed and hospitals faced the possibility of head-to-head competition. This finding is also supported by studies such as those by Starkweather and Carman (73) and Begun and co-workers (74).

The importance of market power considerations in hospital mergers is reminiscent of the turn of the century experience in manufacturing (13). In this context, it is interesting to note that the growth in systems, at least in terms of beds, accelerated between 1983 and 1986 (66) as occupancy rates fell following the introduction of the Medicare PPS.

Turning to the question of financial access, Alexander and colleagues (72) find that favorable access to capital markets has been perceived as a central advantage. And Ermann and Gabel (65) conclude from a review of the literature up to 1984 that a key technical advantage of multihospital systems is their preferred position in capital markets. On the other hand, there is also some conflicting empirical evidence. For instance, for the period during which the Medicare PPS was introduced in 1983, Sloan and colleagues (75) fail to find that multihospital systems enjoyed any clear advantages in debt markets.

To the extent that financial advantages exist, two sources seem possible. One is access to financial expertise. Utilizing national capital markets involves considerable financial sophistication. At least in the 1970s, managers in many hospitals, especially small ones, lacked this sophistication. Mergers provided one way of gaining access to financial expertise. Particularly in the case of for-profit hospitals, whose level of capital investment traditionally was low (25), the growth of multihospital systems appears to have been accompanied by major injections of capital (76), although issues exist about how much of these increases was related to accounting adjustments (35). However, in recent years, the sophistication of hospital administrators has grown, as has the availability of independent consulting services. A second source of financial advantage may be better access to capital due to reductions in risk. Under the Medicare PPS and other forms of risk-based payment, a more lasting motive for integration may be the ability of multihospital systems to pool risks such as those associated with within-DRG variations, which Dada and co-workers (47) suggest may be significant.

In the case of managerial economies, the manufacturing experience suggests possible economies from bulk purchasing, mass marketing, and from the process of diffusing new managerial techniques themselves. Economies of scale from bulk purchasing have long been cited as a possible justification for horizontal integration (44). Hospitals have only recently become involved in marketing activities, but they are burgeoning. Spurred on by increasingly competitive market conditions and the growth of risk-based payment, for-profit and nonprofit institutions alike are aggressively pursuing profitable patients at the same time that they are seeking to avoid unprofitable ones. Disaggregated data are difficult to come by, but increased advertising is certainly one reason why administrative costs are the most rapidly growing area of hospital expenditures, rising at a rate of nearly 20 percent per year between 1980 and 1985 (77).

However, in evaluating the importance of managerial economies in the formation of multihospital systems, the manufacturing experience suggests that it is critical to look at two factors. The first is the extent to which managerial economies transcend the scale of individual production units, here hospitals. The second is the degree to which, if they do, independent organizations cannot perform these functions more efficiently. One obvious case is advertising. If national branding matters, there may be large economies. But recent experience indicates that consumers tend to focus on the reputation of individual hospitals. In fact, attempts by systems such as Humana to achieve national recognition seem to have been more successful for suppliers than for patients (78). This suggests that marketing at the individual hospital level may be quite competitive with marketing by large national systems, especially if a hospital is linked to HMOs. At the same time, bulk purchasing arrangements through groups like the Voluntary Hospitals of America are an alternative to internalizing bulk purchasing in systems. With respect to managerial techniques themselves, as in the case of financial issues, hospital administrators are growing more sophisticated, while expertise is available from outside management consulting firms.

Finally, turning to regulatory issues, Alexander and co-workers (72) suggest that access to managerial expertise on regulatory matters has been a significant factor in motivating hospitals to join systems. However, the same questions exist here regarding the long-run importance of expertise as in the case of managerial expertise. Beyond this, analyzing acquisition patterns prior to 1983, Morrisey and Alexander (79) suggest that the state regulatory environment may have been important. Specifically, acquisitions were less frequent in states with strong rate regulation, which could potentially reduce profitability, while they were more frequent where CON laws tended to create barriers to entry for new hospitals.

## Differences between For-profit and Nonprofit Systems

The discussion above has suggested a number of differences in patterns of growth between for-profit and nonprofit systems. Obvious questions are: (*a*) what do these differences stem from; and (*b*) to what extent are they linked to differences in underlying behavior? For-profit hospital systems presumably exist to make profits. Economic theories regarding the motives of nonprofit hospitals vary and there is no single satisfactory model of their behavior (44, 80). Empirically, significant differences exist overall in both patterns of behavior and the attitudes of administrators between for-profits and nonprofits. Data presented by Lewin and associates (81) indicate sharp differences in the amount of indigent care provided by for-profit hospitals compared with voluntary nonprofits and public hospitals in selected states with high levels of for-profit hospital penetration. Major differences in attitudes also exist. For example, a 1986 survey of health care executives in hospitals, HMOs, and nursing homes by the American College of Health Executives found that 56 percent of executives employed by voluntary nonprofits and 60 percent of those employed by public institutions favored equal access to health care for the entire U.S. population, whereas the percentage for executives employed by for-profit institutions was only 29 percent (82).

Specifically looking at hospital systems, Alexander and associates (72) found that for-profit administrators were primarily concerned about market factors affecting profitability in making acquisitions. Goals in the case of nonprofits were more diverse. For religious systems, acquiring hospitals to maintain or establish a presence in a community was an important consideration. Goals also included possible cross-subsidization between institutions within systems, although in 1985, at the time of the survey, church hospital administrators appear to have been becoming more cautious about taking on unprofitable hospitals.

Behavioral differences are also suggested by data on acquisition patterns collected by Luke and Begun (83) for small systems with less than eight hospitals in the period 1982–83 to 1985. Hospitals in small for-profit systems tended to be geographically spread out and to have no large identifiable "parent" hospital, consistent with what Luke and Begun describe as an "investment" orientation. Both Catholic hospital systems and secular nonprofit and non-Catholic church systems tended to have an identifiable parent hospital. In the case of Catholic systems, hospitals tended to be geographically spread out, consistent with a mission to maintain and expand a presence across communities. In the case of secular and non-Catholic church systems, hospitals tended to be highly geographically concentrated, suggesting market power concerns.

While differences in goals may help to explain historical growth patterns, many questions remain. For instance, it has been suggested that the introduction of

Medicare and Medicaid may have served as a catalyst for consolidation in the for-profit segment of the industry in the late 1960s and 1970s in the face of a large pool of small, undercapitalized for-profit hospitals. For not only did Medicare and Medicaid increase the demand for hospital services, but they lowered financial risks, creating new opportunities for profitable investment (25, 35). But problems with undercapitalization also existed for a substantial number of small nonprofit hospitals. While some were in fact taken over by for-profit systems, no similar burst in growth in nonprofit systems is apparent. Purely on the basis of differences in attitudes towards service roles, it is not obvious why nonprofit systems should not also have emerged. No attempt to resolve this issue is made here. But it is interesting to note that the growth of the large national and international for-profit systems has slowed just as changes in payment systems have increased financial uncertainty, while the growth of local and regional systems has accelerated.

## LESSONS FROM MANUFACTURING

Comparing and contrasting the experiences discussed in the previous section with those in manufacturing at the time of its "corporatization," several features stand out. Unlike manufacturing, large-scale national markets for health care services have not emerged. Rather, markets for hospital services remain primarily local and regional. In smaller markets, market size has limited hospital size, but based on experiences in larger urban markets, so has the lack of internal economies of scale. This suggests that even if national markets were to develop, single hospitals would not expand to serve such markets for most services, except perhaps for highly specialized, low volume services such as organ transplants, unless there were major changes in the organization of production.

Turning to issues of vertical and horizontal integration, from an industrial organization perspective, the local and regional character of hospital markets suggests that the nation as a whole may not always be the appropriate unit for evaluating questions of market power. As discussed in the previous section, vertical and horizontal integration have taken place in the industry not only through the formation of large for-profit hospital systems. Especially recently, locally and regionally oriented small nonprofit and for-profit systems have been growing rapidly. These latter types of systems in many cases may have a greater impact on concentration in specific markets than national chains.

Paralleling turn-of-the-century experiences in manufacturing, the potential for greater control over markets, better access to capital, and managerial economies of scale all appear to have been important in motivating the growth of these systems. However, what are striking by their absence are the kind of very large economies of scale within individual production units that Chandler (5) suggests have been key to the long-run survival of large multiunit enterprises in manufacturing.

A central question is whether this implies that the recent consolidation movement among hospitals will prove transitory. Ermann and Gabel (65) note that in the early 1980s, before the introduction of the Medicare PPS, predictions were being made that 70 percent of all hospitals would be in systems by 1986, more than double what actually happened. Friedman (66) observes that similar predictions still continue, although with longer timetables. If in fact gains from hospital mergers are mostly short-run, these new projections could also prove overly optimistic.

On the other hand, even if nothing happens at the individual hospital level comparable to the emergence of giant plants in industries such as steel, autos, or petrochemicals in the late 19th and early 20th century, there are several factors motivating integration that were not present in manufacturing. One is the growing use of risk-based payment. Assuming this trend is not reversed, this tends to create increasing financial advantages from risk pooling of a sort which, as noted, were in general probably not present for firms in national manufacturing markets. A second feature is the important role of nonprofits in the industry in the context of growing financial problems with care for the indigent and traditional systems of cross-subsidization of services within hospitals. In both cases, gains for institutions from combining resources appear likely to be ongoing even if other types of gains from forming systems prove transitory.

A final issue is the impact of managed care. As discussed elsewhere in this volume (38), its effect on the organization of production so far appears limited. However, recent efforts to develop standardized treatment protocols could have a major impact, especially if they can be successfully combined with so-called "flexible" manufacturing techniques which have recently been developed in an effort to minimize the costs of mass producing customized products (84, 85). Greater routinization of production through these techniques could increase opportunities for competition on a national basis as well as for national branding. If there are also increased internal economies of scale in hospitals due to the use of protocols, these could provide the basis for the type of large integrated firms Chandler (5) describes in manufacturing. However, even if standardized protocols are successfully implemented, their impact on concentration is by no means clear. Combining standardized protocols with flexible production techniques could actually reduce the efficient size of hospitals, where fragmentation could be accelerated if pressures to move services out of hospitals and into ambulatory settings continue, for example as discussed by Goldsmith (86). In any case, if national markets emerge, while significant economies from vertical integration do not, concentration could effectively decline in the hospital industry.

## CLOSING REMARKS

Rather than the culmination of an extended research agenda, this chapter has been deliberately exploratory in nature. It may perhaps most usefully be viewed as a cautionary tale. It is easy to equate many elements of the modern structure of health care with the earlier traditional organization of medicine and then to frame questions about the impact of "corporatization" in terms of rationalization of a system that is preindustrial in origin. But on closer inspection many of the forces at work in manufacturing at the turn of the century also appear to have been at work in medicine. That the results were quite different may say as much about the limitations of centralized corporate forms of organization, mass production, and for-profit institutions in achieving efficiency gains in health care as it does about professional resistance to these forces. If the industrial revolution is indeed "catching up" with the health sector, it may be primarily because mass production techniques are advancing to the point where they can begin to address the extreme heterogeneity of medical services.

As discussed, what the outcome of such changes may be for the organization of the hospital industry and more generally for health care is unclear. The historical experience in manufacturing indicates the potential for great diversity in the future. Far from suggesting that growing integration and concentration in the hospital industry are inevitable, analogies with turn-of-the-century manufacturing point to the need to look carefully at the nature of the gains involved in hospital mergers and consolidations and the extent to which these gains are likely to be ongoing or transitory in nature.

## REFERENCES

1. Salmon, J. W. Special section on the corporatization of medicine: Introduction. *Int. J. Health Serv.* 17(1): 1–6, 1987.
2. McKinlay, J. B., and Stoeckle, J. D. Corporatization and the social transformation of doctoring. *Int. J. Health Serv.* 18(2): 191-205, 1988.
3. Walton, G., and Robertson, R. *History of the American Economy,* Ed. 5. Harcourt Brace Jovanovich, New York, 1983.
4. Hughes, J. *American Economic History.* Scott, Foresman & Company, Glenview, Ill., 1983.
5. Chandler, A. *The Visible Hand: The Managerial Revolution in American Business.* Belknap, Cambridge, Mass., 1977.
6. Noble, D. F. *American by Design: Science, Technology and the Rise of Corporate Capitalism.* A. Knopf, New York, 1979.
7. Ehrenreich, B., and Ehrenreich, R. The professional managerial class. In *Between Labor Markets,* edited by P. Walker, pp. 5-48. South End Press, Boston, 1971.
8. Gray, B. H. *The New Health Care for Profit: Doctors and Hospitals in a Competitive Environment.* National Academy Press, Washington, D.C., 1983.
9. Relman, A. S. The new medical industrial complex. *N. Engl. J. Med.* 303: 963–970, 1980.
10. Galbraith, J. K. *The New Industrial State.* Houghton Mifflin, Boston, 1967.
11. O'Brien, A. P. Factory size, economies of scale, and the great merger wave of 1898-1902. *J. Econ. Hist.* 48(3): 639–650, 1988.
12. Niemi, A. *U.S. Economic History.* Rand McNally, Chicago, 1975.

13. Lamoreaux, N. R. *The Great Merger Movement in American Business.* Cambridge University Press, New York, 1985.
14. Livermore, S. The success of industrial mergers. *Q. J. Econ.* 50(4): 68–96, 1935.
15. Coase, R. The nature of the firm. *Economica* 4: 386–405, 1937.
16. Alchian, L., and Demsetz, H. Production information costs and economic organization. *Am. Econ. Rev.* 62(5): 777–795, 1972.
17. Nelson, R. Assessing private enterprise: An exegesis of tangled doctrine. *Bell J. Econ.* 12(1): 93–111, 1981.
18. Kolko, G. *The Triumph of Conservatism: A Reinterpretation of American History 1900-1916.* Free Press, New York, 1977.
19. North, D. C., Anderson, T. L., and Hill, P. *Growth and Welfare in the American Past.* Prentice Hall, Englewood Cliffs, N.J., 1983.
20. Davis, L. The capital markets and industrial concentration. *Econ. Hist. Rev.* 19: 255–272, 1966.
21. Starr, P. *The Social Transformation of American Medicine.* Basic Books, New York, 1982.
22. Rosenberg, C. E. *The Care of Strangers: The Rise of America's Hospital System.* Basic Books, New York, 1987.
23. Rosner, D. *A Once Charitable Enterprise.* Cambridge University Press, Cambridge, England 1982.
24. Vogel, M. *The Invention of the Modern Hospital: Boston, 1870-1930.* University of Chicago Press, Chicago, 1980.
25. White, W. D. The American hospital industry since 1900: A short history. In *Advances in Health Economics and Health Services Research,* Vol. 3, edited by R. Scheffler and L. Rossiter, pp. 143–170. JAI Press, Greenwich, Conn., 1982.
26. Rorem, C. R. *The Public's Investment in Hospitals.* University of Chicago Press, Chicago, 1930.
27. Berliner, H. *Philanthropic Foundations and the Rise of Scientific Medicine.* Methuen, New York, 1986.
28. Stevens, R. *American Medicine and the Public Interest.* Yale University Press, New Haven, Conn., 1971.
29. Kalisch, P., and Kalisch, B. *The Advance of American Nursing.* Little Brown & Co., Boston, 1978.
30. Flanagan, L. *One Strong Voice: The Story of the American Nurses' Association.* American Nurses' Association, Kansas City, Mo., 1976.
31. Potter, E. Developing standards of accounting and administration. *Mod. Hosp.* 26(5): 389–394, 1926.
32. Hunter, R. W. Standardization of hospital accounting. *Mod. Hosp.* 16(6): 517–520, 1921.
33. Rorem, C. R. *The Quest For Certainty: Essays on Health Care Economics.* Health Administration Press, Ann Arbor, Mich., 1982.
34. Marmor, T. R., Schlesinger, M., and Smithey, R. A new look at nonprofits: Health care policy in a competitive age. *Yale J. Reg.* 3: 313–349, 1986.
35. Hollingsworth, J. R., and Hollingsworth, E. J. *Controversy About American Hospitals: Funding, Ownership, and Performance.* American Enterprise Institute Studies No. 465. American Enterprise Institute, Washington, D.C., 1988.
36. Anderson, O. *Blue Cross Since 1929: Accountability and the Public Trust.* Ballinger, Cambridge, Mass., 1975.
37. Law, S. *Blue Cross: What Went Wrong?* Yale University Press, New Haven, Conn., 1976.

38. White, W. D., Salmon, J. W., and Feinglass, J. The changing doctor-patient relationship and performance monitoring: An agency perspective. In *The Corporate Transformation of Health Care Part 2: Perspectives and Implications*, edited by J. W. Salmon, pp. 195–224, Baywood, Amityville, N.Y., 1993.

39. Navarro, V. Medical history as justification rather than explanation: A critique of Starr's *The Social Transformation of American Medicine. Int. J. Health Serv.* 14(4): 511–528, 1984.

40. Hirschfield, D. S. *The Lost Reform: The Campaign for Compulsory Health Insurance in the United States 1932 to 1943.* Harvard University Press, Cambridge, Mass., 1970.

41. Committee on the Costs of Medical Care. *Medical Care for the American People.* University of Chicago Press, Chicago, 1932.

42. U.S. Bureau of the Census. *Historical Statistics of the United States, Colonial Times to 1970,* p.74. U.S. Government Printing Office, Washington, D.C., 1975.

43. U.S. Bureau of the Census. *Statistical Abstract of the United States: 1988,* Ed. 108, p. 98. U.S. Government Printing Office, Washington, D.C., 1987.

44. Feldstein, P. J. *Health Care Economics,* Ed. 2. Wiley Medical, New York, 1983.

45. Steinwald, B., and Slaon, F. Regulatory approaches to hospital cost containment: A synthesis of the empirical evidence. In *A New Approach to the Economics of Health Care,* edited by M. Olsen, pp. 273–307. American Enterprise Institute, Washington, D.C., 1981.

46. National Center for Health Statistics. *Health, United States, 1987.* DHHS Pub. No. (PHS) 88-1232. U.S. Government Printing Office, Washington, D.C., 1988.

47. Dada, M., White, W. D., and Cooksey, J. The Medicare Prospective Payment System and Financial Risk. Unpublished working paper. College of Business Administration, University of Illinois at Chicago, October 1988.

48. Gabel, J., et. al. The health insurance industry in transition. *Health Aff.* 6(3): 46–60, 1987.

49. de Lissovoy, G., et. al. Preferred provider organizations one year later. *Inquiry* 24: 127–135, 1987.

50. Anderson, G., and Erickson, J. Data watch: National medical care spending. *Health Aff.* 6(3): 96–104, 1987.

51. Guterman, S., et. al. The first 3 years of Medicare prospective payment: An overview. *Health Care Financ. Rev.* 9(3): 67–77, 1988.

52. American Hospital Association. *Hospital Statistics: 1987 Edition.* Chicago, 1987.

53. Guy, B. Return on equity—how much profit must a not-for-profit hospital earn? *Hosp. Top.* 65(1): 9–11, 1987.

54. Roper, W., et. al. Effectiveness in health care: An initiative to evaluate and improve medical practice. *N. Engl. J. Med.* 319: 1197–1202, 1988.

55. Nash, D. Hospitals and their medical staffs: High anxiety. *Front. Health Serv. Manage.* 4(3): 24–26, 1988.

56. Mayer, H. Payers to use protocols to assess treatment plans. *Am. Med. News,* December 9, 1988, pp. 1, 62–64.

57. Prudential sets insurance precedent. *Chicago Tribune,* July 27, 1988, Sec. 1, p. 1.

58. Dranove, D., White, W. D., and Wu, L. An Analysis of Admission Patterns in Local Hospital Markets. Unpublished working paper. Graduate School of Business, University of Chicago, April 1989.

59. Garnick, D., et. al. Appropriate measures of hospital market areas. *Health Serv. Res.* 22(1): 69–89, 1987.

60. Morrisey, M., Sloan, F., and Valvona, J. Defining geographic markets for hospitals and the extent of market concentration. *Law Contemp. Probl.,* 1989, in press.

61. Cowing, T. G., et. al. Hospital cost analysis: Survey and evaluation of recent studies. In *Advances in Health Economics and Health Services Research*, Vol. 4, edited by R. Scheffler and L. Rossiter. JAI Press, Greenwich, Conn., 1983.
62. Mullner, R., and Hadley, J. Interstate variations in the growth of chain-owned proprietary hospitals, 1973–1982. *Inquiry* 21: 144–151, 1984.
63. American Hospital Association. *Directory of Multihospital Systems: 1985 Edition.* Chicago, 1985.
64. American Hospital Association. *Directory of Multihospital Systems: 1983 Edition.* Chicago, 1983.
65. Ermann, D., and Gabel, J. Multihospital systems: Issues and empirical findings. *Health Aff.* 3(1): 50–64, 1984.
66. Friedman, B. Hospital Restructuring Under PPS and Competitive Pressures. Unpublished working paper. Hospital Research and Educational Trust, Chicago, July 1988.
67. Bell, C. 1987: Multi-unit providers. *Mod. Healthcare* 17(12): 37–58, 1987.
68. Greene, J. Multihospital systems: Systems went back to basics in 87, restructuring to stay competitive. *Mod. Healthcare* 18(22): 45–117, 1988.
69. Berliner, H., and Burlage, R. Proprietary hospital chains and academic medical centers. *Int. J. Health Serv.* 17(1): 27–46, 1987.
70. Feder, J., and Hadley, J. A threat or a promise: Acquisition of teaching hospitals by investor-owned chains. *J. Health Polit. Policy Law* 12(2): 325–342, 1987.
71. Kenkel, P. HMOs/PPOs: Multi-unit providers survey: Managed-care growth continued in 1987 despite companies' poor operating results. *Mod. Healthcare* 18(23): 20–89, 1988.
72. Alexander, J., Lewis, B., and Morrisey, M. Acquisition strategies of multihospital systems. *Health Aff.* 4(3): 5–31, 1985.
73. Starkweather, D., and Carman, J. Horizontal and vertical concentration in the evolution of hospital competition. In *Advances in Health Economics and Health Services Research*, Vol. 7, edited by R. Scheffler and L. Rossiter, pp. 179–194. JAI Press, Greenwich, Conn., 1987.
74. Begun, J., et. al. Strategic behavior patterns of small multi-institutional health organizations. In *Advances in Health Economics and Health Services Research,* Vol. 7, edited by R. Scheffler and L. Rossiter, pp. 194–214. JAI Press, Greenwhich, Conn., 1987.
75. Sloan, F., Morrisey, M., and Valvona, J. Capital markets and the growth of multihospital systems. In *Advances in Health Economics and Health Services Research*, Vol. 7, edited by R. Scheffler and L. Rossiter, pp. 83–109. JAI Press, Greenwich, Conn., 1987.
76. Cromwell, J., et al. Comparative trends in hospital expenses, finances, utilization, and inputs, 1970-81. *Health Care Financ. Rev.* 9(1): 51–69, 1987.
77. Anderson, G. F. Data watch: National medical care spending. *Health Aff.* 5(3): 123–130, 1986.
78. Perry, L. Brand names invade the healthcare market: But it takes more than a sleek image to lure consumers. *Mod. Healthcare* 18(21): 22–29, 1988.
79. Morrisey, M., and Alexander, J. Hospital participation in multihospital systems. In *Advances in Health Economics and Health Services Research,* Vol. 7, edited by R. Scheffler and L. Rossiter, pp. 59–82. JAI Press, Greenwhich, Conn., 1987.
80. Jacobs, P. A survey of economic models of hospitals. *Inquiry* 11(2): 83–97, 1973.
81. Lewin, L., Eckels, T., and Miller, L. Setting the record straight: The provision of uncompensated care by not-for-profit hospitals. *N. Engl. J. Med.* 318(18): 1212–1215, 1988.
82. Weil, P., and Stewart, J. Testimony. In *Proceedings: The Corporatization of Health Care: A Two-day Symposium and Public Hearing,* edited by J. W. Salmon and J. Todd, pp. 83–93. Illinois Public Health Association, Springfield, Ill., 1988.

83. Luke, R., and Begun, J. Strategic orientations of small multihospital systems. *Health Serv. Res.* 23(5): 598–618, 1988.
84. McClain, J. O., and Thomas, L. J. *Operations Management: Production of Goods and Services.* Prentice-Hall, Englewood Cliffs, N.J., 1985.
85. Piore, M. J., and Sabel, C. F. *The Second Industrial Divide: Possibilities for Prosperity.* Basic Books, New York, 1984.
86. Goldsmith, J. Competition's impact: A report from the front. *Health Aff.* 7(3): 162–173, 1988.

Originally published in the International Journal of Health Services, Volume 20, Number 1, Pages 85–114, 1990.

# CHAPTER 2

# Walk-In Chains: The Proprietarization of Ambulatory Care

## Howard S. Berliner and Robb K. Burlage

Ambulatory care, after a slower start than acute or long-term care, has become a major target of proprietary firms (1, 2). While it is not difficult to understand why ambulatory care should now be an object for corporatization and proprietarization, the reasons it has lagged behind other dimensions of health services in this regard are more complicated.

Led by the rapid growth of for-profit Health Maintenance Organization (HMO) companies and the diversification of proprietary hospital management corporations into ambulatory care, Wall Street analysts have been promoting and predicting rapid growth and high earnings from this new modality (3).

We examine in particular the growth of free-standing ambulatory care units including urgent care centers, surgi-centers, ambulatory diagnostics and HMOs. We do not address related institutionally based ambulatory care alternatives.

### AMBULATORY SURGERY

Ambulatory surgery was the earliest of the free-standing ambulatory care developments. Its initial growth was spurred largely by technological developments in anesthesia which allowed for complete awakening within twelve hours. Its more recent growth is a result of changes in health insurance policies which now encourage out-of-hospital procedures. The first ambulatory surgery center was located in Providence, Rhode Island, and began operation in 1968. In 1970, the Surgicenter began operation in Phoenix, Arizona, and within two years had performed 70,000 operations with no fatalities and no transfers to a hospital. By

1982 there were between 100 and 150 free-standing ambulatory surgery centers in the United States (4). A 1984 survey of 253 free-standing centers across the U.S. showed 164 were independently owned, mostly by physicians; 64 were owned by chains and 25 were owned by hospitals (5, p. 82). The vast majority of institutional ambulatory surgery (over 90 percent) is still controlled by hospitals however (5, p. 88). Prices for ambulatory surgery average 50 percent of the charges for an in-patient procedure, and for this reason insurance companies are increasingly demanding that subscribers in need of surgery that can be safely performed on an outpatient basis should use such services.

Proprietary surgicenters have been plagued by poor performance and an inability to make profits. Wall Street analysts have been cautioning investors to steer away from these centers until they can demonstrate a better profitability rate (6, 7).

## URGENT CARE CENTERS

Urgent care centers provide episodic and routine care for 12–16 hours per day, seven days per week. The first urgent care center was established in Rhode Island in 1975, and over 2500 units are in existence today (4). Urgent care has seen the greatest growth of all forms of ambulatory care in recent years. Data from the National Association of Freestanding Ambulatory Care (the trade organization which recently changed its name from the National Association of Freestanding Emergency Care after the threat of legal suits by hospitals over the use of the word emergency) indicate an expansion from 1100 urgent care units in 1983 to 2300 in 1984 (8). The sources of support for growth have been varied: approximately 3 percent comes from venture capital, 49 percent from debt finance (in many cases backed by personal or professional assets), 32 percent from internal finances, 14 percent from outside investors, and 2 percent from other sources (6). Most urgent care centers are still owned by their original owners who were primarily physician-entrepreneurs.

The growth of corporate urgent care, particularly subsidiaries of hospital management firms (e.g. Humana's MedFirst chain), has bright prospects ahead according to Wall Street analysts (9). When a large number of units are operated within a discrete geographic area mass advertising becomes cost-effective and certain economies of scale are achieved. This gives impetus to groups with the wherewithal to expand to reach the critical unit size. This movement towards franchising has earned urgent care centers the sobriquet "docs-in-a-box," a phrase as descriptive as it is humorous.

A factor aiding the growth of urgent care is the price. The fees of the average urgent care center are generally 40–60 percent lower than typical emergency room fees and roughly comparable to the charges of solo physicians. The urgent care center, however, features a brief wait to see a physician (generally less than 20 minutes or the visit is free) and the absence of necessity to schedule appointments in advance.

Many urgent care centers have sought to build a steady client base rather than a strict reliance on episodic walk-in patients. This is most particularly true of those centers that are owned by hospitals or by hospital chains, which use the centers as patient feeders or as organizational loci for prepaid insurance schemes. Because urgent care centers tend to be set up in affluent areas and because they require payment at the time of service delivery, even by credit card, they tend to have low bad debt experience. By referring away those patients whose needs are more serious and who may need more intensive and expensive treatment, they tend to be profitable. Despite the ease of making a profit in urgent care, the margins will be higher if the costs can be spread over a larger patient base. Increasing the patient volume also helps in rationalizing staffing patterns and supply schedules. New services that urgent care centers offer include general primary care; pre-exercise program physicals and stress testing; and international traveler checkup and vaccination services (10). It seems likely that the continued growth of urgent care center hybrids will come to look exactly like small group practices (11).

While the origin of urgent care can be found in a rising physician surplus and the high costs of initiating private practice, the proprietary chain penetration of this modality of care leads to its drastic alteration. Rather than keeping people away from the hospital and replacing costly and medically unnecessary emergency room visits, the urgent care centers that belong to hospital chains are explicitly designed to feed patients to the hospitals. This makes the hospitals less dependent on their voluntary attending staff, and shores up declining occupancy rates.

## AMBULATORY DIAGNOSTIC CENTERS

Free-standing ambulatory diagnostic centers have their origins in expanding medical technology and the restrictions placed on hospitals by Certificate of Need (CON) regulations. The computerization and the miniaturization of medical technology has allowed for its deployment outside the hospital. Medical entrepreneurs, seeing the difficulties confronting hospitals petitioning Health Systems Agencies for new equipment such as Computerized Axial Tomography (CAT) scanners and Nuclear Magnetic Resonance (NMR) imagers, began to buy such equipment, hire staff and provide the services themselves without any State regulation.

In some cases it is the access to capital that has fostered the growth of proprietary diagnostic care. Many hospitals have been effectively barred from obtaining new equipment and new technology not so much by CON regulations as by the institution's lack of access to capital. Proprietary firms as well as individual entrepreneurs have moved in to fill the gap. An example of this process is the series of magnetic resonance imaging centers that AMI Corporation has contracted to build and operate for some teaching hospitals that needed the new technology but couldn't afford it, including the University of California and the University of Utah (12; see also 13).

## HEALTH MAINTENANCE ORGANIZATIONS

The first of the proprietary HMO corporations began operation in 1981 having converted from a not-for-profit tax status to be better able to obtain access to capital for expansion (14). By 1984 there were 60 proprietary HMOs (21 percent of all HMOs) (15). The largest, HealthAmerica has over 700,000 enrollees spread over plans in 31 markets in 19 states (16). Recent projections call for proprietary HMOs to have over 50 percent of the HMO market, a market that is expanding at almost 20 percent per year (17–19). Most of the new growth is expected to come from large markets that were previously impenetrable to any extent to prepaid care. There are, for example, 30 different firms currently competing for market share in Chicago with a projected enrollment of 20 percent of the population by 1990 (20). Similarly there are 20 applications pending in New York State by firms interested in establishing HMOs, including 13 by proprietary firms (21). One of these, U.S. Health Care Systems, aims for 800,000 enrollees (almost 10 percent of the market) in New York within 5 years (22).

One reason for the growth of proprietary as well as not-for-profit HMOs has been the push by corporate employers and unions to control costs. Because an HMO's cost to an employer is known in advance, they have become the favorite form of health insurance coverage of benefits managers (23). It was announced recently by General Motors Corporation that workers in the new Saturn plan in Tennessee will not be given traditional health insurance, but will only be able to get HMO care (21).

Proprietary HMOs have the ability to raise capital for startup costs. Because most of these HMOs are of the IPA type, that is they utilize existing physicians offices, their actual physical capital needs are small. Instead they use the capital generated for promotion and advertising and to subsidize the first few years so that they can build market share by under-cutting competitors on a cost basis. Not-for-profit HMOs do not have this advantage and as a result many are switching their status. Alternatively, some not-for-profits have set up proprietary subsidiaries so they can raise capital more easily, without having to change their auspices (24, 25).

The Health Care Finance Administration (HCFA) of the U.S. Department of Health and Human Services in 1985 paved the way for the elderly to participate in HMOs through the Medicare system. HCFA has agreed to pay approved HMOs 95 percent of the average annual per capita cost (AAPCC) that it would pay for a Medicare recipient in a particular region (26). In this manner Medicare feels that it could save money and at the same time provide more complete protection for elderly recipients. Considerable activity has been generated through this mechanism, although it is too soon to have any empirical results. Many states have been attempting to increase the number of Medicaid enrollees in HMOs as well. These two payers may add significant numbers of enrollees to HMOs of all kinds around the country. To date, the experience with such kinds of patients has not been good (27). The elderly and the poor utilize more services and thus are more costly for the HMOs than their typical patient. Moreover, both groups must agree to substantial limitations of their freedom of choice of providers and services if they accept these new arrangements. Whether this will change with new aggressive management techniques or whether enrollment of sufficient numbers of healthy people within HMOs will mitigate the effects of the elderly and the poor remains to be seen.

When the HMO Act of 1973 mandated the dual choice option in areas with federally certified HMOs, it was thought that this form of medical practice would prosper (28). The requirement to offer HMOs as a fringe benefit if any other health insurance was given seemed a sure way to increase the public awareness of HMOs as well as guarantee a substantial marketing edge over indemnity plans. That HMOs did not flourish has been attributed in part to the fact that they were required to price their services on a community-rating basis and were required to offer long open enrollment periods and wide benefits (27). Since that time many for-profit HMOs have either dropped their federal certification or decided not to attempt to acquire it in order to compete more easily with commercial insurance plans, Blue Cross or with other HMOs (29).

## ANALYSIS

Growth prospects for proprietary ambulatory care are rated as extremely good by virtually all Wall Street analysts. Since the ability of proprietary firms to generate capital stems in large measure from the willingness of investors to take risks based on the analysis provided them by market researchers, the importance of such favorable ratings cannot be overstated.

Because favorable growth is so instrumental in selling stock, and in generating publicity about individual companies or industries which leads to further investment, it is easy to speculatively create a boom atmosphere in which growth is self-propelled. To a large extent this is what has been happening over the past year in ambulatory care and is a partial explanation for both the Wall Street downturns of hospital stocks and the upswings of ambulatory care offerings.

One of the major incentives for the growth of proprietary ambulatory care was the Omnibus Tax Reform bill of 1981. This legislation allowed for the accelerated depreciation of commercial properties. Entrepreneurs had found that medical clinics were ideal investments, particularly for smaller scale investors. Widely represented among these entrepreneurs were physicians looking for new investment opportunities in the field they knew best (30). The earliest surgicenters and urgent care centers as well as diagnostic centers were owned by physicians. Their model was emulated by large scale corporate investors or they were bought out by established proprietary firms. Not only were ambulatory clinics more or less outside the purview of health facility regulatory agencies, but there was considerably less public interest in proprietary ambulatory care than in proprietary hospital ownership or nursing home ownership. The benefits of multiple facilities in terms of efficiencies and economies of scale led many individual entrepreneurs to seek other investors in their enterprises as well.

Another factor that aided the growth of ambulatory care was the availability of venture capital and its rapid influx into the health system. Building on the successful base of hospital and nursing home chains, significant sums of money were available to entrepreneurs with new methods and/or skills to market their ideas successfully. Many corporations, seeing rapid and sustained growth in health care, began to make large sums of money available for corporate spin-offs. Hospital management firms also devoted a considerable portion of their available funds to ambulatory care, thinking of vertical integration and new ways to keep their beds filled (31).

The growth in ambulatory care has come at a time when a large surplus of physicians exists in the U.S. It has become increasingly difficult to start a solo private practice today due to the heavy debt that most physicians accrue during medical school and residency and the increasing costs of renting, staffing and equipping an office, not to mention increased malpractice premiums. Thus, for an increasing number of young physicians, the chance to begin their careers on a salary with bonus potentials and little worry about overhead and administrative costs comes as a welcome relief (32). That the large surplus of physicians and the increasing competition for positions has also driven down starting salaries has made it considerably easier for corporate health firms to start ambulatory ventures (33).

For individual entrepreneurs, the drive to ambulatory care has been based on three major factors. (a) The ability to generate profits with relatively small investments. (b) The ability to evade the regulatory (CON) process in those states that restrict entry to the health field. As noted earlier, private clinics and ambulatory facilities are exempt from regulation in most states. Even in states where health facilities are highly regulated, individual physicians or non-physician entrepreneurs have been able to acquire expensive technology while the access of hospitals to the same equipment is restricted. (c) The hope to sell out while the price is still high. Knowing that the large chains are interested in ambulatory care gives entrepreneurs an incentive to establish systems that can be profitably sold to the chains at a later date.

For hospitals the drive to ambulatory care has been based on four major factors. (a) The ability to evade the regulatory process as described above. Hospitals have created spin-off ambulatory care centers that can acquire technology the larger institution is denied. Moreover, the new spin-offs allow the institution to control access to the technology (i.e. require payment for services) that would be difficult within the hospital. (*b*) Profits. The ambulatory centers can be quite profitable and generate revenues that the hospital can utilize to subsidize other less profitable activities. (*c*) Patient capture. If patients utilize ambulatory facilities in which the physicians have affiliations with a particular hospital, they are more likely to use that hospital for their regular inpatient care needs. Hospitals can thus use ambulatory care centers to fill their empty beds by reaching out to areas beyond or outside the traditional service market of the institution. (*d*) Physician capture. Hospitals need physicians to put the patients in their beds and to order the ancillary tests that generate revenues for the hospital. By providing physicians with offices and handling the administrative tasks, hospitals have been able to get physicians to admit their patients exclusively to the responsible hospital.

For proprietary hospital corporations the drive to ambulatory care has been based on all the above mentioned factors as well as two additional ones. (*a*) Because the hospital business is a limited one, proprietary corporations have sought to ensure their survival by becoming insurance firms, that is by integrating health care finance with delivery. To accomplish this, the corporations need a primary care base strategically clustered around their hospitals. (*b*) Brand recognition. The hospital companies have an interest in having their entire system known to the public. Putting their name on primary care centers and diagnostic centers as well as hospitals helps to create a recognition of their name in the public mind. When health care of any type is desired, the various institutions of the corporation will be thought of as able to deliver it.

## PROSPECTS AND IMPLICATIONS

Proprietary ambulatory care, like proprietary hospital care, profits by selective marketing and pricing. It has no interest in poor people, but only in those who can pay best for their services and for the convenience of a fast appointment. Above and beyond the direct evaluation issues of quality, fragmentation and continuity of these ambulatory services, more basic questions must be addressed. How will public hospitals and whatever remaining voluntary institutions provide indigent care handle the load that will be left for them by the new ambulatory-oriented proprietary chains? How will the inevitable market shakeout affect the provision of care to those who have bought into the weaker systems?

In conclusion, while the availability of ambulatory services rather than high technology acute care might in theory be a social good, selective profit-making networking and marketing of ambulatory services could remain part of a doubly obstructed road to social efficiency. Only with public and community based services with universal population coverage can the apparent private efficiencies of appropriate levels of care be transformed fully into a truly socially cost-effective health system.

While over-hospitalization was a major problem in the retrospective cost reimbursement era, the specter of under-care looms large as the problem of today. It is possible that low-income people will face a greater inability to obtain hospital care (through reduced capacity and stricter utilization review) as well as an inability to obtain ambulatory services. With decreasing inpatient capacity and ambulatory care restricted to those who can afford its price, larger numbers of people may be left without services. The problem is potentiated by the increasing number of nonprofit chains and institutions that seek to emulate the financial success of their proprietary counterparts.

Individual state actions aimed at improving access for the indigent are helpful so far as they go. In most states that have instituted bad debt and charity care pools, however, these have been oriented toward inpatient rather than ambulatory care, and in all cases apply only to institutional services. Thus it seems that the states have not learned the appropriate lessons of deinstitutionalization.

Ambulatory care is not exempt from the economic pressures that confront all facets of health care delivery in the U.S. The provision of primary care services through entities organized along profit-making lines is the direct outcome of a system that has placed profits in front of people. Based on all the attention devoted to ambulatory care because of its lower costs, it is highly probable that the trends toward increased proprietary penetration of ambulatory care will continue.

## POSTSCRIPT

Reading the health services literature more recently, after the turn of the decade, one does not find the same number of references to the growth of proprietary ambulatory care as was evident five years ago. In fact, it is fair to say that while ambulatory care is still widely perceived as the major growth area in health services for the '90s, proprietary ambulatory care has definitely been significantly diminished. What are the reasons why an area which showed so much promise only recently has lost its appeal? The remainder of this chapter examines the reasons that proprietary ambulatory care has lost its luster.

### THE DECLINE OF THE FOR-PROFIT CHAINS

Although the proprietary hospital chains were instrumental in lobbying Congress for the passage of PPS because they felt that they could profit from DRGs, they, in fact, did not do very well. The squeeze on the chains, caused by low occupancy rates and then intensified by the reimbursement pressures exerted by PPS, forced all of the for-profit hospital chains into decline. As growth rates fell and earnings tumbled, the chains were forced to divest themselves of their more marginal properties. The ventures in proprietary ambulatory care, not yet generating self-sustaining revenues, were among the first to go. In most cases the ambulatory care units were sold to other buyers—they did not go out of business—but because these ventures are no longer owned by public firms and therefore able to be researched in annual reports and 10K statements, we have lost the ability to follow them as easily.

Some of the ambulatory care operations were bought by the for-profit subsidiaries of not-for-profit hospitals. These units tend to receive almost no publicity so that their organizational connections to the parent firm are not widely exposed. A situation is created in which the activity is present but the tracking of that activity is disabled.

One of the keys to ambulatory surgery was the expectation of reimbursement rates that would support the higher overhead of an ambulatory facility over a physician's office. However, the rates from many payers have not been high enough to generate a significant profit. As a result, much ambulatory surgery occurs in physicians' offices rather than in surgicenters.

The demise of the federal health planning program and the subsequent elimination of CON statutes in many states has allowed facilities to again acquire medical technology without regulatory oversight. As a result, much of the raison d'être of proprietary ambulatory diagnostics may have evaporated. Most people feel more secure receiving high technology services in a hospital, and utilize an ambulatory facility for those services only when a hospital does not have the equipment or provides it in an inconvenient manner. With the hospital's acquisition of the equipment, and the ability to operate on a 24 hour schedule, it is likely that the market for ambulatory diagnostics severely eroded.

The market for branded national ambulatory care is not as large as many may have thought. Health care is a local product and consumers see it in local terms with few advantages accruing to national identity except in those cases where quality is paramount—thus the Mayo Clinic has opened branches in Florida and Arizona—and attracts business based on its name. Hospitals with good local reputations may also be able to capitalize on an ambulatory care market. But the evidence of the past five years would indicate that no firm can garner enough support to make a substantial business in ambulatory care. This is particularly true when firms do not have deep enough pockets to sustain the building of a market over several years. Even in areas where proprietary hospital firms have substantial market share, a movement into ambulatory care provision might threaten physicians and drive them away from the hospital chain, threatening an even larger profit center. Federal regulations now limit the kinds of incentives physicians can receive (and hospitals can provide) to encourage use of a particular hospital. Hospital chains may well have decided that the ambulatory market is not yet mature enough to risk giving up the lucrative inpatient market. Firms which have tried to market ambulatory care services directly to employers have found that there is also less of a market than may have been anticipated. Workers resent such arrangements because they feel that they are getting substandard care and would prefer to receive their care from already established practitioners.

The physician surplus should have been a major factor that would make proprietary ambulatory care a growing operation. If there was a true surplus, corporations could hire doctors to work in primary care settings for a relatively low salary and still charge high enough prices to make a profit. Yet, there seems to be little market for proprietary primary care physicians—physicians seem to prefer the relative freedom of HMOs and PPOs to the stricter regulations of small ambulatory care operations.

Physicians given a financial incentive to produce more have little trouble producing such business. It is possible that patients are aware of this possibility and feel more security in either better established ambulatory care settings or in hospital emergency rooms or outpatient departments.

The numbers of people who can pay for their own care and do not have easy access to a physician are perhaps too few to support a proprietary ambulatory care system. People may prefer to deal with hospitals than to go to physicians working in "docs-in-a boxes." Such physicians may also feel that they are in an unstable environment and choose to move into a more stable type of practice setting. Also, as physicians seek to gain market share from hospitals, they have chosen, in many cases, to resume consumer oriented services such as longer office hours, house calls, and friendlier manners. Thus private practice physicians may be the biggest barrier to the new organization of ambulatory care. It is also possible that local physicians have conspired to collude against docs-in-a-box doctors by denying them hospital appointments and referrals.

It also seems that HMO utilization has peaked with relatively flat membership over the past year. HMOs had about 30 million people enrolled in 1990 and may have reached their limit. Similarly, as corporations begin to doubt the ability of managed care systems to provide cost containment, they are less receptive to these forms of organizations and may no longer be pushing their patients into these systems. The HMO systems that generate profits are typically those with large enrollments—over 350,000 members. It is increasingly difficulty for newer HMOs to compete on a long term basis with already established units. Thus, the engine of growth of ambulatory care since 1981 seems to have sputtered to a stop.

It will require a complete historical analysis to determine the reasons why proprietary ambulatory care was not ascendent in the later 1980s. It seems likely, however, that the reasons presented above will be included in such an analysis.

## REFERENCES

1. Wallace, C. Investors cool off hospital companies while interest in alternatives heats up. *Modern Healthcare* July 1984, pp. 120–121.

2. Punch, L. Ambulatory care industry has financial growth pains. *Modern Healthcare,* April 12, 1985, pp. 65–66.
3. Bernstein, K. The future of health care delivery in America. *Bernstein Research,* July 1985.
4. Moxley, J., and Roeder, P. New opportunities for out-of-hospital health services. *N. Engl. J. Med.,* 310: 193–197, 1984.
5. Olson, L. Providers preparing for major battles over market for outpatient surgery. *Modern Healthcare,* September, 1984, p. 82.
6. Grahm, J. Ambulatory care centers may find public offerings will be hard to sell. *Modern Healthcare,* January 4, 1985, p. 62.
7. Punch, L. Surgical center chain sells stock, plans to use $6.8 million to expand. *Modern Healthcare,* November 15, 1984, p. 104.
8. Business-minded health care. *New York Times,* February 12, 1985, p. A1.
9. Vignola, M. Hospital management: The patient capture initiative. *Medinotes L. F. Rothschild, Unterberg, Towbin,* New York, October 29, 1984.
10. Finding that cuts and bruises can't support business, freestanding ambulatory care centers seek to diversify. *Hospitals,* July 16, 1985, p. 62.
11. Fiscal crisis produces financing hybrids. *Hospitals,* December 1, 1984, p. 46.
12. American Medical International Corporation. *Annual Report,* 1984.
13. Diagnostic center breaks the mold. *Medical World News,* February 24, 1986, p. 86.
14. Iglehart, J. HMOs (for-profit and not-for-profit) on the move. *N. Engl. J. Med.* 310: 1205, 1984.
15. Friedman, E. Investor-owneds enter not-for-profits bastion. *Hospitals,* April 16, 1984, p. 100.
16. Vignola, M. Health maintenance organizations. *Medinotes L. F. Rothschild, Unterberg, Towbin,* New York. December 31, 1984.
17. Outlook good for non-profit HMOs. *Hospitals,* March 16, 1985, p. 36–37.
18. Enrollment in typical HMO up 30% in '84 Survey. *Modern Healthcare,* January 17, 1986, p. 24.
19. HMOs will experience explosive growth. *Modern Healthcare,* July 5, 1985, p. 22.
20. Tatge, M. The battle's on for Chicago customers as new entries offer low cost plans. *Modern Healthcare,* April 26, 1985, p. 37.
21. *Modern Healthcare,* September 27, 1985, p. 12.
22. Richman, D. U.S. health care aims at growth push into New York, Dallas. *Modern Healthcare,* September 27, 1985, p. 50.
23. Freudenheim, M. Surge of prepaid health plans. *New York Times.* December 15, 1984, p. 30.
24. HMOs' needs are few. *Modern Healthcare,* March 29, 1985, p. 102.
25. Harvard community health plan creates investor-owned company. *Hospitals,* March 1, 1985, p. 26.
26. Iglehart, J. Medicare turns to HMOs, *N. Engl. J. Med.* 312: 132–136, 1985.
27. Brown, L. *Politics and Health Organization: HMOs as Federal Policy.* Brookings Institution, Washington, D.C., 1983.
28. Salmon, J. The health maintenance organization strategy: A corporate takeover of health services delivery. *Int. J. Health Serv.* 5: 609–624, 1975.
29. HMO operator HealthAmerica willing to drop federal certification to compete with lower benefit levels by insurance companies. *The Blue Sheet.* November 28, 1984, p. 10.
30. Morris, D. Urgent care centers: Should hospitals beware? *Multis,* February 1, 1985, pp. M31-M34.

31. Humana Corporation, *Annual Report*, 1984. Louisville, Ky.
32. Ginzberg, E. (ed.). *The Coming Physician Surplus*. Rowman, Allenheld, Totowa, N.J., 1984.
33. Trauner, J., and Luft, H. A Lifestyle Decision: Facing the Reality of Physician Over-supply in the San Francisco Bay Area. Paper presented at the 2nd Cornell Conference on Health Policy, New York. February, 1986.

Originally published in the International Journal of Health Services, Volume 17, Number 4, Pages 585–594, 1987.

# CHAPTER 3

# The Profitization of Health Promotion

## Nancy Milio

The attention of U.S. health policy in the 1980s has been on the problems of health care delivery, specifically the Federal costs of reimbursement, and not the prospects for Americans' health. In spite of mushrooming problems that bode ill for a large share of the population, Congressional hearings, legislation, policy newsletters and press discussion have focused on medical economics. Across most of the political spectrum, answers to the problems of high medical care costs and of the promotion of health have been sought in the marketplace. Yet, the public consistently supports a strong Federal role in health and thinks the government should do more to promote people's health (1).

The marketplace is an ineffective arena for health development; it generates decision-making paths that obscure the perspective and directions that can best promote Americans' health. In an era of "exporting" U.S. ideas for health care reform to other nations, the prevalent U.S. brand of "health promotion" ought not to be "sold" abroad without a critical examination and awareness of alternatives.

### DEPTH OF THE HEALTH PROBLEM

For too many Americans, the conditions for health have deteriorated and the problems of health have increased in the last decade:

- Low birthweight and infant mortality continue as serious problems, with higher risks of cumulative illness in later years for survivors (2–5);
- Young and old have more disabling chronic illness than 15 years ago (6);

- Income gaps are widening and unemployment continues its untoward effects on health (7–12);
- Public income maintenance programs and minimum wage levels retain people below poverty (13);
- Compensatory jobs, food, and nutrition programs decline in real terms as the numbers of the poor increase (14);
- Well over 35 million people have no health insurance and less than half of the poor are covered by Medicaid (15, 16);
- In spite of publicity about Americans' growing interest in "healthy lifestyles" and "self-responsibility" for health, in the last 10 years, a larger share (a 28 percent increase, especially the poor) are drinking more heavily, becoming obese (a 10 percent increase, especially the affluent and men), and reducing their physical activity (a 12 percent increase in sedentary living, mainly the affluent and women) (17).

## THE MARKETPLACE SOLUTION

In recent years, the answer to this set of problems among policymakers, and a growing share of professionals (18), has been not just privatization, deflecting government responsibility (if not resources) in the nonpublic sector, but more precisely, profitization often extending to corporatization. The assumption is that the "invisible hand" of the marketplace will hone an efficient, cost-controlling health care delivery system for the ill and effectively disseminate the message of self-responsible health promotion for the well. This marketplace version of privatization tends to undermine a sense of collective responsibility and to mask the socioeconomic, occupational, and ecological sources of both health and illness. It thereby casts a further shadow on the prospects for health, especially among disadvantaged groups who do not have the means to enter the market in the first place.

The untoward effects of a market-oriented personal health care system have been widely noted and bear little repeating here (19–23). An important impetus to the recent revolutionary changes in health care financing and organization has been a plethora of Federal policies whose apparent intent is to contain *Federal* costs, without equal regard to non-Federal financial and social costs. Among the less well-known consequences of the privatization of health care have been the increase in self-insurance by corporations, allowing them to avoid premium taxes and mandatory benefits provisions in State laws, and reducing coverage for women, minorities, and the poor (15); the shift to more profitable services by providers (24, 25); the contraction or termination of health care facilities without public or even physician consultation (26); and a growing role by corporations as both purchasers and providers of care in shaping the composition, distribution, and pricing of health services (27). As the Institute of Medicine concluded in its review of profit-making in health care, the once-assumed provider responsibility for meeting community health needs may be disappearing (28).

## A NEW BRAND OF HEALTH PLANNING FOR PROMOTION

As the share of care controlled by corporate systems enlarges, public and especially community involvement in decision-making is becoming increasingly difficult; citizens cannot claim the right to due process in profitized systems as they can from publicly controlled systems and programs. Profitization, especially in its large corporate forms, is becoming a de facto system of nationwide health planning, with new institutions (ranging from Health Coalitions, to manufacturers, financial firms, and advertising agencies) and new decisionmakers accountable to national investors (29); new "target populations" (e.g., the young, "upscale" well); new objectives (e.g., efficient delivery of harm-free services while raising profits); and new strategies. One such strategy is "health promotion," which itself reflects the new style of planning.

## "HEALTH PROMOTION"

With a focus on the well majority of Americans, "health promotion" is the rubric for a range of activities intended to avoid illness and the added burden to the medical care system, among other purposes. These programs are increasingly a 1980s' marketplace variant of health education adopted by the new breed of health decisionmakers, and using methods appropriate to their entrepreneurial experience.

About half of the Fortune 500 have "Wellness" programs, costing them 0.1 percent of net profits, in contrast to their costs for employee health insurance coverage at 24 percent of profits (30). The extent of this attempt at cost reduction nationwide involves as many as two-thirds of worksites with over 50 employees which report having health promotion programs (31).

### Decision Apparatus

Such programs are adopted not by community health, public, or consumer boards but by high level corporate managers who wish to recruit and retain expensive personnel, lower their medical care outlays, and increase worker productivity (32–34); by private and commercial insurers who can increase their own revenues up to 45 percent by offering Wellness coverage to employers (30, 35); and by multi-hospital system marketing directors who seek public "name-recognition" of their "products" and opportunities to "sell" their expensive inpatient services (36).

Further, a new generation of "participatory" planning organizations, the local Health Coalitions, has sprung up in the 1980s, following the demise of Federally supported health systems agencies (HSA). There were 163 of these private equivalents of HSAs in 1986, almost all (96 percent) of which included employers; most included hospitals (75 percent), medical societies (72 percent), and commercial insurers (60 percent); just over a third (36 percent) included labor unions. Their main sources of financing were business, hospital, and health insurance firms. Collectively they "represented" 25 million employees and dependents. Among those who have joined together to help shepherd these coalitions are the American Hospital Association and Washington Business Group on Health, an offspring of the influential corporate body, the Business Roundtable (37). One recent event that may be an augur for the future tenor and make-up of Coalitions was the Washington, D.C., Coalition's decision to place its medical, labor, and consumer groups in an advisory role, so that its remaining business and employer members could more aggressively pursue deregulation and other issues to lower costs (38). Most of the agendas of these coalitions focus on monitoring and reducing personal health care costs, but half are also involved in legislative activities and half also deal with health promotion and Wellness program issues.

A survey of 400 California firms with over 99 employees showed that those most often involved in the decision to adopt Wellness programs were chief executive officers (75 percent) or personnel heads (70 percent); employee benefits (85 percent) and personnel offices (63 percent) were most commonly involved in operating them. Only in a minority did health and safety (37 percent) or medical departments (28 percent) run the programs or take part in the adoption decisions (12 percent of companies) (39). Apparently, there were no questions in the survey about employees, their involvement in program design, or whether they wanted such programs as an option to other benefits.

Two-thirds had one or more health promotion activities, the largest firms having the most. Their main sources of program information were insurance brokers (68 percent), and professional media (57 percent) or associations (40 percent). The implications drawn by the researchers included advice to public health professionals to "promote" health promotion to targeted audiences, such as personnel managers and insurance brokers. No mention was made of labor unions or employee groups (39).

This pattern of Wellness programming by large corporations and commercial insurers is revealed in other studies showing that management and insurer decisions to use Wellness activities are based on hopes for medical cost containment (40), setting program priorities according to economic criteria (41). One large evaluation survey aimed at measuring both the impact of preventive education on individual worker behavior as well as organizational barriers to preventive interventions, paradoxically included no questions related to environmental problems or needed changes, nor were questions directed to management personnel (42). This, in spite of trade union collaboration in the study design.

Yet the thrust of workers' responses among 13 plants covering 124,000 blue collar personnel showed their greater concern over workplace than lifestyle issues, greater confidence in Health and Safety Committees in making needed changes than in management, and interest in worksite programs rather than lifestyle programs—except for stress management, which could be viewed as a sign of environmentally induced problems (42).

There is at least some evidence to suggest that employer interests in employee health and job commitment might be better rewarded by giving attention to job characteristics—such as greater autonomy and supervisory support—rather than specific worker behaviors to defend against risky environments that require change (43, 44).

*Program Design*

The typical approach to worksite health promotion focuses on changing the individual worker's habits rather than the conditions under which she or he works. They mainly consists of designs that bring the best short-term gains to the sponsor, not necessarily the largest gains in health for the workers. For example, the most popular (among employers) of large corporations' Wellness programs are physical examinations. Risk reduction programs tend to be single component, top-down designs known to be least effective for long-term behavior changes (32, 45). A recent and rare controlled study of a competitive/incentive worksite quit-smoking program concluded that "long term [non-smoking] maintenance will be as difficult as it is for clinic-based" interventions. Despite special relapse-prevention measures, there was no difference between experimental and control groups (46, p. 14).

*Delivery Channels*

Consistent with the marketplace mentality, health promotion is literally being commodified, packaged, brand-labeled, and sold or franchised through advertising techniques. The entrepreneurs of these licensed "products" are hospital corporations, insurance firms, or other corporations such as Control Data (47).

Marketing departments in the largest health care corporations are more likely to use commercial techniques, advertising through the electronic media and by direct mail (36). The trademark "Balance," for example, sells a counseling service for eating disorders; a hospital can buy the license for this "product" for a year at $25,000, which includes marketing materials and an advertising campaign. An "Ask a Nurse," advertising a hospital information service, successfully added 100 telephone inquiries per day, and generated increased patient volume per month of 100 emergency room visits, 10 hospital admissions, and 150 physician referrals (36).

This selling of promotion and its "feeder" effects into medical services— arguably not contributing to cost containment—has been indirectly supported by the deregulatory and privatizing policies of the Federal Trade Commission,

Federal Communications Commission, and the burgeoning of the new information technologies (48, 49). Not only are multi-state corporations knit together by telecommunications and computers, but they also have become a market themselves for health-related software and hardware, expected to reach $2 billion by 1990. Corporate employers, for example, are buying more health software than are health care institutions and physicians combined, and health-related interactive video training systems are being used for executives, staff, consumers, patients, and students (50).

## Target Populations

The varieties of health promotion programs do not necessarily focus on high risk groups. Wellness programs of corporate employers and insurers are mainly for low risk, young, upper middle class and/or unionized personnel (45, 51). Such programs overall affect less than 5 percent of the labor force (30, 52).

Programs are also aimed at consumer "markets" in affluent communities, such as a franchised 10 month exercise "package" offered by hospitals to pregnant women for $450 as a "turnkey operation" to fill obstetrical beds, or CPR courses offered by hospitals for similar purposes, and health fairs designed as sites to promote HMO sales (36).

In effect, to whatever extent Wellness programs improve health, they are addressed to those groups who need them least but who can most readily enter the market (or by their insured status are part of the market).

## New Training and Personnel

Taken together, this proliferation in program development and distribution suggests an acceleration of Health Promotion as a "growth sector" in the health business. Another prognostic sign and indicator of active entrepreneurial interest is a joint project of the Federal Bureau of Health Professions and the American College of Preventive Medicine, financed by a large commercial insurer, Equitable, and the largest U.S. for-profit hospital chain, Hospital Corporation of America. The three-year effort developed Recommendations and Strategies for Educating Health Professionals (53) in "health promotion," a term which was not defined. Among the guidelines were educational collaboration and coordination with industry, including internships, field placements, and curriculum development based on, among other things, employers' needs for certain types of health promotion skills for their prospective health professions employees.

## ALTERNATIVE VIEWS AND DIRECTIONS

Education in health promotion, for health professionals, the rest of the workforce, or the consuming public, may become another pleasant-sounding addition to the vocabulary of the American Way. The growing entrepreneurial interest in activities that carry this label, and growing health care system collaboration with industry interests at all levels of development and delivery, warrant caution about the principal aims and subsequent results of this marketable form of health promotion. Is the emphasis *health* or (commercial) promotion? (54).

One minimum assumption must be that profit-oriented interests would not be involved unless they expected an acceptable return on investment. Whether their profits are also in the public's health interest is an issue to be judged by the evidence. However, relatively little empirical data currently exist, or they are difficult to obtain, not being in the public domain. Further, few companies have devoted adequate resources to systematically evaluate their health promotion programs (55).

Individual programs are most often evaluated according to short run economic returns (mainly derived from reduced absenteeism) rather than the effects upon people's health. When health or behavior changes have been assessed, the effects, as suggested above, have been temporary, equivocal, neutral or maintained only when direct economic incentives were continued for workers (35, 51, 56, 57).

There has been no definitive study showing the cost-effectiveness of such programs. Large, white collar employers, such as Prudential Life Insurance, claim 40–60 percent reductions in absenteeism for fitness program participants. Other large financial and manufacturing firms report $2 to $6 in benefits over program costs, although the National Heart Lung and Blood Institute could demonstrate only $1.60 in benefits from hypertension control programs (47, 58). Individual company studies show small and unimportant health benefits (e.g., the loss of one pound in overweight participants after 5 years) or higher gains for more favored (e.g., salaried vs. blue collar) workers (59). Some studies show employer health care cost reductions but cannot relate them to improvements in employee fitness. These findings have led to speculations that a "Hawthorne effect" is operating and that an equal employer investment in other types of employee benefits would yield similar results (60).

*Some Uncosted Consequences*

The profitization of "health promotion" has had some untoward effects. It has contributed to making the North American meaning of "health promotion" not a goal but a product; not a process to engage people in finding individual and collective ways to improve health, but an attractive, saleable package to be "added on" to consumers' lives; not a means to direct health-giving resources toward vulnerable groups and communities, but rather the focusing of information resources on the relatively affluent; not a set of health-effective program strategies but an income-preserving and income-producing technique for investors.

The presumed efficacy of the marketplace seems also to have been "sold" to many health professionals, who have taken on its marketing jargon and methods in academic, research, and service programs (54, 61). This occurs as public health in the U.S. itself has become more narrowly focused, personal health services-oriented, and less environmentally sensitive, if the *American Journal of Public Health* is an effective monitor of trends (62). Even health departments, under the prevention/promotion label, are using relatively ineffective single-risk factor "targets" and more informational and media methods instead of population-based planning, organization, and advocacy (45, 63). For example, posters, brochures, and public service announcements in the media exhort women to seek early prenatal care, to eat a balanced diet, and to avoid smoking. A more health-effective effort might extend prenatal care programs, food programs, and designated-smoking-area laws, and develop the organizational constituency needed to have such policies reach fiscal priority, locally and nationally. A report by the Centers for Disease Control suggests that restrictive smoking policies have broader, longer lasting effects than individualistic methods. They may not only reduce a health hazard for smokers and nonsmokers, but also foster long-term acceptability of further policy changes, discouraging potential smokers. Further, the current increase in smoke-free worksite policies has occurred not because of employer initiative but more often because of local or state public policy requirements (64).

Individual-oriented and information-driven health strategies may be comparatively low cost in economic and political terms, but they also displace attention and resources from such profoundly health-important workplace problems as, for example, unemployment, or control over the adoption and use of new technologies (65, 66). One job-related, modestly health-promoting action, for example, was suggested by a recent study for Congress on worker support during plant closings. It showed that most (76 percent) of some 1.3 million displaced employees (during 1983 and 1984) were from larger firms (with over 99 workers), and that two-thirds of the companies gave workers less than 15 days advance notice, but shorter notice, and less financial and reemployment help, if any, to blue collar and non-unionized workers (67). Public policy requiring reasonable advance notice and transition support to buffer the health-damaging strains of job loss (68, 69) may well do more to promote the health of more employees and their families than such health promotion programs as stress management classes alone.

The current official Federal policy view of "health promotion" is institutionalized in the Office of Disease Prevention and Health Promotion. It retains an individualistic focus, in which the main resource distributed to promote health is information (70). Not surprisingly, given this view and the other policies noted at the outset, many of the 1990 Health Promotion Objectives, concerning disadvantaged groups in particular, are almost certainly unattainable (16, 70).

*Other Directions*

Some nations, less imbued with faith in individualistic strategies, are both advocating (71–73) and adopting far broader approaches to the promotion of health (74–76). They are using not the marketplace but the arena of public policy as the more effective ground on which collective choices can be made about—and called to account for—the collective lifestyle that sets the terms for producers' and consumers', organizations' and individuals' choices (77).

One example of the integration of health criteria into other sectors of public policy is Sweden's Work Environment Act (78). In this Act, occupational safety and health is not restricted to conventional clinical and educational services, but rather is encompassed in a mandate that employers and employees cooperate to establish a good working environment. This is interpreted to mean that working conditions must be adapted to physical and mental capacities in ways that can be co-determined by employees and employers. These adaptations concern such issues as working hours, work organization, job security, specific safety and health measures, and consideration of the effects of piecework on health and safety.

The organizational machinery to deploy this policy involves elected safety delegates, joint labor-management committees, and funding for training, information, research, and evaluation of decision-making and of workplace issues. This is financed by a payroll tax and administered by a national Work Environment Fund. A recent evaluation showed that the safety officers had assumed that activation of the workers would result automatically from the provision of adequate information on health hazards (79). It was found, however, that workers' initiative would develop only if the provision of information was accompanied by dialogue, exchange of experiences, joint problem-solving and participation in decision-making. Efforts were therefore made to take account of workers' experiences and knowledge through group discussions in which the safety officers took part.

There are, of course, people and communities that are unwilling to accept a narrow, individualistic meaning of health promotion (80–82). For example, at least some questions of worksite health promotion have been raised by trade unions, based on the potential for worker coercion, and more so, on the "fundamental shift of responsibility" from employer to employee for health protection (83, p. 70). Again, the issue of priority between individual and environmental change is questioned. The view is that (83, p. 71):

> health-promotion programs can be best conducted by non-profit university, government or community health organizations. The best of these programs will be those that emphasize a wholistic approach to health and look at the whole person—job and community exposures, job and home stress, economic status, existing health problems, lifestyle, and heredity. Ultimately, it is this comprehensive approach which will achieve the healthiest outcome for the largest number of participants.

Within the delivery system, there have been efforts to reorganize and redirect substantive resources toward health-supporting programs and processes, such as a community health center HMO (84) and universal, prevention-oriented, health-advocating service systems (85, 86). These are likely to remain concepts for the near term.

It is perhaps not too much to say that the United States, with its diversity, wealth, and size, is resplendent with creative ideas for healthful change. The problem is to translate those ideas into a social reality that can be collectively and equitably shared. This task cannot be achieved spontaneously; it requires organization, funds, committed people, relevant information, and time. Clearly, where such conditions exist locally, one usually finds communities that promote people's health: the "haves" are also the most likely to "have" health. But these oases are not reachable by the "have-nots," whether they are the poor, minorities, women, or elders.

The only way to ensure equitable access to the conditions that promote health (e.g., decent housing, income, education, health care, and safety and security) is through public policy (77). However imperfect, public policy is the only instrument that can create health-promoting options for those groups that do not have the wealth or power to create their own, to devise a social reality of their choosing. When the living conditions for health exist for groups of people, then perhaps "health promotion" is also less likely to have a "victim-blaming" effect, which is a current and persistent threat.

Health, to be promoted beyond hype, requires a broader view at the level of public policy. The "risk factors" chosen for the focus of attention of "health promotion" have been biological and behavioral. Yet, as noted, more fundamental risks to health are poverty, discrimination, poor living and working conditions, and inadequate education, health care, and community resources. Health proponents could develop a broader agenda, as women's, minority, children's, and environmental advocates have done over the last decade. Even the Committee for Economic Development, composed of the largest U.S. corporations, has, for its own reasons, recognized that the health and well-being of children begins with a broad spectrum of federal policies providing for the schooling of prospective mothers, and support through to birth, early child daycare programs, and primary education. They propose that such options be universally available (87).

But to begin to be effective, an agenda for health, developed and moved by health-concerned organizations, must become part of public policy agendas in such areas as housing, employment and economics, agriculture and environment, transportation, education, communications, and not least, health care. At a minimum, such an effort would begin the long-term task of "re-educating" the gatekeepers to the public mind— namely, the mass media and policymakers.

There is some evidence that public and policymaker "information campaigns" stressing policy level (rather than personal) issues for the promotion of health can be effective and acceptable (88–90). Such efforts would most likely eventuate in shifts of resources toward more health-promoting uses of the nation's land, food, facilities, and human energy.

## SUMMARY AND CONCLUSION

The current and still-growing trend in finding ways to improve Americans' health is a narrowly defined, individualistic "brand" of "health promotion." It has taken on an increasingly commercial character, often being shaped and delivered by and for entrepreneurial interests with little evidence of or effort in enhancing the public's health interests. At the same time, there is evidence to show that substantial improvement in the prospects for health, especially for the disadvantaged groups that are at higher-risk, could be achieved by granting access to the conditions of living that promote health, ranging from housing and health care to job and community security. This approach to the promotion of health requires placing the public's health interests on the agendas of a broad spectrum of public policy areas.

Too often "health promotion" in the United States has meant more hype than health. The health of Americans, especially those most burdened by the policies of the 1980s, will be best promoted by centering decision-making in public and collective arenas, with involvement by those whose health interests are at stake, and grounding health in policies and programs that can establish and safeguard the social and other environmental conditions conducive to health.

## REFERENCES

1. Shapiro, R., and Young, J. The Polls: Medical care in the U.S. *Public Opinion Q.,* 50: 418–428, 1986.
2. National Center for Health Statistics. Annual summary. Births, marriages, divorces and deaths, U.S. 1985. *Monthly Vital Statistics Report,* September 19, 1986.
3. National Center for Health Statistics. Advance report. Final mortality statistics, U.S. 1984. *Monthly Vital Statistics Report,* September 26, 1986.
4. Milio, N. *Primary Care and the Public's Health.* Lexington Books, Lexington, Mass., 1983.
5. Olshansky, S. J., et al. The Fourth Stage of the Epidemiologic Transition: The Age of Declining Mortality in Advanced Ages. Paper presented at the Annual Meetings, American Public Health Association, Washington, D.C., November 19, 1985.
6. Rice, D., and LaPlante, M. The Burden of Multiple Chronic Conditions: Past Trends and Policy Implications. Draft report. Paper presented at the Annual Meetings, American Public Health Association, Las Vegas, October 1, 1986.
7. Office of Policy. *Studies in Income Distribution: Changes in the Money Income of the Aged and Nonaged, 1967-1983.* Social Security Administration, Washington, D.C., September, 1986.
8. Belous, R., et al. Middle class erosion and growing income inequality: Fact or Fiction. *Congressional Research Service,* #85-203E. Washington, D.C., November 28, 1985.

9. Congressional Budget Office. *The Changing Distribution of Federal Taxes: 1975-1990.* Congress, Washington, D.C., October 1987.
10. Smith, R. Bitterness, shame, emptiness, waste: An introduction to unemployment and health. *Br. Med. J.* 291: 1024–1027, 1985.
11. Joint Economic Committee. *Economic Change, Physical Illness, and Social Deviance.* Congress, Washington, D.C., June 15, 1984.
12. Westcott, G., Svensson, P. G., and Zollner, H. (eds.). *Health Policy Implications of Unemployment.* World Health Organization, Copenhagen, 1985.
13. Danziger, D., Haveman, B., and Plotnick, S. *Antipoverty Policy: Effects on the Poor and the Non-poor.* Institute for Research on Poverty, University of Wisconsin, Madison, 1985.
14. Friends Committee on National Legislation. *Survival of Programs for the Poor.* Washington, D.C., November 1986.
15. Farley, P. Private health insurance. In *The U.S. National Medical Care Expenditure Survey.* National Center for Health Services Research, Washington, D.C., September 1986.
16. Children's Defense Fund. *Medical and Health Perspectives,* 1, February 22, 1988.
17. National Center for Health Statistics. Trends in smoking, alcohol consumption, and other health practices among U.S. adults, 1977 and 1983. *Advance Data,* June 30, 1986.
18. Ruderman, A. Marketing health promotion in Canada: An idea whose time has come. *Can. J. Public Health,* 77: 315–317, 1986.
19. General Accounting Office. *An Aging Society: Meeting the Needs of the Elderly While Responding to Federal Costs.* Congress, Washington, D.C., September 1986.
20. National Center for Health Statistics. Aging in the 1980s. Preliminary data. *Advance Data,* September 30, 1986.
21. General Accounting Office. *Posthospital Care.* Congress, Washington, D.C., January 23, 1987.
22. Fisher, M., et al. DRG Consequences for Home Health Nursing Care. Paper presented at the Annual Meetings, American Public Health Association, Las Vegas, September 28-October 1, 1986.
23. General Accounting Office. *Medicare Home Health Care.* Congress, Washington, D.C., 1986.
24. Shortell, S., et al. Diversification of health care services: Effects of ownership, environment, and strategy. In *Advances in Health Economics and Health Services Research,* edited by L. Rossiter, and R. Schechter. JAI Press, Greenwich, Conn., 1986.
25. Light, D. Corporate medicine for profit. *Sci. Am.* 255(6): 38–45, December 1986.
26. Manheim, L., et al. *Impact of HCA Hospital Acquisitions: Structure, Process, and Outcomes.* Northwestern University Center for Health Services and Policy Research, Chicago, October 1986.
27. Fruen, M. and DiPrete, H. *Health Care in the Future.* John Hancock Mutual Life Insurance Company, Boston, 1986.
28. Institute of Medicine. *For-Profit Enterprise in Health Care.* National Academy Press, Washington, D.C., 1986.
29. Siegrist, R. Wall Street's view of the for-profit hospital corporations. In *The New Health Care for Profit,* edited by B. Gray. National Academy Press, Washington, D.C., 1983.
30. Wellness industry. *Health Business.* August 1, 1986, p. 2T.
31. Office of Disease Prevention and Health Promotion. *National Survey of Worksite Health Promotion Activities.* Department of Health and Human Services, Washington, D.C., October 1987.

32. Hertzlinger, R., and Calkins, D. How companies tackle health care costs III. *Harvard Business Review.* January-February, 1986, pp. 70–77.
33. Hallett, K. Smoking intervention in the workplace: Review and recommendations. *Prev. Med.* 15: 213–231, 1986.
34. Strunkard, A., et al. Mobilizing a community to promote health: The Pennsylvania County Health Improvement Program (CHIP). In *Prevention in Health Psychology,* edited by J. Rosen and L. Solomon. University Press of New England, Hanover, N.H., 1985.
35. Reed, R. *Health Promotion Services: Evaluation and Impact Study.* Blue Cross Blue Shield, Indianapolis, April 1985.
36. *Winning Health Care Strategies.* Health Policy Week, Bethesda, 1986.
37. Office of Health Coalitions. *Summary Statistics, 1985-86 Survey.* American Hospital Association, Chicago, 1986.
38. Health coalitions address local concerns, but may face change. *Qual. Care Insights* 1(3): 6, Fall 1987.
39. Bulow-Hube, S., and Marisky, D. The innovation-decision model and workplace health promotion program. *Health Ed. Res.* 2(1): 15–25, 1987.
40. Annual Claim Facts Survey. *Medical Benefits,* October 15, 1987, pp. 7–8.
41. Wickizer, T., and Samuelson, M. Using claims data to set health promotion goals. *Business & Health,* October 1987.
42. Schenck, A., et al. A labor and industry focus on education: Using baseline survey data in program design. *Health Ed. Res.* 2(1): 33–44, 1987.
43. Yelin, E. The myth of malingering: Why individuals withdraw from work in the presence of illness. *Milbank Mem. Fund Q.* 64(4): 622–649, 1986.
44. Karasek, R. A., Schwartz, J. E., and Pieper, C. A New Job Analysis System for Predicting Productivity, Health, and Wellbeing Correlates of Work Activity. Part I. Unpublished paper, Columbia University, Department of Industrial Engineering and Operations Research, New York, 1982.
45. Glasgow, R. E., and Klesges, R. C. Smoking intervention programs in the workplace. In *Surgeon General's Report, The Health Consequences of Smoking: Cancer and Chronic Lung Disease in the Workplace,* pp. 473–515. Government Printing Office, Washington, D.C., 1986.
46. Klesges, R., et al. Competition and relapse prevention training in worksite smoking modification. *Health Ed. Res.* 2(1): 5–14, 1987.
47. Wang, P., et al. A cure for stress? *Newsweek,* October 12, 1987, pp. 64–65.
48. Folland, S. Effects of health care advertising. *J. Health Policy Polit. Law,* 10(2): 329–342, 1985.
49. Milio, N. Telematics and the future of health care. *J. Prof. Nursing,* February 1986.
50. Sk & A Research, Inc. *Interactive Video. Training Market Evaluation for Health-Related Applications.* Sk & A Research, Falls Church, Va., 1985.
51. Conrad, P. Who comes to worksite wellness programs? A preliminary review. *J. Occup. Med.* April 1987.
52. Warner, K., and Murt, H. Economic incentives and health behavior. In *Prevention in Health Psychology,* edited by J. Rosen and L. Solomon. pp. 325–353. University Press of New England, Hanover, N.H., 1985.
53. National Council for the Education of Health Professionals in Health Promotion. *Recommendations and Strategies for Educating Health Professionals.* NCEHPHP, Washington, D.C., 1987.
54. Milio, N. Promoting health promotion: Health or hype? *Community Health Studies,* Winter 1986, pp. 490–496.

55. Iverson, D. Making a case for health promotion: A summary of the scientific evidence. *Corporate Commentary: A Worksite Health Evaluation Report* 1(2): 7, 1985.
56. Weinstein, M. *Health Policy and Lifestyle Change in the Workplace.* Health and Education Department, World Health Organization, June 3, 1983.
57. Michigan Health Care Education and Research Fund. *Go to Health.* December 1985.
58. American Heart Association, Greater Boston, The Corporate Heart. Nedham Mass., 1986.
59. Bly, J., et al. Impact of worksite health promotion on health care costs and utilization. *JAMA*, 256: 3235–3240, 1986.
60. Shepherd, R., et al. Impact of changes in fitness and lifestyle upon health care utilization. *Am. J. Public Health* 74: 51–54, 1983.
61. Health policy agenda for the American people. *JAMA* 257(9): 1199–1210, 1987.
62. Percentage distribution of subject matter, AJPH 1911-1980. *Am. J. Public Health* July 1986, p. 812.
63. Kottke, T. Disease and risk factor clustering in the U.S.: Implications for public health policy. In *Integration of Risk Factor Interventions,* pp. 1–62. Office of Disease Prevention and Health Promotion. Department of Health and Human Services, Washington, D.C., 1986, 1–62.
64. Rigotti, N. A. Policies restricting smoking in public places and the workplace. In *Surgeon General's Report, The Health Consequences of Involuntary Smoking,* pp. 261–334. U.S. Government Printing Office, Washington, D.C., 1986.
65. Weinstein, M. Lifestyle, stress, and work: Strategies for health promotion. *Health Promotion 1(3):* 363–371, 1986.
66. Milio, N. Healthy nations. *Can. J. Public Health,* May/June 1985, pp. 79-87.
67. General Accounting Office. *Plant Closings.* U.S. Congress, April 17, 1987.
68. Karmaus, W. Working conditions and health: Social epidemiology, patterns of stress and change. *Soc. Sci. Med.* 19: 359–372, 1984.
69. World Health Organization. *Unemployment, Poverty, and Quality of Working Life— Innovative Interventions to Counteract Damaging Health Effects.* World Health Organization, Copenhagen, 1987.
70. McGinnis, J. The United States' Public Health Policy Managed by Objectives. Paper presented at the Second International Conference on Health Promotion, Adelaide, South Australia, April 5–10, 1988.
71. Daneff, T. *Preventing Illness: Strategies for a Preventive Health Policy.* Social Democratic Party Health Campaign, London, November 1984.
72. Draper, P. A *New Vision of Health.* Labor Party, London, August 1985.
73. Marks, L. Public health and agricultural practice. *Food Policy,* May 1984, pp. 16–21.
74. Catford, J. Take heart: A consultative document on the development of community-based heart health initiatives within Wales. *Heartbeat Wales.* Wales, U.K., September 1985.
75. Milio, N. Promoting health through structural change: Norway's farm-food-nutrition policy. *Soc. Sci. Med.* September-October, 15A: 721–734, 1981.
76. National Nutrition Council. *The Norwegian Diet and Norway's Nutrition Policy.* Oslo, August 1986.
77. Milio, N. *Promoting Health Through Public Policy* (softback edition). Canadian Public Health Association, Ottawa, 1986.
78. Swedish Work Environment Fund. *Working Environment in Sweden.* Stockholm, 1987.
79. World Health Organization. Health Promotion in the Working World. Report of a Joint Meeting in Cologne, October 7–9, 1985. Copenhagen, 1987.

80. Arlington County Board. *Adopted Policy for Grocery Stores.* Arlington County, Va., October 5, 1985.
81. Martin, M. J., and Silverman, M. F. The San Francisco Experience with Regulation of Smoking in the Workplace. Paper presented at the Annual Meetings, American Public Health Association, Washington, D.C., November 20, 1985.
82. Gurian, G. A Community-Based Approach to Achieving this Nation's 1990 Health Objectives. Paper presented at the Annual Meetings, American Public Health Association, Las Vegas, September 28-October 2, 1986.
83. Gordon, J. Workplace health promotion: The right idea in the wrong place. *Health Ed. Res.* 2(1): 69–71, 1987.
84. Platt, L. Proposal for a Community Health HMO. Unpublished paper. U.S. DHHS, Region X, December 1986.
85. H.R. 200. U.S. Health Program Act. Congress, Washington, D.C., January 6, 1987.
86. Massachusetts Health Security Program Act. Boston, Mass., Legislature, January 1987.
87. Committee for Economic Development. *Children in Need.* New York, 1987.
88. Steward, L., Ransom, R., and Casswell, S. The Community Action Project. Activities of Community Organizers. Research Report, Alcohol Research Unit, Auckland University School of Medicine, Auckland, N.Z., February 1987.
89. Jeffery, R., et al. Community Attitudes Toward Public Policies to Control Alcohol, Tobacco, and High Fat Food Consumption. Research Report, University of Minnesota School of Public Health, 1987.
90. Puska, P., et al. The community-based strategy to prevent coronary heart disease: Conclusions from 10 years of the North Karelia Project. *Annu. Rev. Public Health 6:* 147–193, 1985.

Originally published in the International Journal of Health Services, Volume 18, Number 4, Pages 573-585, 1988.

# CHAPTER 4

# The Corporate Compromise:
# A Marxist View of
# Health Maintenance Organizations
# and Prospective Payment

## David U. Himmelstein and Steffie Woolhandler

The dominance of economic imperatives in health care and the corporate transformation of American medicine is strikingly congruent with Karl Marx's century old description of the development of a capitalist industry. This chapter presents a Marxist view of current U.S. health policy. We argue that the growth of prospective payment can be traced to an implicit compromise between cost-conscious corporate purchasers of care, and corporate health care providers struggling to expand profitability and to assert control of medicine.

Marx emphasized that technological progress in the 18th and 19th centuries changed not only the processes of production, but also power relations in industry. As the cost of the tools of manufacture (capital) rose to exceed the means of individual producers, the owners of capital gained power, since producers without modern equipment could not compete. The dominance of the owners allowed them to depress wages and command profits, which in turn paid for the ever larger investments needed to remain competitive, investments increasingly unthinkable for ordinary workers. Thus, owners of capital came to control production (often from afar), as well as the profits which became new capital. Through these powerful levers they shaped much of society.

The history of health care's emergence as a capitalist industry reads like a modern textbook of Marxist economics. Small scale owner/producers (doctors) initially came together in workshops (hospitals). Technical development made access to large concentrations of capital (buildings and machines) indispensable for medical practice and increased the power of those who controlled health care capital. Simultaneous with this increasing accumulation of capital, control of health care institutions shifted from public hands. Today in medicine, the power of those who control capital is reflected in the rising influence of hospital administration, corporate executives, insurance bureaucrats, and other functionaries unfamiliar with the clinical encounter, but well versed on the bottom line.

The recent conversion of health care from public service to private industry has brought those who profit from providing health care into conflict with industries for whom health care (viz. employee health benefits) is a cost of production. This inter-corporate conflict powerfully shapes health policy. It has caused the rapid proliferation of health maintenance organizations (HMOs) and other forms of prospective payment which establish incentives for cost containment but allow health institutions to remain profitable, and has hastened the decline of physician dominance in both health policy and clinical decision making.

## HEALTH CARE AND THE PROFITABILITY OF INDUSTRY

Marxists view medical care as an industry analogous to other industries. Medicine is not an autonomous discipline guided solely by scientific discoveries or idealistic concerns. Rather health care is one sector of economic production which responds to the economic and political needs of the capitalist system as a whole.

Marxists hold that the drive for profit and expansion is the main determinant of the development of any capitalist industry. However, some industries that would not be viable in a purely market driven economy are necessary for the profitability of other industries, or the stability of the system as a whole. In such cases the government, which Marx referred to as "a committee for managing the common affairs of the whole [corporate class]" (1), may step in to assure that needed functions are carried out. The provision of roads, water and sewage systems, public education, and other public services are examples. Similarly, in our view the impetus for government programs to improve medical care for the poor is not primarily humanitarian. It is in the main a response to fears of popular unrest, an effort to increase the productivity of current and future workers, and a means of channeling money to the profitable drug, medical supply, and hospital construction industries. Thus an analysis of health care must encompass its impact on the profitability of other industries as well as the growth of production for profit within medicine.

Health care facilitates profit-making in three ways. First, many illnesses which sap the productivity of workers can be cured or managed. To quote Charles Eliot, a 19th century President of Harvard University: "The objective of research in medicine is to prevent industrial losses due to sickness and untimely death among men and domestic animals" (2). Second, medicine is an important psychological tool for the maintenance of the domestic tranquility and social stability needed for production and profit; in Marxist terms this is the ideological role of medicine. Since Bismarck's introduction of health insurance for German workers in 1883, governments have used health care to ameliorate the conditions of working class life, simultaneously responding to popular demands and forestalling more radical ones (3). Third, the medical care industry has itself become an important field for investment and profit.

While the first two of these roles for health care (often perceived as public service and charity) have a long history, the last (pecuniary interest) only recently emerged as a driving force for health care expansion. Within the past few decades medicine has become not only a service for the rest of industry and society but a major profit producing industry in its own right. Health care, initially an adjunct to production in other sectors, has itself come into the age of capitalist production. Previously, the corporate class was most concerned with the products of health care, biological and ideological. The transformation of the past few decades is making profit, rather than health or ideology, the major objective of production in this field. Ultimately, to paraphrase Marx's *Capital*, in health as in other industries, capitalist production is indifferent to the particular product produced. Increasingly the sole purpose of production is to secure profits (4).

## FROM PUBLIC SERVICE TO PROFITABLE INDUSTRY

At the turn of the century public health and sanitation measures dramatically increased life expectancy (5). By contrast most curative medical therapies were useless or worse (5). A doctor could serve as a comfort in the face of suffering but offered little of use to patients besides sympathy and morphine. Individual (physician) producers who required few tools to ply their trade dominated medical care. For less than a dollar a day hospitals provided room, board and quarantine, but little specialized equipment or personnel (6, 7). Some cities had established public hospitals for the poor. Most "private" hospitals were small charitable enterprises aided by state and local governments. The distinction between private and public hospitals was blurred and relatively unimportant since the total amount of money spent on hospitals was small ($29 million in 1903, 0.08 percent of the Gross National Product (GNP)) (6, 7).

The first half of this century saw a gradual and accelerating growth in medical knowledge and technology, and with it an increase in the capital needed to practice medicine. By 1950 the nation's hospital bill had climbed to $3.7 billion (1 percent of the GNP) (8), and such items as x-ray departments, laboratories, and surgical suites were considered a necessity for every hospital (net fixed hospital assets grew from $2.8 billion in 1950 to $48 billion in 1980 (9)); hospital boards and administrators who controlled capital came to command greater power. The need for ever-expanding investment to maintain state of the art facilities gradually eroded the former charity and service orientation of hospital managers, and fostered an entrepreneurial mentality even in many nominally non-profit institutions (10). Thus philanthropy and local government grants accounted for more than 90 percent of hospital investment capital in the 1920s (9), and philanthropy remained the largest single source of hospital capital until the mid 1960s (11). Yet by 1973 charitable donations accounted for only 10 percent of construction funds, while debt financing contributed 58 percent of the total (9). In 1983 debt and philanthropy financed 70 and 4 percent, respectively, of hospital capital (9).

The corporate class as a whole supported the expansion of health care by providing health insurance for employees of large firms. Government encouraged these employer-paid health benefits by exempting them from taxes, and, during World War II, freezing wages but not benefits. Employers welcomed this development for several reasons. Health insurance was popular with workers, improved their productivity, and gave corporations additional leverage over workers by tying health care to employment, while maintaining lower standards of care for the unemployed, retired and disabled. Whereas the labor movement in the rest of the developed world demanded and won universal health insurance, organized labor in the U.S. abandoned this demand and accepted health benefits negotiated on a contract by contract basis.

Blue Cross, founded in 1929 by hospitals, became the model for all subsequent employee health plans. Blue Cross paid hospitals for whatever services and equipment they deemed necessary and specifically included payment to cover all capital costs (12). Thus any hospital which could raise the down payment for new acquisitions was given a blank check to cover the mortgage, with patients footing the bill for the accumulation of hospital capital under private control. In 1946 the federal government intervened to solve the problem of raising down payments with the passage of the Hill-Burton program which gave billions of dollars in grants to hospitals for capital projects (13).

These financial encouragements assured the post-war expansion of the medical industry. Hospitals added over 40 percent of current total inpatient capacity during the 1950s and 1960s. The U.S. went from a shortage to a surplus of hospital beds (reflected in a sharp drop in occupancy rates) (14, 15). Dozens of expensive new machines and medical techniques were widely adopted, often without proof of efficacy (16). However, the large number of uninsured poor and retired people who could not afford to purchase the increasingly costly services limited the further growth of the industry.

The movements for civil rights and social justice of the 1960s provided additional impetus to remove this barrier to the growth of the medical industry. Responding in classic "Bismarckian" fashion to the threat of social unrest, Congress established the Medicare and Medicaid programs. These programs were a cornerstone of the expansion of the social welfare system and constituted a real victory for the health of the poor and elderly (17). However, both programs helped not only the poor and elderly but also the health care industry, by dramatically increasing and radically reorienting government spending on health care. Spending which had hitherto been concentrated in direct grants to public health programs and public hospitals skyrocketed and was devoted to the purchase of care in the private sector (18–20). The programs were closely modeled after (and often administered by) Blue Cross, and included virtually unlimited payments to hospitals for capital expenditures. While noisily proclaiming the benefits of Medicaid and Medicare for the poor and elderly, government quietly added its signature to the blank check for private hospital expansion.

## PUBLIC MONEY, PRIVATE CONTROL

After the passage of Medicare and Medicaid, private hospitals moved to capture the newly insured patients from public hospitals (19, 21), while often refusing to care for the millions of non-elderly poor who were eligible for neither program (10, 21–24). Since insurance paid for almost any service provided, insured patients received an increasing number of tests and interventions, many of them of uncertain value (25). Public hospitals remained the low-tech institutions of last resort for the uninsured (26, 27). The non-profit status of most private hospitals proved small hindrance to profit making. While non-profit hospitals could not themselves reap profits, the cost-plus payments provided by government and private insurance made them ideal conduits for the profits of drug companies, equipment manufacturers, construction and real estate firms, banks, and insurance companies (10, 28, 29). The situation was somewhat analogous to the defense sector in which suppliers are paid on a cost-plus basis and reap profits, while the military itself is operated as a non-profit "public service." Health related industries have been extraordinarily profitable. For example, the profit rate of pharmaceutical firms has for decades ranked first or second among the 47 U.S. industry groups (30, 31). The incentives to raise the cost of hospital care and thereby expand the market for medical products led to the seemingly bizarre result that during the 1970s the lowest cost hospitals were the most likely to be driven out of the market (32).

Since 1965 government subsidies to private hospitals have become the financial backbone of the industry. The Medicaid and Medicare programs contributed 38 percent of hospital revenues, $63 billion in 1985 (33). Tax exemptions for health insurance and non-profit hospitals indirectly contribute tens of billions more (34–37). Finally, tax exempt bonds have financed much recent hospital expansion. In 1981 alone hospitals sold over $5 billion in such bonds, which was 17 percent of all tax exempt bonds issued, 7 percent of the total bond market, and represented a loss in taxes to the federal treasury of $1.5 billion (11). Overall, the proportion of hospital capital funding supported by federal subsidies (direct or indirect) increased from less than 20 percent in 1968 to more than 80 percent in 1976 (9). Private hospitals receive more than 60 percent of revenues from government sources, a government subsidy which far exceeds the budgets of public hospitals (18).

By the early 1980s private health insurance and government support had fostered the emergence of health care as one of America's largest industries (38). Between 1950 and 1983 national health expenditures increased more than 25 fold, reaching $357 billion per year, and the proportion of the GNP accounted for by the health sector increased from 4.4 to 10.8 percent (33). During the 1970s health care employment increased from 4.2 to 7.2 million workers (8), accounting for one seventh of all new jobs in the U.S. Hospitals expanded so rapidly that by 1980 the average age of hospital capital assets stood at an all time low of 7 years, as compared to 15 years for the service sector as a whole and 23 years for capital in manufacturing industries (39). Whereas between 1946 and 1950 public hospitals accounted for 32 percent of new hospital capital, between 1970 and 1974 this figure had fallen to 16 percent (40).

While private hospitals vied to purchase the latest technology and provide the greatest number of profitable services, public hospitals were left as pitiful remnants of their former selves, housed in aging buildings, equipped with outdated machines, serving largely uninsured patients (27, 41, 42). The average age of public hospital capital assets exceeds 12 years, almost twice the average for private hospitals (27). Since 1965 six of New York City's 19 public hospitals have closed, as have 29 of California's 66 county hospitals (43) and the only public hospitals serving Detroit and Philadelphia (41, 44). Further cuts in New York's public hospitals, including those in medically underserved areas, are being considered. Meanwhile private hospitals in bed-rich Manhattan neighborhoods have embarked on extensive new construction projects.

THE BUCKS STOP HERE:
THE RISK OF PROFIT-MAKING PROVIDERS

The copious flow of funds for private health services eventually convinced entrepreneurs that hospitals and HMOs need not be mere non-profit conduits for the profits of other industries, but could themselves be operated as profit-making (proprietary) entities. While proprietary hospitals and HMOs are not eligible for tax exemptionism, they can tap capital markets (by issuing stock) unavailable to non-profit hospitals. Moreover, both government and private insurance programs virtually guaranteed the profitability of proprietary hospitals, including profit as an allowable (and reimbursed) cost. Proprietaries able to "market" services to the well-insured underwent rapid expansion.

Between the founding of the first for-profit hospital company in 1960 and the reorientation of hospital payment heralded by the passage of the Medicare DRG program, the number of corporate owned proprietary hospitals grew to more than 1000. By 1982, Hospital Corporation of America, the largest proprietary chain, owned 351 hospitals with 50,200 beds producing revenues of $3.5 billion (45).

Among HMOs, U.S. Health Care Systems was the first, in 1983, to convert to for-profit status, go public and offer stock (46). Today 431 of the 650 HMOs in business are proprietary (47). Interestingly, in 1983 even the enormous profits of proprietary hospitals ($1.2 billion) (48) were still dwarfed by those of suppliers of drugs ($5.6 billion) (31) and medical equipment ($2.8 billion) (29).

## THE INTER-CORPORATE CONFLICT

In the past the corporate class was virtually unanimous in the support for the expansion of health care. However, divisions have emerged as employee health benefit spending has become a major cost of production. By 1983 U.S. corporations were spending more than $89 billion a year for employee health benefits (49). Health care costs were not only eating into profits, but also compromising the international competitiveness of U.S. industry. For example, in 1983 Ford Motors spent $5300 per employee for health care, while Mitsubishi spent only $815 (50). As soaring health care costs have become a major concern for non-medical corporations, they have moved to curtail the assured profits and rapid expansion of the health sector (51–53). In the Marxist analytic framework, this process is viewed as a result of the tendency toward equalization of profit rates across different sectors of industry (4).

Already in 1970 Fortune magazine had sounded the corporate alarm, editorializing that: "The management of medical care has become too important to leave to doctors. . . . The majority of physicians constitute an army of pushcart vendors in an age of supermarkets" (54). In 1981 the Business Roundtable, an organiztion of the most powerful corporate executives, declared the control of health care costs a top priority and formed a health task force headed by Citibank President Walter Wriston. Its decision to get serious about hospital costs marked a turning point: until then, the issue was the province of insiders with a stake in the continuing expansion of the health care industry. Business-sponsored coalitions devoted to health care costs grew in number from 25 in 1982 to over 200 in 1986 (53), and now operate in at least 43 states. Eighty percent of the members represent business, and one-third of the "coalitions" allow only corporate members (53). Many corporations have restructured health insurance benefits to force providers to lower prices and shift costs to employees through co-payments and deductibles (55–58). By 1984 corporations in Arizona were engaged in open warfare with the hospital industry, placing a stringent cost-control measure on the ballot and spending millions of dollars campaigning for the measure. In Massachusetts in 1982, representatives of the hospital industry, insurance firms, and the Business Roundtable rewrote the state's hospital reimbursement laws with no input from patients, physicians or even politicians (59).

Simultaneously, government has moved to end the privileged position enjoyed by the health care industry. Phase-out of Hill-Burton grants for hospital capital projects began in 1975 (13). In 1971 the Nixon administration made support for

HMOs (previously reviled as incipient socialized medicine) the centerpiece of its health policy, presaging a major shift in the structure of the health industry (60, 61). A decade later the passage of the Medicare Diagnosis-Related Group (DRG) program and widespread corporate advocacy of HMOs firmly entrenched "prospective payment" as both government and corporate policy (53, 62).

PROSPECTIVE PAYMENT:
THE CORPORATE COMPROMISE

The growing conflict between corporate providers and purchasers of care has given rise to prospective payment schemes which are acceptable to both groups but exact a toll from patients and physicians. Two principal variants of prospective payment have emerged. Capitation schemes pay the HMO (or other provider) a fixed annual fee per enrollee to cover all care. In contrast, per case schemes, such as DRGs, pay the provider a fixed fee to care for a single episode of illness (e.g., a hospital stay). Both HMOs and DRGs untether payment from actual resource use (63, 64). Previously, profitability depended on recruiting well-insured patients, and maximizing the services provided to them. Prospective payment preserves the incentive to serve only the well-insured, but rewards minimization of services and/or their cost. This latter feature may bring the financial interests of physicians and health institutions into conflict. Under DRGs, reduced resource use lowers physician income but benefits hospitals. In HMOs, doctors' incomes are subtracted directly from the bottom line. With both HMOs and DRGs, institutional profitability, expansion and even survival hinge on administrative control of physician behavior. The result has been an enormous expansion of the administrative apparatus of health care, which now consumes about 22 percent of all health expenditures (29, 65). The premium on administrative control has hastened the shift of power from physicians to those who manage and own the massive concentrations of capital now needed to practice medicine.

Corporate *purchasers* favor the incentives under prospective payment for providers to curtail care and its costs. Additionally, since HMOs provide virtually no care to the uninsured, they eliminate the cross-subsidy for "free care" incorporated into Blue Cross and commercial insurance rates.

For corporate *providers,* prospective payment has allowed increased profits even in the face of constrained revenues since reimbursement is disconnected from resource use (66–68). While this incentive rewards efficiency, it also rewards less desirable behaviors. Thus HMOs selectively enroll the healthy— marketing to employee groups with low health care utilizations rates, and on occasion even going so far as to place enrollment offices on the upper floors of elevator-less buildings (69–71). HMOs may also profit by discouraging enrollees from seeking care or curtailing physicians' ordering of needed tests, hospitalizations, etc. (69, 70). Indeed, the Rand Health Insurance Experiment found that

HMOs decrease appropriate medical admissions as much as inappropriate ones, though they do selectively discourage unnecessary surgery (72).

Under DRGs, hospitals can prosper by encouraging the admission of patients likely to require little care (73); discharging patients prematurely (67, 74, 75); avoiding patients whose DRG payment is likely to be less than the cost of care, e.g., the seriously ill, patients admitted emergently or cared for by more experienced surgeons, the poor, or those with inadequate home supports who may require longer lengths of stay (76–79); or "gaming" the system by miscoding patient diagnoses into a higher-paying DRG (80). Conversely, institutions unwilling or unable to alter patient mix, physician behavior, or diagnostic coding face financial ruin. Thus under the DRG program average hospital profits on Medicare patients soared (66), doubling in the first year of prospective payment to $5.5 billion (67, 68). Meanwhile the financial situation of many rural and inner city hospitals has deteriorated (27, 77, 81, 82).

Indeed, the gap in profit margins between hospitals that are doing well (the top 5 percent) and those that are doing poorly (the bottom 5 percent) has increased by 37 percent under DRGs (82). While other health policies might be acceptable (or even preferable) to corporate providers and purchasers separately, prospective payment is uniquely acceptable to both. Unfortunately, this policy option poorly serves many patients and providers. By curtailing cost shifting it even more rigidly excludes the 37 million uninsured from the medical mainstream. HMO enrollees, particularly of low income, may be unable to obtain needed care due to the "gate-keeping" essential for HMO profitability (70, 83). In extreme cases, such as International Medical Centers, the largest Medicare HMO, the drive for profitability has caused fraud and outright patient abuse (84). Even in high quality HMOs patients routinely suffer disruptions of doctor/patient relationships with job change, retirement, or if their employer decides to change health plans. At one Boston-based HMO 35 percent of members disenroll annually, and annual disenrollment figures as high as 42 percent have been reported (85). The doctor/patient relationship is often further compromised by patients' fears that their doctor may be rewarded for skimping on care (86, 87). A spate of anecdotal reports as well as a few careful studies raise concern that DRGs have compromised the quality of care (67, 74, 75).

As prospective payment increasingly dominates the policy landscape, physicians find many satisfying aspects of their traditional role challenged—their position transformed from independent small producer to highly paid foreman in a medical factory. Long-term relationships with patients are arbitrarily disrupted; doctor/patient confidentiality is routinely violated by financial reviewers; productivity standards constrain human interactions; decisions on new programs and equipment become the prerogative of a management increasingly divorced from clinical care; even the right to waive fees for the needy is usurped. Physicians are losing their former control of medical production; they are being "proletarianized"

(88)—a process vividly described by Marx: "The [corporate class] has stripped of its halo every occupation hitherto honored and looked up to with reverent awe. It has converted the physician, the lawyer, the priest, the poet, the man of science, into its paid wage-laborers" (1).

More than a century later, Ellwood coined the term Health Maintenance Organization and sold the concept to President Nixon as a policy alternative to blunt the drive for national health insurance (61). Ellwood's prediction of the effects of the policy is striking both for its accuracy and its congruence with a Marxist formulation. "[HMOs] could stimulate a course of change in the health industry that would have some of the classical aspects of the industrial revolution—conversion to larger units of production, technological innovation, division of labor, substitution of capital for labor, vigorous competition, and profitability as the mandatory condition of survival" (89).

## PROSPECTIVE PAYMENT AND
## THE DISSOLUTION OF HEALTH PLANNING

While prospective payment imposes tight regulation on clinical practice, it undermines broader health planning. The increasing economic rationality of each production unit (i.e., the individual HMO or hospital) fosters the irrationality of the system as a whole—a phenomenon Marx labelled "the anarchy of capitalist production."

Rational health planning should allocate new capital based on health needs. But prospective payment makes profitability rather than need the implicit basis for allocating new capital. Profitable hospitals and HMOs not only have their own profits to reinvest, but also can attract additional money from outside banks and investors. Resource allocation decisions are made in the board rooms of profitable firms, or of non-profit institutions with a surplus of revenues over expenditures. These decisions must be bent towards the narrow institutional goal of profitability, since future modernization, expansion, and even survival depend on a continuing surplus. Hospitals lacking a surplus (whether because of poor management, spendthrift physicians, or uninsured or unprofitably sick patients) are likely to be those most in need of new investments. Unable to modernize, such hospitals often enter a downward spiral toward closure (27, 90–92). Meanwhile, hospitals in highly competitive markets vie to provide profitable services, causing wasteful, and sometimes dangerous duplication of lucrative "product lines" such as coronary angioplasty (93), and irrationality in the distribution of health resources—a surfeit of expensive facilities in some areas and continuing shortages in areas of greatest need.

## CONCLUSIONS

The past thirty years have seen an enormous accumulation of capital in health care institutions, the emergence of medical production for profit, and the rapid rise of administrative dominance of clinical practice. The health sector's explosive growth, in the past encouraged by the entire corporate class and fueled by government funds, now threatens the profits of other capitalist industries. Prospective payment with providers permitted to retain any surplus is an inter-corporate compromise which maintains profitability, reinforces private control of health care capital, and accelerates the trend toward bureaucratic and corporate dominance of medical care.

This is not the only, and certainly not the best, possible direction for health policy, even within the context of capitalism. The Canadian single payer National Health Program has assured access to care, preserved clinical freedom, and contained costs by constraining corporate dominance and rationalizing health resource (capital) allocation.

Health policy in the U.S. has hitherto been shaped largely by the interests of the corporate class, a process that threatens many valuable traditions in medicine. The enormous sums spent on health care are sufficient to provide high quality services to all, improve prevention, nurture research, and assure providers adequate income. However, the imperatives of corporate profitability now foster massive irrationality and waste: $50 billion devoured annually by the insurance industry and armies of administrators (65, 94), and billions more squandered on profits and advertising for health care corporations (29, 30). Finally, allocating new capital on the basis of profitability to private providers pursuing narrow institutional goals assures massive duplication and maldistribution of facilities.

A reorientation of policy will require an alternative coalition capable of resisting the imperatives of pecuniary interest. The growing movement for a single-payer National Health Program may provide such a force.

## REFERENCES

1. Marx, K., and Engels, F. The manifesto of the Communist Party. In *Selected Works,* pp. 35–63. International, New York, 1970.
2. Eliot, C. W. "The qualities of a scientific investigator," an address delivered May 11, 1906, quoted in Brown, E. R. *Rockefeller Medicine Men*, p. 118. University of California Press, Berkeley, Cal., 1979.
3. Roemer, M. I. Social insurance as leverage for changing health care systems: International experience. *Bull N.Y. Acad Med* 48: 93–107, 1972.
4. Marx, K. *Capital*, Volume 3. Charles Kerr, Chicago, 1909.
5. Powles, J. On the limitations of modern medicine. *Science Medicine, and Man*, 1973, pp. 1–30.
6. Stevens, R. A poor sort of memory: Voluntary hospitals and government before the depression. *Milbank Mem. Fund Q.* 60: 551-584, 1982.
7. U.S. Bureau of the Census. *Historical Statistics of the United States, Colonial Times to 1957.* U.S. Department of Commerce, Washington, D.C., 1960.
8. National Center for Health Statistics. *Health, United States, 1982.* DHHS publication no. (PHS) 83–1232. U.S. Public Health Service, Washington, D.C., 1982.
9. Cohodes, D. R., and Kinkead, B. M. *Hospital Capital Formation in the 1980s.* Johns Hopkins University Press, Baltimore, 1984.

10. Ehrenreich, B., and Ehrenreich, J. *The American Health Empire*, p. 48. Random House, New York, 1971.
11. Wilson, G., Sheps, C. G., and Oliver, T. R. Effects of hospital revenue bonds on hospital planning and operations. *N. Engl. J. Med.* 307: 1426–1430, 1982.
12. Law, S. A. *Blue Cross: What Went Wrong?* Yale Univ. Press, New Haven, Conn., 1976.
13. Feshbach, D. What's inside the black box: A case study in allocative politics in the Hill-Burton program. *Int. J. Health Serv.* 9: 313–339, 1979.
14. American Hospital Association. *Hospital Statistics, 1986 edition.* Chicago, 1986.
15. Hospital occupancy rate hits a record low at 63.6%. *Mod Healthcare* 11, 1986.
16. Waitzkin, H. A Marxist view of the growth and development of coronary care technology. *Am. J. Public Health* 69: 1260–1268.
17. Davis, K., and Schoen, C. *Health and the War on Poverty.* Brookings Institution, Washington, D.C., 1978.
18. Woolhandler, S., et al. Public money, private control. *Am. J. Public Health* 73: 584–587, 1983.
19. Piore, N., Leiberman, P., and Linnane, J. Public expenditure and private control? Health dilemmas in New York City. *Milbank Mem. Fund. Q.* 55: 79–116, 1977.
20. Goldfarb, M. G., et al. Health care expenditures. In *Health, United States, 1980.* DHHS publication no. (PHS) 81-1232, pp. 101–116. U.S. Public Health Service, Washington, D.C., 1980.
21. Roemer, M. I., and Mera, J. A. Patient dumping and other voluntary agency contributions to public agency problems. *Med. Care* 11: 30–39, 1980.
22. Institute of Medicine. *Health Care in a Context of Civil Rights.* National Academy Press, Washington, D.C., 1981.
23. Himmelstein, D. U., et al. Patient transfers: Medical practice as social triage. *Am. J. Public Health* 74: 494–496, 1984.
24. Schiff, R. L., et al. Transfers to a public hospital: A prospective study of 467 patients. *N. Engl. J. Med.* 314: 552–557, 1986.
25. Fuchs, V. R. *Who Shall Live?* p. 74. Basic Books, New York, 1974.
26. National Council on Health Planning and Development. Proceedings: Meeting on capital, financial and organizational issues facing health care organizations in the 1980's. July 8-9, 1982. U.S. Department of Health and Human Services, Washington, D.C., 1982.
27. Gage, L. S., Andrulis, D. P., and Beers, V. *America's Health Safety Net: A Report on the Situation of Public Hospitals in Our Nation's Metropolitan Areas.* National Association of Public Hospitals, Washington, D.C., 1987.
28. Kotelchuck, D. (ed.). *Prognosis Negative.* Vintage, New York, 1974.
29. Himmelstein, D. U., and Woolhandler, S. Socialized medicine: A solution to the cost crisis in health care in the United States. *Int. J. Health Serv.* 16: 339–354, 1986.
30. Silverman, M., and Lee P. R. *Pill, Profits and Politics.* University of California Press, Berkeley, Cal., 1974.
31. Bureau of the Census. *Quarterly Financial Report for Manufacturing, Mining, and Trade Corporations, Fourth Quarter 1983.* U.S. Department of Commerce Publication No. QFR-83-4. Washington, D.C., 1984.
32. Sager, A. Survival of the fattest: Part 2. *Health PAC Bull.* 12(8): 26, 1981.
33. National Center for Health Statistics. *Health, United States, 1986.* DHHS Pub. No. (PHS) 87-1232. Public Health Service. U.S. Government Printing Office,Washington, D.C., 1986.
34. Wilensky, G. R. Government and the financing of health care. *Am. Econ. Rev.* 72: 202–207, 1982.

35. Enthoven, A. C. Consumer choice health plan. *N. Engl. J. Med.* 298: 650–658, 1978.
36. Klarman, H. E. The financing of health care. In *Doing Better and Feeling Worse,* edited by J. H. Knowles. Norton, New York, 1977.
37. Brandon, W. P. Health related tax subsidies: Government handouts for the affluent. *N. Engl. J. Med.* 307: 947–950, 1982.
38. U.S. Bureau of the Census. Statistical Abstract of the United States: 1987 (107th edition). Washington, D.C., 1986.
39. Cohodes, D. R. Review of capital needs study (letter). *Health Aff.* 1(4): 111–115, 1982.
40. American Hospital Association. *Hospital Statistics: 1975 Edition.* Chicago, 1975.
41. Wolfe, S., and Sherer, H. R. *Public General Hospitals in Crisis.* Coalition of American Public Employees, Washington, D.C., 1977.
42. Wolfe, S., et. al. *Report of the Task Force on Public General Hospitals of the American Public Health Association (APHA).* American Public Health Association, Washington, D.C., 1978.
43. Blake, E., and Bodenheimer, T. *Closing the Doors on the Poor: The Dismantling of California's County Hospitals.* Health Policy Advisory Center, San Francisco, 1975.
44. Friedman, E. Demise of Philadelphia General an instructive case; other cities treat public hospital ills differently. *JAMA* 257: 1571–1575, 1987.
45. Hospitals: A proprietary interest. *Washington Report on Medicine and Health,* 1983.
46. HMOs grow and change. *Washington Report on Medicine and Health,* July 1, 1985.
47. HMOs: At the crossroads. *Washington Report on Medicine and Health,* April 25, 1988.
48. Federation of American Hospitals. *Statistical Profile of the Investor-owned Hospital Industry, 1983.* Washington, D.C., 1984.
49. Employee Benefit Research Institute. *Employee Benefit Notes.* February 1986.
50. Cronin, C. Next Congress to grapple with U.S. health policy, competitiveness abroad. *Business and Health* 4(2): 55, 1986.
51. The Business Roundtable. *An Appropriate Role for Corporations in Health Care Cost Management.* New York, 1982.
52. Bradbury, R. C., and O'Connor J. T. *Health Care Costs in Massachusetts.* The Massachusetts Business Roundtable, Waltham, Mass., 1982.
53. Bergthold, L. A. Business and the pushcart vendors in an age of supermarkets. *Int. J. Health Serv.* 17: 7–26, 1987.
54. It's time to operate. *Fortune* 81(1): 77–80, 1970.
55. Hewit Associates. *Salaried Employee Benefits Provided by Major U.S. Employers: A Comparison Study, 1979 through 1984.* Lincolnshire, Ill., 1985.
56. Workers pay bigger cut of health benefits: Poll. *Mod. Healthcare,* November 17, 1982.
57. Kittrell, A. Employers turn to managed care, utilization review to control costs. *Mod. Healthcare,* 1986, pp. 96–98.
58. Gibson, L. Employers lean on employees in fight against rising healthcare costs. *Mod. Healthcare,* 1984, pp. 50–54.
59. Woolhandler, S., and Himmelstein, D. U. Terms of endowment: Prospective hospital reimbursement in Massachusetts. *Health PAC Bull.* 15(2): 13–16, 1984.
60. Mayer, T. R., and Mayer, G. G. HMOs: Origins and development. *N. Engl. J. Med.* 312: 590–594, 1985.
61. Brown, L. D. *Politics and Health Care Organization; HMOs as Federal Policy,* pp. 157–172. Brookings Institution, Washington, D.C., 1983.
62. Iglehart, J. K. Medicare turns to HMOs. *N. Engl. J. Med.* 312: 132–136, 1986.
63. DRGs change hospital organization, management. *Washington Report on Medicine and Health,* 37(22), 1983.
64. Morone, J. A., and Dunham, A. B. The waning of professional dominance: DRGs and the hospitals. *Health Aff.* 3(1): 73–87, 1984.

65. Himmelstein, D. U., and Woolhandler, S. Cost without benefit: Administrative waste in U.S. health care. *N. Engl. J. Med.* 314: 441–445, 1986.
66. Feder, J., Hadley, J., and Zuckerman, S. How did Medicare's prospective payment system affect hospitals? *N. Engl. J. Med.* 317: 867–873, 1987.
67. Iglehart, J. K. Early experience with prospective payment of hospitals. *N. Engl. J. Med.* 314: 1460–1464, 1986.
68. Hospitals' 1984 PPS profits totaled $5.5 billion—study. *Mod. Healthcare* 21, 1986.
69. Luft, H. S. Health maintenance organizations and the rationing of medical care. *Milbank Mem. Fund Q.* 60: 268–307, 1982.
70. Carnoy, J., Coffee, L., and Koo, L. Corporate medicine: The Kaiser health plan. In *Prognosis Negative*, edited by D. Kotelchuk. Random House, New York, 1976.
71. Hellinger, F. J. Selection bias in health maintenance organizations: Analysis of recent evidence. *Health Care Financing Rev.* 9(2): 55–63, 1987.
72. Siu, A. L., et al. Use of the hospital in a randomized trial of prepaid care. *JAMA* 259: 1343–1346, 1988.
73. Carter, K. Majority of hospitals consider DRG 104 to be a moneymaker *Mod. Healthcare*, 1986, p. 84.
74. Fitzgerald, J. F., et al. Changing patterns of hip fracture care before and after implementation of the prospective payment system. *JAMA* 258: 218–221, 1987.
75. Sager, M. A., Leventhal, E. A., and Easterly, D. V. The impact of Medicare's prospective payment system on Wisconsin nursing homes. *JAMA* 256: 1762–1766, 1987.
76. Rhodes, R. S., Krasniak, C. L., and Jones P. K. Factors affecting the length of hospital stay for femoropopliteal bypass: implications of the DRGs. *N. Engl. J. Med.* 314: 153–157, 1986.
77. Munoz, E., et al. Source of admission and cost: Public hospitals face financial risk. *Am. J. Public Health* 76: 696–697, 1986.
78. Munoz, E., et al. The financial effects of emergency department-generated admissions under prospective payment system. *JAMA* 254: 1763–1771, 1985.
79. Epstein, A. M., et al. The association of patients' socioeconomic characteristics with the length of hospital stay and hospital charges within diagnosis-related groups. *N. Engl. J. Med.* 318: 1579–1585, 1988.
80. Hsia, D. C., et al. Accuracy of diagnostic coding for Medicare patients under the prospective payment system. *N. Engl. J. Med.* 318: 352–355, 1988.
81. Ashby, J. L., and Palmer, C. L. The impact of Medicare prospective payment on central city and suburban hospitals. *Health Aff.* 4(4): 99–107, 1985.
82. Guterman, S., et al. The first three years of Medicare prospective payment: An overview. *Health Care Financing Rev.* 9(3): 67–77, 1988.
83. Ware, J. E., et al. Comparison of health outcomes at a health maintenance organization with those of fee-for-service care. *Lancet* i: 1017–1022, 1986.
84. Fackelmann, K. A. Peer review of ambulatory care. *Medicine and Health* 41(35), 1987.
85. Shimshak, D. G., et al. An analysis of HMO disenrollment data. *GHAA Journal* 8(1): 13–22, 1987.
86. Hillman, A. L. Financial incentives for physicians in HMOs: Is there a conflict of interest? *N. Engl. J. Med.* 317: 1743–1748, 1987.
87. Losek, J. B., Wlash-Kelly, C. M., and Altstadt, J. F. HMOs and pediatric emergency care. *Pediatric Emergency Care* 3: 79–82, 1987.
88. McKinlay, J. B., and Arches, J. Towards the proletarianization of physicians. *Int. J. Health Serv.* 15: 161–195, 1985.
89. Ellwood, P. M., et al. Health maintenance strategy. *Med. Care* 9: 291–298, 1971.
90. Whiteis, D., and Salmon, J. W. The proprietarization of health care and the underdevelopment of the public sector. *Int. J. Health Serv.* 17: 47–64, 1987.

91. Sager, A. Why urban voluntary hospitals close. *Health Serv. Res.* 18: 450–475, 1983.
92. Hernandez, S. R., and Kaluzny, A. D. Hospital closure: A review of current and proposed research. *Health Serv. Res.* 18: 419–436, 1983.
93. Robinson, J. C., Garnick, D. W., and McPhee, S. J. Market and regulatory influences on the availability of coronary angioplasty and bypass surgery in U.S. hospitals. *N. Engl. J. Med.* 317: 85–90, 1986.
95. Lee, S. S. Health policy, a social contract: A comparison of the U.S. and Canada. *J. Public Health Policy* 3: 293–301, 1982.

Reprinted with permission from Annals of Internal Medicine Volume 109, Number 6, Pages 494–501, September 15, 1988.

# PART 2

# Implications for the Medical Profession

Prevailing analyses of the changing organization of health care in America have failed to capture the magnitude and severity of the true crisis. The rapidity of change inside the health sector since the mid 1960s, with its direct stimuli from larger economic forces, necessitates a clearer understanding of current dynamics and future possibilities.

Over the past decade, managed care—bringing with it what Relman called that "revolution in assessment and accountability"(1, p. 1220)—has taken on a different tone from the earlier prepaid group practice notion. The once passive public and private payors have become more aggressive in monitoring the clinical, as well as financial, performance of health care providers. Provider organizations— hospitals, health maintenance organizations, and others that contract for physician services—are seeking to hold individual practitioners accountable to newly formulated standards of practice.

The immediate consequence is that medical practice decisions, employment opportunities, compensation, and more are now subject to bureaucratic supervision by managers in large corporate hierarchical entities which pay, and arrange, for the provision of care to insured groups. The individual doctor is less autonomous, has less control over his/her own patients, and increasingly yields on issues of professional loyalty to the employing organization. This shift holds profound implications for professionalism.

The chapters in Part 2 go far in describing what is happening to doctoring, though the explanations differ as to the origins and course of the directions, and their causes and consequences. The authors hold varying assumptions, but all have reflected upon the nature of recent medical practice. Together they offer a departure from previous academic medicine and sociology representations, which have focused upon the changing medical knowledge and technology, the increasing subspecialization of medicine, the growth of bureaucratic forms, the hierarchical extension over the work of other practitioners, among other preoccupations found in exploring medicine as a "social institution." While still relevant, these issues do not capture the political economy of pending professional problems.

The individual chapters that follow provide a combination of views, which significantly illuminate the contextual developments surrounding medical practice. While a few cover similar ground, the seven selections go far in preparing for needed critical research about how these structural changes in health care will affect the future of health workers in America (2).

In the first selection, "Reflections on Modern Doctoring," Stoeckle notes that the doctor-patient relationship has evolved with changing conditions of practice. He sums up how this key relationship has been viewed at different points in time, and he dissects the elements of satisfaction in medical work today. The current impact on medical work as perceived by physicians is a change in the nature of practice from a "calling" of the 1900s, to a "service" in the 1930s, and to a "job" in the 1980s. Physician satisfactions seem diminished whether these are institutional (power), interprofessional (collaborative work), or interpersonal (patient attachments). Stoeckle's opening questions on the physician-patient relationship pave the way for the subsequent inquiries.

In "The Futures of Physicians: Agency and Autonomy Reconsidered," Salmon, White, and Feinglass continue to focus upon the physician role in the context of larger health care delivery. They historically trace these dialectics, identifying costs, corporatization and "a quiet revolution from the use of patient care information to expand the range of options for imposing standards" upon physicians. This analysis broadens Stoeckle's points by directly showing how payment and reimbursement for services shaped the delivery system's directions and its organizational structures. The authors emphasize that the growing pressures by corporate and government payors for cost containment necessitate scrutiny over physician performance, timed with the introduction of information technologies throughout the health sector. This monitoring provides the means for another cost control attempt, where planning, regulation and competition have failed as past strategies. Salmon, White, and Feinglass speculate about alternative futures for physicians, mentioning the rising ethical dilemmas surrounding incentives in how physicians are paid.

Next, Feinglass and Salmon concentrate upon medical management information systems applications, ongoing and potential, as means to propel financially motivated utilization management interventions. The introduction of such systems came with the databases constructed by health care payors, and the resulting scientific exploration of wide variations in the practice of medicine. This chapter examines how innovations in medical management information systems enable greater monitoring of practitioners' clinical decisions in order to improve the productivity of physicians and other health care personnel. As this systems technology shifts power from previously autonomous physicians to corporate health care managers, all of the health professions are likely to be subjected to far more administrative and bureaucratic controls than conceivable even a few years ago.

Light and Levine go on to explore theoretical issues addressing the changing character of the medical profession. From Parsons through Freidson, they point out differences in the dominant sociological perspective that came into favor. Light and Levine rely heavily upon the cultural context, which they see as serving a fundamental source of professional power. These authors discuss three critiques of Freidson's view, which seriously challenge his paradigmatic approach. Freidson still adheres to the assumption that the legal empowerment of the medical profession to make decisions and oversee the medical work of others is key. Light and Levine provide pointed criticisms from the perspectives of: (*a*) deprofessionalization (where Haug maintains that the loss of the monopoly over knowledge, the decline in public esteem for the profession, and the lessening of work autonomy and authority are in evidence); (*b*) proletarianization (where McKinlay, Arches, Stoeckle and others argue that the relations between the medical profession and capitalism are essential to understanding the changed standing of the physician); (*c*) corporatization (where a number of analysts explain how physicians are subjected to forms of corporate control within complex organizations and financial arrangements, also tied to the nature of capitalist development).

In "Professional Dominance or Proletarianization? Neither" Navarro speaks to evidence on the declining power of the medical profession amidst the enormous advances in the production of medical knowledge and technology. Navarro disputes that the profession ever was the dominant force shaping medical practice, its organization, or medical knowledge. This chapter points to a more central role by the dominant class in the political economic and social functioning of the United States. He argues that medicine must be placed in this proper relation to class, gender, race and other power relationships for a fuller understanding of its past and present, and its future directions. This selection clarifies the emerging debate, and challenges the initial assessments about the medical profession's "proletarianization."

In the following chapter, "The Changing Doctor-Patient Relationship and Performance Monitoring: An Agency Perspective," White, Salmon, and Feinglass seek to complement existing analyses on the future of physicians by drawing on an agency framework. The economic theory of agency suggests that problems with monitoring the performance of physicians have been a significant factor in shaping the traditional doctor/patient relationship. Recent expansion of payor and provider monitoring appears to have been triggered primarily by cost containment policies. But refinements in assessment techniques to improve their efficacy and potentially upgrade standards of care are emerging as an important force for further expansion. Expanded monitoring may not only curtail physician autonomy and attenuate relationships between doctors and patients, but undermine systems of professional values and self-regulation, according to these authors. This could create unanticipated quality problems and generate demands for yet further monitoring simply to maintain the existing quality of care.

The final chapter discusses aspects on the above-described debate on professionalism, applied outside the United States. In "Canadian Medicine: Dominance or Proletarianization?" Coburn speaks to the conceptual difficulties in varying theoretical perspectives on medicine. His analysis applied to his own country demarcates stages of development, where in the last stage beginning around 1962, there are increasing signs of professional decline and a beginning "proletarianization." While Canadian medicine, in Coburn's view, has not changed much politically and ideologically, it faces powerful encroachment upon its privileges and prerogatives. This author joins others who regard the position of medicine as "dependent on the broader class struggles." Future analyses applied to a number of nations with advanced health care industries must begin with assessments of the conditions under which medicine is reproduced and transformed. Such intellectual work must become a continuous process because the entirety of the development has not reached its historical maturity. As McKinlay (2, 3), Navarro (4), Salmon and others (5) maintain, the ongoing corporate transformation of health care entails powerful structural and ideological strictures, which cannot be neglected in their organizational expression in medical practice and health care delivery. These await more thorough investigation.

## REFERENCES

1. Relman, A. S. Assessment and accountability: The third revolution in medical care. *N. Eng. J. Med.* 319(18): 1220–1222, 1988.
2. McKinlay, J. B. Introduction: The changing character of the medical profession. *Milbank Mem. Fund Q.* 66(2): 1–10, 1988.
3. McKinlay, J. B. (ed.) *Issues in the Political Economy of Health Care.* Methuen, New York, 1984.
4. Navarro, V. *Crisis, Health, and Medicine.* Routledge and Kegan Paul, New York, 1986.
5. Salmon, J. W. (ed.). *The Corporate Transformation of Health Care, Part I: Issues and Directions.* Baywood Publishing Co., Amityville, New York, 1990.

# CHAPTER 5

# Reflections on Modern Doctoring

## John D. Stoeckle

Yesterday, medical education and training were problematic; today, medical practice is. Looking backward to the 1950s, expanding medical schools and teaching hospitals promised to develop more doctors who would provide quality care over their long lives. To deal with increased specialization and technology, a new generation of students, competent in both the technical and humane care of patients, became the focus of attention.

The teaching and training programs of medical schools and hospitals were then closely examined, first by policy groups and medical sociologists as outsiders (1, 2) and then, somewhat later, by the insiders, the students and residents, who produced their own autobiographical, often alienated, accounts of the experience of becoming a doctor (3). Those initial studies counted importantly in a renewal of education in "comprehensive medicine" for students (4) and of the training of generalists in family medicine, primary care internal medicine, and pediatrics for residents. In this reform of education and training (and of future care), practitioners were seen as a lost cause, organization was largely ignored, and few studies were undertaken (5).

Today, doctoring and the doctor are the focus of attention to education and training, not the student and resident. The conditions of assumptions about medical work are now being questioned, reexamined, and transformed, but without the benefit of empirical studies. The new conditions are changes in the organization of practice; the new assumptions hold that organization determines physician behavior and the quality of care that once was promised by properly educated physicians alone. For understanding the modern work of the doctor and, in turn, practitioners' thinking and feeling about this job, three organizational changes are selected for illustration from among many others that could also be discussed.

These changes are: (a) the rapid, competitive corporatization of practice, (b) an increased use of medical technology, and (c) a new use of information technology. In brief, as practice is corporatized in a more bureaucratic/industrial mode, the doctor becomes an employee and the doctor-patient relationship responds to corporate interests; as clinical work uses more medical technology it becomes not only more technical and specialized but also more divided and "deskilled"; and as information systems monitor the doctor's work, it becomes more standardized and prescribed.

## CORPORATIZATION

Large numbers of medical practitioners—now approaching 60 percent—have moved into group practices of various forms, as corporate group organization becomes the major mode of medical work (6, 7). The most widely discussed form of practice is the prepaid group health maintenance organization (HMO), in which the doctor is a salaried employee. This group-practice corporatization is driven by a variety of forces, perhaps the most important of which is for efficiency to reduce the costs of care (or increase profits) through economies of scale, alternative modes of care (outpatient vs. hospital), nonphysician health workers, and programs to reduce the use of medical services. This corporatization/group-practice trend, of course, is not new, but is only now readily accepted and expanded. The idea and its major goal, efficiency, have been argued ever since the 1900s by early reformers of medical practice.

### The Promises

The early proposals that would reform solo medical practice from "a cottage industry" into salaried group practice were derived from similar reforms of industrial production, namely "Taylorism" (8), that was introduced in the Progressive Era of 1900 to 1920. Manufacturing was broken down into "piece work," and specialized workers for separate tasks were coordinated in a production line that increased efficiency and output. This process was also proposed for organized (group) medical practice (9–11). Medical work, like its industrial counterpart, could be "deskilled" by the transfer of tasks to less highly trained professionals and then reorganized into faster production "teams" for patient care. This organizational efficiency promised additional improvements: (a) the doctors would have more time to care for more people, increasing access; (b) the uncertainty about the doctors' availability for "the sick poor" would be reduced as their work in charity clinics would no longer be "voluntary" but paid for and assigned; (c) the salaried doctor in the community, freed from running a practice, would also have more time to devote to his/her patient's expense; (d) the salaried clinician-researcher in the medical school would not be diverted from laboratory investigation and student instruction by lucrative private practice. Moreover, in that era, the notion was that the doctor's employers (medical schools, hospitals, and groups) would do more social good than the doctor working alone (12) for they were then driven by a religious and civic ethos that promised service to patients, not by business profits of the doctor's "fees for service."

If, in the 1990s, organized practice was under religious and civic ideals that promised more service to patients of all kinds, those conditions do not exist today (13). The current corporatization of medical practice is driven by efficiency for profit, or, if not for profit, the drive is for the reduction of health care costs for the payers, namely government and industry who view them as a burden on the budget or on production (14).

*The Consequences*

This old utopian effort to industrialize medicine's cottage industry with group practices was resisted. The doctor, it was argued, would have divided loyalties to the patient and to the organization, posing an ethical dilemma that was inconsistent with the ideal of the professional as the patient's advocate. The patient would also be lost sight of in a shuffle between specialized members of the health care team, resulting in a loss of therapeutical responsibility. The physician, now more distanced from the patient, might also lose his/her commitment to patient care. Such were the early professional critiques of group work.

Besides this historical resistance to the corporatization of medical practice, later sociological writings critiqued long-stay treatment institutions, though not medical groups or acute hospitals that were the doctor's workshop. These studies noted the impersonality of large-scale organizations, namely those early public-service corporations, the tuberculosis sanatoria (15) and mental hospitals (16), and how their bureaucratic rules and staff behaviors impaired the care of the individual, and indeed, might become victimizing. While these descriptive/critical writings focused on care in long-stay institutions, the problems that these writings addressed may reappear in today's short-stay hospitals. Now that these institutions are more efficiency-driven internally and are externally regulated by public authorities, they, in turn, may demand behaviors of medical staff—e.g., quick discharges of patients—that can impair patient functioning and recovery.

Despite these old critical commentaries, some theorists argue today that modern corporate competition will prevent victimization in treatment institutions and assure more civil and personal treatment. In theory, patients (or customers) may readily exit from a practice (or practitioner) if their interpersonal and medical needs are not met. Practitioners are then pressured into better doctoring and doctor-patient relations in a competitive search for patients. Witness the "we care" adds of corporate practice itself and the external program of the Health Care Financing Administration to publicize "good and bad" performance of hospitals and doctors (17).

## MEDICAL TECHNOLOGY

Technology is a second powerful influence on modern medical work. Today, medical technologies are everywhere—in the patient's home, the doctor's office, the hospital, commercial laboratories, and out-of-hospital free-standing centers of all sorts.

Whether located at hospitals, offices, or multiple sites in the community, medical technologies promised to make the doctor's diagnosis and treatment more accurate, and, even though they are costly, they will be more effective in reducing disease and disability. The technologies also bring specialization of medical work which, in turn, may divide the doctor-'patient relation, or, when technology use is transferred on to nonphysician health workers, the doctor-patient relation may be diminished and, sometimes, even by-passed by use of tests alone. Indeed, the modern patient often has not one but several doctors, along with many non-physician health workers (18); the doctor, in turn, may function as a technician, attending only to the patient's disease with procedures, rather than as a traditional professional attending to both the patient's disease and illness. Moreover, with more diagnostic testing transferred outside the hospital (19) to multiple, divided and specialized sites—imaging centers, free-standing surgical, ambulatory and cancer centers, rehabilitation centers, walk-in units for stroke prevention, and mammography and cancer prevention—testing may even precede the consultation with the doctor. In sum, over the patient's lifetime, each of several interchangeable and complementary specialized practitioners and health care workers provide bits and pieces of medical diagnosis, treatment, and psychological care. The care of the individual has become a more divided task and, under the best of circumstances, a collective collaboration, as has the doctor-patient relationship as well.

There are several consequences of greater and greater technology use. Might the patient be neglected as the doctor pays more attention to machines at the bedside than to the patient (20), or, with the "absentmindedness of specialization," the needs of the patient be ignored in the clinical focus on disease (21)? After such early critiques come more modern ones. As information for diagnosis can be had from tests on patients rather than by talking with them, might the time for learning patients' views then be abbreviated? As more technology moves from the hospital to the medical office, will the encounter with the doctor (and that relation) be perceived as a mere location for patients to receive some medical commodity: diagnostic tests for "check ups," dialysis "for my kidneys," prescriptions tests for "stroke potential"—forms of packaged care for relief, cure, prevention and rehabilitation rather than a service between persons: the doctor and the patient? Finally, will the many items for medical testing be deskilled to other health workers than the doctor, avoiding the medical encounter altogether? This avoidance has already happened as screening and diagnostic tests performed by technicians or doctor-managed technicians are marketed directly to consumers;

the negative results are then communicated to the customer, as are the positive results too, but with the advice to "see your doctor" (22).

## INFORMATION TECHNOLOGY

Compared to the technologies for diagnosis and treatment, the information technology that supports decision systems has new, distinctive implications. In the language of technology assessment, medical technologies may be assessed to be effective (or not) for diagnosis or treatment; in practice, they will then be applied (or misapplied) to the patient by the doctor, illustrating the traditional themes about the doctor's work—the technical (science) and the humane (art). In stark contrast, information technologies are applied not to patients but to doctors, i.e., to their decision making and their medical acts (23).

### The Promises

In effect, decision making about diagnosis and treatment and about medical work may now be prescribed. No longer is the individual doctor expected to continue to dispense knowledge and skills learned during his/her socialization in medical school, hospital training, or even practice. Now a well-defined decision/support system can dictate the flow of events, prescribe optimal information, and provide standards for proper clinical decisions (or standards to judge clinical performance as quality assurance) that the practitioner must meet (24). While these decision/support systems may appear to be for meeting the diagnostic and treatment needs of the patient via the doctor-patient relation, they may be more concerned with meeting corporate needs of accountability, profitability, insurability, and bureaucratic standards. Such use of information technology has an impact on the doctor's job.

### The Consequences

The doctor's job can be viewed as a large and varied number of decisions that are discretionary, based on the physician's individual judgment. Discretionary decisions have been a hallmark of professional autonomy that traditionally doctors have highly valued. Of the multitude of discretionary decisions in practice, those concerning choices in clinical diagnosis and treatment are the most studied—e.g., the diagnostic algorithm for chest pain with its decision trees defining the nature and scope of the patient's workup and treatment. In contrast, management efforts (and their information systems) for controlling the costs of care—e.g., by reducing operations and tests—have an impact on, in turn, not only the clinical decisions of doctors but the doctor/patient relationship and the requests of patients.

Not only for monitoring clinical decisions, information systems can also be used to specify them so that professional actions may be increasingly standardized and routinized, leaving fewer for discretionary judgments. Besides diagnostic and treatment decisions, many other categories of decisions impinge on the doctor-patient relationship and on the work of practice. In comparison to decisions on diagnosis and treatment, those about the work of practice have been infrequently studied, being largely taken for granted because the doctor traditionally made them when "running" his/her own practice. Such work decisions are now made in corporate practices and concern the following issues: (*a*) accountability; (*b*) defensive medicine; (*c*) patient and family requests; (*d*) hospital admission/discharges; (*e*) preventive medicine practices; (*f*) organizational arrangements (the hours to work, the availability of practice sessions, the degree and mode of personal access to the doctor, fees for service, etc.); (*g*) interprofessional practice (referral, consultation, transfer, and consultant care decisions); and (*h*) patient communication, education, and information transmittal decisions. These caretaking discretionary decisions can now be subject to monitoring, if not control, in corporate practices.

In sum, medical practice is now more commercial, competitive, and corporatized, with physicians hired as employees to provide services, a trend fostered by a larger supply of physicians than in the past; more treatment is being used with more physicians' work becoming only technical in nature, "deskilled," and no longer a mix of science and art; and, finally, more of the doctor's decision making is being standardized and monitored, and is no longer discretionary and personal.

## THE PROFESSIONAL RESPONSES: THOUGHTS, FEELING, AND ACTIONS

What then is happening to medical practitioners and how do they think and feel about practice? Of course, professional opinions is these changing times may differ widely depending on such variables as the practitioner's generation, specialty, and practice location, to mention but a few. Despite the limited, specific survey research (25–27), some common views can be identified from a wide variety of sources.

Today's literature on the work and experience of the practitioner, however, is largely anecdotal. Unlike those old empirical studies on education and training, the new sources are the medical throwaways (such as "Private Practice"); the bulletins and newsletters of professional societies (such as the American College of Physicians, Family Medicine, and American Society of Internal Medicine); newspaper accounts; the gossip about professional life at reunions, medical conventions, and staff meetings; and interviews with students, residents, and fellows, along with the experience of practice itself. Such glimpses into modern practice give a hint of the feelings and thinking of practitioners in their adaptation, accommodation, or resistance to changes in organization, technology use, and information systems.

*Professional Thoughts and Feelings*

The modern themes of medical work concern job satisfaction. While variable, overall, it seems less and different. The elements of satisfaction are power, pay, status, control, mission, and rewards that are institutional, interprofessional, and interpersonal.

*Power.* Older clinicians complain about the external bureaucratic regulations of practice that promote short hospital stays and limit admissions, preventing them from meeting the needs of patients. Physicians in preferred provider organizations (PPOs) complain about approvals (and paperwork) for referrals and admissions, explicit restrictions that are part of cost controls in competitive health care plans. These restrict their usual discretionary decisions. In turn, they see themselves as externally regulated, having less power in the control of their practice (28).

*Pay.* Practitioners in primary care specialties—such as internal medicine, pediatrics, and family practice—complain about pay. Their financial rewards (fees from third parties) are diminished as compared to those of their specialty colleagues (29). Physicians, in general, have also seen their income as measured against purchasing power decline. In response, many are increasing their work load (visits per doctor per hour) to maintain income, which can conflict with professional standards. The doctor is prevented from having enough time with the patient to do good clinical work. Pay may not only be less, but jobs—or ideal ones—are harder to find. To the extent that income confers status in the public's view, the practitioners' perception is that their status has declined as, indeed, surveys have also reported (30).

*Control.* In the matter of job satisfaction, the control or management of practice itself was a traditional reward as physicians "ran their own practice (31). But as employees, physicians today may have little participation in or control of practice management. Medical staff complain of "being told what to do" by institutional administrators who may reach decisions that impinge on professional life (for example, practice fees) without discussion or consultations (32).

*Mission.* Besides the professional complaints about bureaucratic and institutional controls that limit discretionary decisions and participation, some sense of loss has come to the mission of practice itself. The older mission of medical institutions and practices has changed from service to individuals and communities to one of marketing technologies and medical commodities to targeted consumers. The rhetoric and advertising are here (33) and many are comfortable with it. Yet, many other practitioners feel a loss of their passion for professional work so defined, wondering if they can keep their old idea of "commitment to service" that had, if only in their mythical belief about their work, unexpressed religious roots. The older view that provision of care in society was a civic and religious service seems out of tune with the newer, secular image of medical work as a corporate job for the distribution of medical products.

*Institutional Rewards.* Besides diminished financial rewards, the quality-assurance reviews of hospitals make physicians feel constantly and publicly observed, not for the steady quality of their performance but for errors, which, in turn, sets them up for criticism and shame, possible loss of jobs and license, and malpractice charges. Even failure to attest records can result in loss of privileges and reports to medical registration boards. Medical staffs are presumably like other workers, producing more and better care with recognition and praise; unfortunately, such communication and notification of quality are not items addressed by quality-assurance management committees in their search for clinical error. The reward of institutional approval for clinical performance has been diminished by such management tactics (34).

*Interprofessional Rewards.* Still other features of practice lessen satisfaction, namely, interprofessional work that has become more controlled and uncertain. In the first instance, for example, payers try to limit consultations as being too costly (except when requiring second opinions for surgery); in the second, emerging health professions stake out therapeutic domains that avoid "Working under (or with) the doctor"—for example, independent nursing practices, physical therapy, and pharmacy. Despite assertions of team work, modern conditions of competition may promote less cooperative work, and less interprofessional interaction, than came from patient exchanges among colleagues in the past (35).

*Interpersonal Rewards.* Regardless of outside (regulations) or inside (management) control of professional life in institutions, the experience of the doctor/patient encounter seems altered. Practitioners complain that the relationship, too, brings diminished rewards, many of which were interpersonal. Historically the relation has been cherished because it is essential to the tasks of doctoring—diagnosis, treatment, communication, support, and prevention—and because it also inspired, gratified, developed and rewarded the doctor.

In the Hippocratic theory of illness, the relation was essential for the medical tasks and for personal care of the person seeking help (36). Since illness arises out of a unique, individual life, knowing the patient through the relation was a necessity for accurate diagnosis and appropriate medical action. The relation was also inspired with those religious and ethical ideals about the rights and duties that define human caring in society (37). It gratified the practitioners, as their autobiographies testify, with the exercise of clinical skill and the therapeutic attachment (38), if not the cure or improvement, of the patient. After medical training, the relation also fostered the development of the doctor on-the-job, continuing the practitioner's life-long learning from experience in the healing science. It could also develop the practitioner's humane qualities as the doctor confronted the suffering of the sick. W. Somerset Maugham (39), as medical student, and William Carlos Williams (40), as practitioner, praised the relationship for the privilege it gave for learning about how others live and suffer—about human nature. Finally, the relation paid off; it was the nexus of the fee-for-service, that monetary exchange for the treatment provided the patient. Paid or not, practice was seen to be altruistic since medical aid always contained a promise that the relief of bodily and mental ills would better the individual—and so benefit society as well. A healthy body and mind made a productive citizen. Moreover, this socially valued work of professional expertise and the recompense for it became a public reward of another kind—status, especially in a society that esteemed financial success.

Given these rewards and interactions, doctors and patients alike have, until recently, celebrated the relation regardless of its public health outcomes on morbidity and mortality—whether or not diseases were always prevented or cured. After all, doctors enabled patients to cope with their disease, disability, and dying. Praise of the relationship also continued even though critics and social science scholars, concerned with the asymmetry in power between doctor and patient, decried doctors' social control of the patient (41, 42) and their dominance in decision making.

Today, however, the relation and the practitioner's feelings about its rewards have changed. The modern experience of doctoring has affected the doctor. Thus, the relation seems, on the one hand, less celebrated and cherished, on the other more alienated and criticized. For example, the patient's communication of information about illness may seem less essential for diagnosis when tests can provide more information on symptomatic and asymptomatic disorders than talking with patients. Doctors report diminished gratification from the encounter as patients are sometimes more adversarial, critical of doctors and less inclined to long-term attachments. The relation is less promising as a life-long phenomenon for learning by doing in one's own practice when new technologies demand study courses and certification outside of one's practice. Praise for professional altruism is gone with everyone—or nearly everyone—a paying (or paid for) patient.

*Professional Actions*

Despite the many changes in organization, technology, and management of practice, the profession has taken few new directions on its own. The mission of practice has not been reinterpreted. Rather, in some instances, the profession has joined hospitals in joint ventures to assure an economic base, or developed competitive , alternative, free-standing physician-run sites for diagnostic testing. National unions have not been formed. Amidst greater regulation and management control, new forms of professional participation and organization have not been invented nor has work been reconsidered and redesigned. Some renewed interest in the views, preferences, and requests of patients is evident in courses on decision making, ethics, and interviewing, if only for "loss-control prevention" in malpractice. As the regulatory and administrative bureaucracy within and outside treatment institutions expands, more professionals seek careers in management that take them away from direct patient care.

## THE FUTURE

Despite these organizational and technological changes that induce professional angst, not all the satisfaction in medical practice has been taken away. Moreover, some new adaptations and accommodations are beginning to emerge, and, in this transition, both younger and older established practitioners now count importantly since the changes going on do not wait on another generation of students to be graduated. Among the continual satisfactions is the exercise of technique and skill. The application of technology to relieve suffering still continues to gratify even as its clinical performance is publicly monitored, graded, and criticized. Another gratification is derived from eliciting patients' preferences and values, and evaluating them before making medical choices from the wide range of technical, diagnostic, and treatment options available. That process requires an intimate, knowing interaction of doctor and patient, one that can be as important as traditional questioning for diagnosis, and one that can be inspiring to both as patient and doctor become engaged in more joint decision making. While much of the privacy and attachment of the therapeutic relationship is often diminished, patients now live so long that each relationship becomes an extended one, with husbands, wives, daughters, and sons attending. Even though the interactions are subject to public review, much medical, educational, and psychological work nonetheless still goes on in the dyadic exchange. For example, since most patients seek an improved quality of life even with disability and chronic disease, their "illness experience" and functional assessment need review.

In medical work, the redesign of the hierarchical corporations of the hospital and group practice into more cooperative work places has been considered, even if it is yet to be implemented. Professional values and perceptions of the professional self continue to change as there is more employment and less upward mobility. Practitioners now search for a job and lifestyle, not a "service commitment" of the 1900s. In the mission of practice, patient-care values may also reappear and be restated despite the present efficiency-driven institutions and regulations. Looking ahead, the old passion, romance, power, money, charisma, and status—mythical as they might all have been—are now going out of doctoring. Yet, as it becomes the newest of the white-collar corporate jobs, doctoring can certainly emerge as a "good job"—if not a profession.

## REFERENCES

1. American Medical Association. *Report of the Citizens Commission on Graduate Medical Education.* Chicago, 1966.
2. Merton, R., Reader, G. G., and Kendall, P. L. *The Student-Physician.* Harvard University Press, Cambridge, 1987.
3. Stoeckle, J. D. Physicians train and tell. *Harvard Med. Alumni Bull.* 61: 9–11, 1987.
4. Reader, G. G., and Goss, M. E. W. *Comprehensive Medical Care and Teaching.* Cornell University Press, Ithaca, 1967.
5. Friedson, E. *Doctoring Together.* Elsevier, New York, 1975.
6. McKinlay, J. B., and Stoeckle, J. D. Corporatization and the social transformation of doctoring. *Finnish J. Soc. Med.* 24: 73–84, 1987.
7. Emmons, D. N. *Changing Dimensions of Medical Practice Arrangements.* American Medical Association, Office of Socioeconomic Research, Chicago, 1987.
8. Zuboff, S. *The Work Ethic and Work Organization in Work Ethic: An Analytical View.* The Industrial Relations Research Association, Madison, Wisconsin, 1983.
9. Cabot, R. C. Suggestions for the reorganization of hospital out-patient departments with special reference to the improvement of treatment. *Maryland Med. J.* 1: 81–91, 1907.
10. Cabot, R. C. What dispensary work should stand for. *Mod. Hosp.* 7: 467–468, 1916.
11. Davis, M. M., and Warner, R. *Dispensaries, Their Management and Development.* Macmillan, New York, 1918.
12. Stoeckle, J. D. Working on the factory floor. *Ann. Int. Med.* 107: 250–251, 1987.
13. Starr, P. *Social Transformation of American Medicine.* Basic Books, New York, 1982.
14. Peterson, P. G. The morning after. *Atlantic* 260: 43–69, 1987.
15. Roth, J. A. *Timetables.* Bobbs-Merrill, New York, 1963.
16. Goffman, E. *Asylums: Essays on the Social Situation of Mental Patients and Other Inmates.* Doubleday Anchor, New York, 1961.
17. Higgins, L. C. Federal data bank may do harm. *Med. World News* 29(11): 17–18, 1988.
18. Stoeckle, J. D., and Twaddle, A. Non-physician health workers. *Soc. Sci. Med.* 8: 71–76, 1974.
19. Health Industry Manufacturers Association. *Alternate Site Provider Report: An Update.* Washington, D.C., 1988.
20. Reiser, S. J. *Medicine and the Reign of Technology.* Cambridge University Press, Cambridge, 1977.
21. Cabot, R. C. Humanizing the care of the sick poor. *City Club Bull.* 4: 113–118, 1911.
22. Fentiman, I. S. Pensive women, painful vigils: Consequences of delay in assessment of mammographic abnormalities. *Lancet* 2: 1041–1042, 1988.
23. Lorch, S. Technology and the work of the doctor outside the hospital. *Int. J. Technol. Assess. Health Care* 5: 43–52, 1989.
24. Goldman, L., et al. A computer protocol to predict myocardial infarction in emergency department patients with chest pain. *N. Engl. J. Med.* 318: 797–808, 1988.
25. Colombots, J., and Kirchner, C. *Physicians and Social Change.* Oxford University Press, New York, 1986.
26. Rubin, W. Survey shows increasing unhappiness of internists. *Int. Med. News* 21: 1, 11, 19, 28, 1988.
27. Derber, C. Physicians and their sponsors: The new medical relation of production. In *The Political Economy of Health Care,* edited by J. B. McKinlay, pp. 217–254. Tavistock, New York, 1984.

28. Lachine, Y. A. From the trenches: Strangled by rules and regulations. *Int. Med. News* 21: 52–53, 1988.
29. Burdell, G. P. The plight of primary care physicians. *Am. Coll. Phys. Observer* 5, March 1987.
30. Blendon, R. J. The public's view of the future of health care. *JAMA* 259: 3587–3589, 1988.
31. Mechanic, D. The growth of medical technology and bureaucracy: Implications for medical care. *Milbank Mem. Fund Q.* 55: 61–79, 1977.
32. Sheldon, A. *Managing Doctors*. Dow Jones-Irwin, Homewood, Ill., 1986.
33. Field, M. G. Turf battles on Medicine Avenue. *Society* 25: 12–17, 1988.
34. Weinstein, M. Policing the profession. *Am. Coll. Phys. Observer* 1: 10–11, 1988.
35. Physicians woes are pervasive. *Med. World News* 28(7): 14, 1987.
36. Osler, W. *Aequaminitas*. Blakiston, Philadelphia, 1952.
37. Percival, T. *Medical Ethics*. J. Johnson and J. Bickerstaff, London, 1803.
38. Hertler, A. E. *The Horse and Buggy Doctor*. Harper and Brothers, New York, 1938.
39. Maugham, W. S. *The Summing Up*. Heineman, London, 1938.
40. Williams, W. C. *The Doctor Stories*. New Direction Books, New York, 1954.
41. Zola, I. K. Medicine as an institution of social control. *Sociol. Rev.* 20: 487–504, 1972.
42. Illich, I. *Medical Nemesis*. Pantheon, New York, 1976.

Reprinted with permission from The Milbank Quarterly, Volume 66, Supplement 2, Pages 76–91, 1988.

# CHAPTER 6

# The Futures of Physicians: Agency and Autonomy Reconsidered

## J. Warren Salmon, William D. White and Joe Feinglass

After half a century of relative stability, dramatic changes are occurring in the delivery and financing of medical care in America. No longer a cottage industry, it is now big business, symbolized by the ascension of regional, national and multi-national organizations. Over only the last twenty years, large for-profit corporations have secured a major position in hospitals, nursing homes, Health Maintenance Organizations (HMOs), home care and other service areas.

Medical care has moved out of the patient's home into huge medical complexes. A physician transported in time from the early part of this century would be amazed by the size and sophistication of the modern hospital. He would also certainly be bewildered by the complexity in how physicians are compensated for their services. One aspect of the organization of care he would find familiar, however, would be his own role.

Despite the enormous changes in health care, the role of physicians has remained remarkably the same (1). At the turn of the century, physicians acted as their patients' agents. Final responsibility was vested in them for the coordination of care, whether provided at home, in the office, or in the hospital. As independent agents, they were usually subject only to informal review, by their peers and their individual patients.

A majority of physicians still operate within this old basic framework. Acting as the autonomous agent of their patients, the physician has been the titular "captain of the health care team." Most physicians continue to be paid on a fee-for-service basis, albeit through often third party intermediaries. The primary method of quality assurance remains self-regulation.

125

However, the physician's role in modern medicine is finally being altered; there is now an increasing move to hold physicians accountable for their clinical decisions. Escalating costs from the mid-1960s brought a corresponding increase in governmental cost containment policies and regulatory safeguards for the quality of care. Today physicians are subject to sometimes stringent monitoring by "outside parties," including not only government regulators and purchasers of employee health care benefits, but also managers and administrators in settings where doctors have traditionally practiced unencumbered. A growing number of physicians are salaried employees or dependent on some form of contract for "managed care". Those who continue to practice on a fee-for-service basis increasingly must answer to public and private payors for financial implications of their medical decisions.

As Winkelwerder and Ball have stated, "The physician-patient relationship—once based on a covenant whereby the patient trusted the physician to do what was best for him or her—is being transformed into a contractual relationship in which the physician provides a specified, measurable service at a negotiated price. . . . Increasingly, the ideals of competition, efficiency, risk-taking, profit, and market-derived concepts of quality service are determining priorities. A critical question is how much the values of physician-patient trust and doing what is best for patients can be maintained in such an environment" (2, p. 317).

This chapter explores what may be the twilight years of the doctor we have known since the historic Flexner Report of 1910. We examine forces behind these developments and speculate about implications for the future. The growing literature on the changing position of physicians has focused on: first, the impact of rising costs, efforts to contain them, and changes in the objectives of payors and providers, and second, the corporatization of the health care industry, partly as a result of penetration of large-scale for-profit firms, but also as result of the increasing adoption of corporate managerial techniques by "not-for-profit" providers (3, 4).

We also see a third, more subtle factor as crucial: a quiet revolution from the use of patient care information to expand the range of options for imposing standards (5). Physicians have long defied attempts at standardized health services, claiming the highly individualized, complex nature of medical problems makes assembly line techniques impractical except for the most rudimentary care. Indeed, the traditional methods of peer review and professional self-regulation in medicine have been predicated on individualized care to assure quality. Organized medicine's efforts to preserve a one-on-one patient relationship have also contributed to this status quo. But basically, its survival has reflected the absence of any feasible alternative. External monitoring of physicians' clinical performance has never offered a practical substitute to professional control over quality assurance within the context of American medicine—until now.

## HISTORICAL BACKGROUND

The modern role of the physician as the patient's autonomous agent is rooted in the late 19th century. Characterized as a "cottage industry," medicine consisted of solo practitioners, who provided care out of their own homes and in patients' homes for fees and sometimes barter. Little support staff or capital equipment was required. Before the scientific advances and medical discoveries which marked the latter part of the century, the physician (overwhelmingly male in gender) could carry most of his technology around in his black bag. Medical training itself was highly variable. There were a large number of medical schools, many operated on a proprietary basis, and their quality was often dubious. But while many schools were recognized as substandard, there was little consensus on what constituted appropriate standards for medical education as homeopaths, allopaths, eclectics, and later osteopaths clashed.

Hospitals (under 200 existed in the early 1870s) were primarily places to die, housing the urban poor and working class who could not afford private practitioners. Partly motivated by professional altruism, physicians often donated services part-time in hospital dispensaries set up in larger cities. But hospitals also provided new opportunities in practice, and significant prestige. Voluntary religious and charitable organizations, founded and administered early hospitals, paying the nursing and non-nursing professional staff. While medical care was usually free, patients who could afford private physicians generally avoided hospitals.

Licensure laws introduced in the late 19th century gave physicians a monopoly and provided a framework for attempting to ensure competence through entry examinations and educational requirements. By the end of the century, members of the American Medical Association (AMA) and the medical specialty societies, marching under the banner of "scientific medicine," emerged as a dominant force within the profession. Reform efforts culminated in the Carnegie Foundation-sponsored Flexner Report of 1910 and the subsequent reorganization of medical education with substantial Rockefeller Foundation funding (6, 7). These interventions coincided with the closing of many existing schools, and the upgrading of medicine to a graduate course of study. Physicians' economic status increased as the number of graduates declined.

The professionalization of medicine involved attempts to raise not only standards of competence, but also performance, and to develop a clear sense of collective identity within the occupation. Two of the foremost tenets of these efforts were: (*a*) that the medical profession should be self-regulating; and (*b*) that physicians should remain autonomous fee-for-service agents.

To a large degree, the history of medicine before the 1930s is the history of the rise of the modern hospital and the growth of medical specialties (8). Around 1900 the hospital began to shed its image as a place to be avoided and emerged as the doctor's workshop, a symbol of the achievements of modern scientific medicine. Patient payments to hospitals were limited to room and board, supplies and drugs; physician fees were excluded. Private patients continued to pay their doctors directly, just as they did on an outpatient basis, while physician services for the poor continued to be donated.

The economic independence of physicians from hospitals was paralleled by a basic managerial split within these institutions. Hospitals provided capital and support staff, including nurses and a wide range of technical support personnel, such as radiologic technologist and laboratory technicians. While (increasingly) the role of physicians shifted from the direct providers of care to the coordinators of the production of complex services using resources provided by hospitals, there was no corresponding shift in clinical accountability to the administration of the hospital. Rather, physicians remained directly accountable only to their peers and their patients.

Over the years doctors vehemently opposed efforts to turn them into employees, and organized medicine worked diligently to preserve physician autonomy and the fee-for-service system. The dramatic successes of scientific medicine, at least as perceived by the public, lent a powerful legitimacy to medicine's claims for the superiority of professional self-regulation. In addition, in the face of clinical successes, there was a strong sense that "more was better." This became the hallmark of our fee-for-service system, which created incentives to overprovide care, particularly care based on technologically defined procedures. Derber maintains: "The traditional privileged and personal relation between physicians and patients created a critical market leverage for physicians that prevented either the private hospitals which capitalized them or the third parties which carried out other market-mediating functions for them from consolidating full control" (9, p. 219).

When voluntary health insurance took hold under Blue Cross-Blue Shield plans in the late 1930s, they ushered in major organizational changes. At first, physicians feared that third party payors of any sort could compromise their autonomy, but eventually they accepted indemnity insurance under physician control which preserved patients' "freedom of choice" by ruling out any restriction on providers, effectively restricting prepaid group practice plans.

With a paucity of external cost or utilization controls, a natural incentive for physicians existed to extend state-of-the art diagnostic and therapeutic technology consistent with a general perception of the "best" care as the most care. Not surprisingly, indeed as hospitals had hoped with Blue Cross, open-ended private insurance coverage served to buoy demand as an endless bounty for pharmaceutical firms and hospital equipment and supply companies. Between 1950 and 1965, health care spending rose from 4 percent of Gross National Product to 5.9 percent, an increase of nearly 50 percent (10).

In the heyday of the Great Society of the 1960s, the budgetary ramifications of providing a blank check for providers were greatly underestimated under

Medicare and Medicaid. Between 1965 and 1975, the share of GNP spent on health care rose from 5.9 percent to 8.2 percent, while today at over 12 percent, it is nearly double its 1965 level (10). Some expansion can be attributed to increased access to care for those who previously lacked means for payment. However, more stems from the greater intensity and complexity of medical care to patients from whom to extract revenue.

Nevertheless, the underlying organizational structure of health care changed remarkably little. Until the 1970s, physicians retained their autonomous role as independent coordinators of patient care, their authority largely unchallenged by either hospital administrators, third party payors, or the public or private sectors. The internal composition of hospitals had continued to allow physicians control over resources with minimal managerial oversight.

## COST CONTAINMENT: FROM THE 1970s

The Nixon proclamation of a "health care crisis" in 1969 ushered in a new era in American health care policy; its central feature was to move away from concerns about access towards an emphasis on cost-containment. Underlying this shift were the explosive growth in health care expenditures and a general slowing in the rate of overall economic growth. Subsequently, public and private sources of funding forced a major reevaluation of the open-ended payment policies of the 1960s. On the one hand, policymakers puzzled over whether efficiency could be improved (i.e., get the same services using less resources). On the other hand, some critics questioned whether the issue was not also too many services, challenging the notion that "more was better."

The early 1970s saw restrictions on cost-based reimbursement and efforts to directly promote innovations; by the 1980s, there was an attempt to restrain costs by "making the market work" through pro-competitive policies based upon shifting financial risks to providers and consumers. The collective failure of the former became the ammunition for the market advocates.

Ironically, the implementation of these 1980s Reagan policies increased the level of (public and private) regulation hitherto unimagined. The center piece—the Medicare Prospective Payment System (PPS)—shifted financial risks from the government to individual hospitals. Here the notion was by tying hospital reimbursement to the average nationwide costs of providing Medicare "product lines" (i.e., Diagnosis Related Groups, DRGs), economic incentives would induce efficiency. A second component was more political cost containment—cutbacks in Medicaid spending and greater consumer cost sharing under Medicare. Finally, there was major new utilization review through government Professional Review Organizations (PROs) and private payors. A growing shift towards corporate self-insurance then spurred changes in previously placid private health insurance. Employers and insurers have both brought their market power to bear through Preferred Provider Organizations (PPOs) and other managed care plans, with ever more stringent utilization review guidelines, for example, requiring preadmission certification before non-emergency hospital care, and denying payment when inappropriate care is given (11).

The combined effect of these private and government efforts has been a massive increase in data reporting requirements and large-scale review of the clinical and financial aspects of patient care, though the financial impact of public and private cost containment efforts in the 1980s remains debatable. Local and regional concentration increased with the consolidation of for-profit and "not-for-profit" hospital and HMO chains. Long standing systems of cross-subsidization for hospital care have collapsed, leading to significant reshuffling of indigent patients among providers, often "dumped" on public hospitals and clinics (12). Yet health care expenditures have continued to increase at a rapid rate, outpaced by the growth in administrative waste related to the corporatization of care (13). Alper wrote in 1984: "The transformation of the hospital from a traditionally altruistic and humanistic institution into a series of profit centers has barely begun. . . . I have trouble understanding how management can grow so rapidly in the face of a falling patient census. . . .Discussion of consumer demographics, target populations, product lines, and marketing compete with traditional concerns over service and the quality of care. Talented people from industry are being hired at high salaries in the hope of acquiring a magic money-making touch. These newcomers speak of focus groups and pretesting and of advertising and image building. They tell of the way in which appliances are sold. Those who have a background in health care are intimidated. At meetings of their own, they are learning to parrot the jargon and fit in with that new thought process. Already accustomed to vague titles and sanitized job descriptions, they are perhaps less resistant to dubious new ideology and its human representatives" (14, p. 1250).

## INFORMATION SYSTEMS MONITORING: THE QUIET REVOLUTION

With the enactment of Medicare in 1965, hospitals were required to establish utilization review committees to review care for the elderly, and eventually for participants in Medicaid. Later, mandated Professional Standards Review Organization (PSROs) extended the scope of quality monitoring to a regional level. In these early years, the process focused on four criteria: (a) the necessity or appropriateness of the admission, (b) the length of stay, (c) services ordered and provided, and (d) discharge practices or the outcome of the episode of care.

As more detail became required and the amount of case mix information needed for hospital strategic planning increased, more sophisticated analytical methods were developed using computer databases to examine patterns of medical practice. The PSROs, however, lacked sufficient clout and resources to have other than minimal impact from the outside.

Quietly, without the fanfare that accompanied either the Nixon administration restructuring or the pro-competitive policies of the Reagan administration, all this has changed. Beginning in the late 1970s, monitoring mushroomed. Three factors have provided the impetus. First, the assembly of computerized data bases in conjunction with cost containment led select state agencies, the federal government, PROs, and private purchasers and payors to require substantial reporting of patient data as a condition for reimbursement. The Health Care Financing Administration's Medicare statistics are the best known of these huge data files, but many others exist as well. At the same time, computing costs declined rapidly; what was once an expensive project for a mainframe computer can now be accomplished on some desk top models. The combined effect has been to make enormous amounts of information available at relatively modest cost. Finally, as researchers and bureaucrats began to explore this burgeoning clinical and cost data, findings from the data set up a powerful dynamic themselves. For as research has progressed, it has become apparent that huge variations exist in resource utilization that do not appear directly linked to patient care outcomes. This has created a crippling challenge to traditional quality assurance and legitimized experimentation with stricter modes of monitoring.

New computerized databases have been designed to yield analysis of the financial implications of (a) the diagnostic process, hitherto the exclusive domain of the physician, including new knowledge-based approaches to clinical decision analysis, (b) the specific decisions physicians make for therapeutic services, including the potential to utilize computerized prediction rules and treatment algorithms, and (c) patient outcomes, which can be assessed over time to determine the cost effectiveness of clinical interventions by treatment patterns and by specific physician.

While research on physician practice variations is quite recent, it provides the basis for a third wave of regulation in health care. Studies on geographic variation in the per capita consumption of medical services have emphasized the discretionary nature of medical decision-making, particularly in differential rates of hospitalization and surgery which appear unrelated to illness rates, demographic or socioeconomic characteristics, insurance coverage, or access to services (15). A Study of Maine hospital service areas demonstrates the magnitude of the variations phenomenon. Between 1980 and 1982, 85 percent of all hospital admissions (adjusted for care received out of area) fell into DRGs with higher variations than hysterectomy, a surgical procedure which is known to have a four-fold variation between similar populations (16).

Hospital lengths of stay are particularly targeted. Studies of inappropriate lengths of stay, extensively reviewed by Payne (11), have found between 12 and 39 percent of acute care days to be medically unneeded. The financial implications of such practice variations are revealed in research on annual Medicare expenditures per beneficiary, which were found to be 66 percent above the national average in the Miami metropolitan area, but only 7 percent above average in the Tampa-St. Petersburg metropolitan area 250 miles away (17).

Coming at a time of disenchantment with both direct cost controls and market incentives, physician practice variation studies give ammunition to policymakers and administrators for a major assault on the doctor as the autonomous coordinator of care. The logic is disarmingly simple: because some physicians are able to provide quality care for less, others should too. The level of cost variations discovered are so vast that they overshadow any quibbles about quality standardization.

In and of themselves, the variations studies' results have not provided a solution to the problem they have identified. Most theoretical explanations emphasize discretionary physician practice habits combined with supply factors (i.e., availability of hospital beds or surgeons). The questions are: What constitutes optimal practice standards, and how can they be implemented?

One of the foremost authorities on variations in medical practice, Wennberg asserts: "The nation's growing demand for improved quality, efficiency, and equity in its health care system is thus hostage to unresolved theories about correct practice. The unsettled nature of contemporary medical opinion on correct practice, the high prevalence of the underlying conditions that reasonably fit theory, and the steady growth in the numbers of specialists trained in invasive technologies merge to insure the continued increase in the per capita cost of care" (18).

As PROs and "managed care" initiatives grapple with both, there has been a strong tendency to evolve towards defining the "best" medical care as that which is parsimonious: order fewer tests, defer hospitalizations, and get the patient out of the hospital quickly—all within the framework of cost effectiveness. However, broad consensus on quality standards is hard to achieve. Scientific and epidemiological evidence about the medical effectiveness and the appropriateness of common diagnostic and therapeutic interventions often remains negligible (19).

Nevertheless, the feeble educational and monitoring programs of the 1970s, symbolized by the ambiguous legacy of the PSROs, have been superceded by ever more stringent *utilization management* strategies. Physicians are now finding themselves subject to unprecedented efforts to constrain their patient care decisions with numerous care-avoidance incentives for cost control. The computerization of medical records, which is following the automation of laboratory, pharmacy, radiology and other ancillary service orders, has made possible sophisticated tracking techniques focused on physicians' differential "test-treatment thresholds" and individual physician practice profiles. Sophisticated software is being developed to integrate patients' registration, billing, utilization, diagnostic, demographic and clinical status. Combining outpatient and inpatient records with prospective problem-oriented reminders may enable a new breed of physician administrator to preside over clinical cost and quality algorithms, and to review the clinical productivity of their "peer" subordinates. Surveillance of physician orders has become a major activity of management in hospitals, HMOs, and PPOs.

Beyond this, new policy initiatives at the federal level to brake escalating costs of Medicare Part B may greatly accelerate the trends towards automated records described above.

## THE FUTURES OF PHYSICIANS

Reconsideration of traditional agency and autonomy issues in medicine comes along with the failings of scientific medicine to "cure" the bulk of chronic degenerative conditions—the specific diseases from which our aging population increasingly suffers. Chronic diseases often involve huge treatment costs over a lifetime. Generations of Americans who have come to expect eventual "conquests" of these "epidemics of modern civilization" now are being told that remedies have become too costly, requiring rationing to reduce expenditures (20). Limitations on payment have already lessened discretionary authority in patient care decisions in may settings, most notably for HMOs and PPOs and exclusions under private indemnity insurance, as well as Medicaid programs.

Numerous well-publicized studies by physicians find their peers guilty of substantial inappropriate use of medical and surgical proceedures, from laboratory tests and X-rays to coronary bypass surgery and pacemaker implants (21). Policymakers are weighing the advisability of restricting the use of many "medical advances" which were often never properly studied in the first place, but became dispersed throughout the health care system (in no small part due to handsome reimbursement of physicians and drug and medical equipment firms). New technology introductions are being cost-scrutinized rather strenuously.

Moreover, a wide range of iatrogenesis (i.e., doctor-inflicted disease) has also been revealed, much of which inevitably results from application of increasingly powerful, often dangerous, drugs and technologies. Academic studies and emotional allegation alike get into the popular and business media coverage (22). Whether referred to as "adverse medical outcomes," "excess mortality," or "cascade iatrogenesis," patients, and payors, have taken heed of the estimated 200,000 Americans each year who are harmed during medical encounters. The "sacred trust" given doctors becomes questionable when a large scale RAND Corporation study found that 17 percent of coronary angiography, 32 percent of carotid endarterectomy, and 17 percent of upper gastrointestinal endoscopy procedures were performed inappropriately (23). Similar reports propel the Health Care Financing Administration's release of Medicare data on individual physician performance profiles (as it has for hospital mortality rates) as part of a preferred provider program designed to lead patients to avoid certain practitioners and institutions.

Unprecedented reactions by private payors reveal an even greater impetus toward limiting physician autonomy. Widely disseminated throughout the business press, Allied Signal Corporation in New Jersey limits payment of their employees' health care to a closed panel of pre-determined physicians and hospitals, about whom they secured performance data through CIGNA, now the largest health insurance firm in the nation. Prudential, the second largest, is channeling its 20 million clients to pre-selected hospitals that have met its quality and cost standards for transplants. Stemming from computerized data analyses of existing providers, additional actions are now commonplace. As payor determinations are implemented, choice of provider is increasingly limited for both the patient and the patient's physician who may wish to recommend a referral if payment is to be forthcoming.

Malpractice acts as well as cases, inappropriate utilization, and medical avarice will all be targeted through more sophisticated surveillance. Doctors will have greater reason to feel disenchanted with their "calling" to a profession increasingly finding its ethics dictated by financial constraints. The profession's own lack of more responsible and effective leadership has provoked those outside the house of medicine to directly challenge physician behavior and decision making (24). The former editor of *The New England Journal of Medicine*, admonishes: "As we try to deal with all the issues raised by the new economics of medical practice, we would do well to keep this guiding principle in mind: Doctors, whether salaried or not, must first of all be advocates for their patients. The economic interests of an employer should not be permitted to interfere with a physician's ability to meet that basic responsibility. Neither, of course, should the economic interests of the physician. Salaried practice has much to recommend it, but like the fee-for-service arrangement . . . it must retain the ethical priorities on which the profession of medicine is based"(25).

Coincidentally serving to undermine autonomy is the sheer growth of the profession—from 142 professionally active physicians per 100,000 population in 1950 to 180 in 1975 and 228 in 1985, with 260 projected for the year 2000 (26). Likewise, the number of group practices, where physician-managers help to socialize their colleagues into acceptance of clinical limitations, has grown from 6,371 in 1969 to 10,762 in 1980 to 17,556 in 1986. Of the non-federal physicians in practice today, nearly one-fourth are salaried. As the average debt of medical school graduates (measured in constant dollars) climbed from $19,700 in 1981 to $28,000 in 1986, most graduates found few options other than salaried slots. More and more dependent upon the purpose and character of the employing organizations, physicians face such trends contributing to their "deprofessionalization," or a "proletarianization" of physicians (27, 28).

Looking to the future, we see three broad areas emerging for the profession within the context of expanding "managed care systems" based on new information technologies. The first continues a patient's agency relationship, but with the doctor in the service of another master, the third party payor through the managed care intermediary. Besides the Independent Practice Association (IPA) form of HMOs, Preferred Provider Organizations (PPOs) have become models under pre-arranged, fee-for-service payment. Hospital executives have in place rudimentary physician practice profiles based on DRGs. With the introduction of a Medicare relative value scale payment of doctors (29), entrepreneurial physician groups may become more involved in peer review and utilization monitoring as brokers to insurers and purchasers.

The tone of such arrangements may vary from cooperative to adversarial, depending upon both the organization's auspice and the immediacy of a funding crunch. A major issue discussed by various physicians—from academic specialists doing costly referrals to fee-for-service stalwarts—has been the degree of relative autonomy permitted in such a managed care framework. Under stringent utilization controls and/or denial of payment where care is ruled unnecessary or inappropriate, conflicts will escalate. Ethical dilemmas may be felt by old-line physicians when determining the patient's needs versus what gets paid for.

In areas of routinized technical services, the physician as a skilled supervisory employee may emerge as a second career path, most likely as in radiology, pathology, and certain procedural medical subspecialties where the hold of fee-for-service has lately been tenuous. These tasks lend themselves to standardized protocols, usually performed or assisted in by subordinate allied health specialists. High-cost diagnostic and therapeutic services are easily brought under tight control; these are the areas where hospital management can best appropriate productivity increases as profit. Here tools and methodologies for data collection are quite advanced, and managerial pressures for cost-savings are great. It seems likely that such physicians, many salaried, will be integrated completely into centralized hierarchies in hospitals, where the notion of the doctor as the patient's independent agent has already eroded.

A third area of change will occur where a high-level of protocol regimentation is possible, a new kind of "medical modularization" not necessarily limited to just primary care. Any clinical endeavor subject to similar, repetitive tasks for patients, where physician judgment is not highly developed, can be subjected to instantaneous reviews of clinical input and physician treatment decisions. Computerized expert systems, now in experimental stages, are being developed and introduced with advances in the technology; they incorporate demands by management for greater standardization in handling complex problems and reducing excessive utilization. Analogies can be found beyond medicine, to case workers in child welfare and criminal justice activities. Assessing quality, often conveniently defined as implementing uniform policy, may be made a much more easier task if clinical algorithms are in place.

An immediate application of this last area might be in public sector medicine. Twenty-some years after the enactment of Medicare and Medicaid, a multitiered distribution of medical care is being openly discussed as a matter of public policy. The sort of "no frills" care evolving under such strategies could become synonymous with rigid limitations of the latitude of physicians caring for Medicaid and uninsured patients. This could be accomplished by a mixture of budget constraints (already in place thanks to the Reagan-Bush policies and state and local fiscal limits) and calculated clinical algorithms for rationing services for these so-called "unproductive" elements in our society. It can now be observed that such constraints have profoundly alienating effects, transforming medicine from a professional pursuit to a mere job in huge, impersonal bureaucracies. Beyond this, such surveillance and fiscal limitations by protocol, even for those practicing in less strict frameworks, are likely to have a deleterious impact on professionalism (30).

On the more positive side, great strides in improving quality, eliminating much inappropriate and unnecessary care, and lessening harmful malpractice may all be possible under the developing interventions to change physician practice patterns. By scrutinizing patient care encounters on a mass scale, the potential is there to know in a broader sense—and to implement uniformly across the health care system—what constitutes both efficacy and cost-effectiveness. This would be especially relevant to pharmaceutical care interventions.

Nonetheless, the institutional and organizational setting bears powerfully on clinical decisions, and observers, as well as medical practitioners, are noting numerous ethical dilemmas arising out of the rapid changes. Given current public policy in the United States, which tolerates vast inequities in the distribution of care and fosters the pursuit of profit over patient care and community needs, one must pause to seriously ponder the obvious ethical responsibility facing professionals today.

While debate ensues in medical journals over the conflicting obligations of physicians to corporate employer or to clients, perverse economic incentives still either reward physicians for overzealous services, or lead providers to withhold care when paid prospectively. The contradiction between producing medical services based on profitability, and physician's traditional commitment to healing and maintaining health should be the focus of discussion.

## REFERENCES

1. White, W., and Dranove, D. Agency and the organization of health care. *Inquiry* 24: 405–415, 1987.
2. Winkelwerder, W., and Ball, J. R. Transformation of American health care: The role of the medical profession. *N. Engl. J. Med.* 318: 317–319, 1988.
3. Salmon, J. W. (ed.). *The Corporate Transformation of Health Care, Part I: Issues and Directions.* Baywood Publishing Co. Amityville, N.Y., 1990.
4. Salmon, J. W. (ed.). *The Corporate Transformation of Health Care, Part II, Reflections and Implications.* Baywood Publishing Co., Amityville, N.Y., 1993.
5. Feinglass, J., and Salmon, J. W. Corporatization of medicine: The use of medical management information systems to increase the clinical productivity of physicians. *Int. J. Health Serv.* 20: 233–252, 1990.
6. Berliner, H. S. *A System of Scientific Medicine.* Tavistock Publications, New York, 1985.
7. Brown, E. R. *Rockefeller Medicine Men.* University of California Press, Berkeley, 1979.

8. Starr, P. *The Social Transformation of American Medicine*. Basic Books, New York, 1982.
9. Derber, C. Capitalism and the medical division of labor: The changing situation of physicians. In *Issues in the Political Economy of Health Care*, edited by J. B. McKinlay, pp. 217–256. Methuen, New York, 1984.
10. Freeland, M., and Schendler, C. Health spending in the 1980's: Integration of clinical practice patterns with management. *Health Care Financ. Rev.* 5: 1–68, 1984.
11. Payne, S. M. C. Identifying and managing inappropriate hospital utilization: A policy synthesis. *Health Serv. Res.* 22: 709–769, 1987.
12. Ansell, D. A., and Schiff, R. L. Patient dumping: Status, implications, and policy recommendations. *JAMA* 257: 1500–1502, 1987.
13. Himmelstein, D. U., and Woolhandler, S. Cost without benefit: Administrative waste in US health care. *N. Engl. J. Med.* 314: 441–445, 1986.
14. Alper, P. R. The new language of hospital management. *N. Engl. J. Med.* 311: 1249–1251, 1984.
15. Shaheen, P., Clark, J. D., and Williams, D. Small area analysis: A review and analysis of the North American literature. *J. Health Polit. Policy Law* 12: 741–809, 1987.
16. Wennberg, J. E., McPherson, K., and Caper, P. Will payment based on diagnosis-related groups control hospital costs? *N. Engl. J. Med.* 311: 295–300, 1984.
17. McClure, W., and Shaller, D. Variations in medical expenditures. *Health Aff.* 3: 120–129, 1984.
18. Wennberg, J. E. The paradox of appropriate care. *JAMA* 258: 2568–2569, 1987.
19. Eddy, D. M., and Billings, J. The quality of medical evidence: Implications for quality care. *Health Aff.* 7: 19–32, 1988.
20. Feinglass, J. Variations in physician practice and covert rationing. *Theor. Med.*, pp. 31–45, 1987.
21. Eisenberg, J. M. *Doctor's Decisions and the Cost of Medical Care: The Reasons for Doctor's Practice Patterns and Ways to Change Them*. Health Administration Press Perspectives, Ann Arbor, 1986.
22. Otten, A. L. How medical advances often worsen illnesses and even cause death. *Wall Street Journal*, July 27, 1988, p. 1.
23. Chassin, M. R., et al. Does inappropriate use explain geographic variations in the use of services? A study of three procedures. *JAMA* 258: 2533–2537, 1987.
24. Salmon, J. W. The medical profession and the corporatization of the health sector. *Theor. Med.* 8: 19–29, 1987.
25. Relman, A. S. Salaried physicians and economic incentives. *N. Engl. J. Med.* 319: 784, 1988.
26. Kletke, P. R., Marder, W. D., and Silberger, A. B. *The Demographics of Physician Supply: Trends and Projections*. American Medical Association Center for Health Policy Research, Chicago, 1987.
27. Ritzer, G., and Walczak, D. Rationalization and the deprofessionalization of physicians. *Social Forces* 67: 1–22, 1988.
28. McKinlay, J. B., and Stoeckle, J. D. Corporatization and the social transformation of doctoring. In *The Corporate Transformation of Health Care, Part I: Issues and Directions*, edited by J. W. Salmon, pp. 133152. Baywood Publishing Co., Amityville, N.Y., 1990.
29. Christensen, C. Developing a relative value scale for physician payments. *The Internist: Health Policy in Practice* 28(3): 6–9, 1987.
30. White, W. D., Salmon J. W., and Feinglass, J. The changing doctor-patient relationship and performance monitoring: An agency perspective. In *The Corporate*

*Transformation of Health Care, Part II: Reflections and Implications,* edited by J. W. Salmon. Baywood Publishing Co., Amityville, N.Y., 1993.

Reprinted with permission from Theoretical Medicine, Volume 11, Pages 261–274, 1990, Klumer Academic Publishers.

# CHAPTER 7

# The Use of Medical Management Information Systems to Increase the Clinical Productivity of Physicians

## Joe Feinglass and J. Warren Salmon

Unlike engineers and other scientific and technical personnel employed in manufacturing, physicians have long resisted their reduction to paid employees. In the United States, the medical profession has won an unprecedented measure of autonomy from outside interference in medical practice. The profession's ideological hegemony in the health care delivery system has rested upon its highly specialized knowledge, requiring lengthy training and decision-analytical methods presumed to be inaccessible to nonprofessionals (i.e., only members of the profession can evaluate the value of each others' work). Physicians remain perhaps the most stereotypical representatives of the professional-managerial class, whose relationship to the productive process has been defined as the reproduction of social life, popular and material culture, and the mechanisms of social control (1).

However, the era of professional dominance of the U.S. health care system is passing. Health policy in the 1980s has been largely shaped by demands of business and government health insurance purchasers for market-oriented standards of economic efficiency and productivity enhancement. These standards of efficiency, imposed through the health care financing mechanisms of third-party payors, have come into sharp conflict with the previously dominant values and culture of professional-managerial class health care practitioners. "Blank check," fee-for-service reimbursement for physicians and retrospective cost reimbursement for the physician-controlled "not-for-profit" hospital industry had been the highest achievements of an autonomous medical profession at the peak of its power and prestige. A counterattack began throughout the 1970s and early 1980s; an unceasing stream of government and foundation-funded policy literature exposed the chaotic, wasteful, duplicative, and irrational aspects of the old physician-dominated organizational model. The capture of key government health care financing agencies within the Reagan administration represented a decisive victory for those sectors of capital seeking to stem the rise of health care outlays for both the business and government. This was the beginning of the end of the "golden era" of fee-for-service, cost-reimbursed U.S. medicine.

Today, control of the delivery system by an autonomous professional-managerial class of physicians (and allied groups of mission-oriented philanthropic administrators) is more than ever seen as intolerable under the new economic ground rules. By reversing the cost-increasing and access-expanding incentives of the past, advocates of market-oriented health care have succeeded in inducing price and product competition and aggressive for-profit management into the hospital sector, a process now being repeated in the market for physician services (2). The process of corporatization is transforming all health care providers into inherently bottom-line operations, with professional altruism and institutional purpose rapidly fading into historical artifacts.

Large corporate health care firms—both explicitly for-profit and their so-called "not-for-profit" counterparts—are spearheading a rapid rationalization and restructuring of the production of medical services. In this chapter we examine one aspect of these changes: the role of technical innovations in medical management information systems (MMIS) in spearheading far-reaching changes in the practice of medicine. Information system technologies are already reshaping medical practice and the working relationships between health practitioners and corporate managers. As cost containment pressures intensify under the aegis of a corporate-based health care system, numerous signs point toward a new era of health policy implementation focused on standardized clinical decision making. The claims of scientific expertise and the ethical standards of public service long cherished by the medical profession will be put to their most severe historical test.

## THE PROMISE OF INFORMATION TECHNOLOGY

Over the last decade, a dazzling series of technological innovations has reshaped information system technology. These innovations include the development of advanced telecommunications, fiberoptic cabling and local area networking, new magnetic and optical data storage technologies, new print graphics, optical scanning and video display capabilities, speech recognition and voice synthesis methods, new structured query languages, self-documenting fourth-generation languages designed for rapid screen-generating and menu-driven report capabilities, and new integrated operating system software. The application of these technologies in the health care industry promises to revolutionize the practice of medicine and the medical workplace (3–5). New mainframe-mini-microcomputer interfacing standards, more flexible microcomputer local area network connectivity protocols, new telephone data transmission techniques, and the development of cheap, portable microcomputers have major health industry applications (6). Perhaps within a few years, most major hospitals will have bedside computer terminals, with voice input devices or highly customized data entry screens, and a host of logical audit functions for interpreting medical staff orders, storing clinical data, and providing uniform standards of quality assurance and risk management. Knowledge-based diagnostic and artificial intelligence programs will eventually be used on line with computerized records; expert advice and critiquing systems are already assisting physicians in various aspects of medical problem solving, while posting reminders about patients' risk factors, the predictive value of laboratory tests, and the proper scheduling of preventive care (7–15).

Diversified access to large automated data bases (using increasingly standardized object codes and data dictionaries) is becoming a practical means to solve previously intractable quality-of-care measurement problems. Computerized claims systems are being used to overcome one of the most fundamental stumbling blocks in the epidemiological analysis of medical care: the absence of valid case mix adjustments (particularly for ambulatory care). The lack of measures for patients' illness severity leads to difficulties in risk-adjusting evaluations of medical interventions (16). By storing individual patient data on ever more complex sociodemographic and clinical indicators, new health care data bases are producing more refined severity-of-illness adjustments, thus providing fuller estimates of the relationship between medical resource inputs and patients' health outcomes (17–19).

Given present directions, the large scale epidemiological data used to evaluate medical practice will be interfaced with computerized licensure and performance data and computerized medical records (11, 20–22). Automated medical records, including optical scans of patient waveforms, on-line computational imaging, and videotaped history and physicals, promise to provide more valid estimates of hospital and physician performance and patient satisfaction than traditional manual chart reviews (23, 24). MMIS data will also serve as the central components of new operations research, strategic planning, risk management and decision support software, which is being viewed as essential for providers to limit malpractice liability and to score favorably on publicly disseminated quality indicators (25).

## THE ADVANCE OF INFORMATION TECHNOLOGY IN THE AGE OF HEALTH CARE CORPORATIZATION

The on-going corporatization of the U.S. health care delivery system is accelerating the development of medical information technology. These technological advances are allowing new interventions in the practice of medicine, most of which involve particular MMIS applications for corporate health managers seeking to maximize profits or survive in an ever tightening reimbursement climate. As business purchasers and public and private payors demand greater accountability for their health care outlays, the increasingly concentrated set of providers is using information systems to restructure the labor process in medicine.

In the past, requirements for flexible responses to patients and the information-intensive aspects of clinical encounters have retarded the process of business concentration in the health sector. Physicians have long asserted that medicine is too much of an "art" to be subject to standardization by "outsiders." This view was eloquently expressed by surgeon John Hornsby, speaking at a 1917 meeting of the American College of Surgeons on hospital standardization (quoted in 26, p. 169):

> We all know you cannot standardize an art. The efficiency engineers have a place with us; there is no doubt as to that, but they will have to study our problems from the standpoint of the medical profession before they can set mathematically guiding lines for us. These men are laymen; they are business people. They have not the slightest conception of what takes place in a hospital, and consequently have a very limited knowledge upon which to base suggestions for administrative methods. They know nothing about surgery, and consequently could not possibly be the agents through which surgery could be standardized.

Computerized MMIS technology, with its increasing capabilities for expert knowledge and decision analysis modeling, will inevitably undermine Hornsby's arguments. New information technologies have been a prerequisite for the most recent phase of horizontal and vertical integration in the health care industry, marked by the emergence over the last decade of multihospital systems and health maintenance organizations (HMOs). As the for-profit drive became pervasive for most providers, investor-owned and otherwise, economies-of-scale and access to capital have increasingly favored larger enterprises and systems. However, as recent financial declines among certain for-profit hospital and HMO chains suggest, centralized management strategies may fall short when the complexities of highly specific local markets are not well understood. Just as project-oriented information technologies are eliminating various layers of middle management in U.S. industry as a whole, new health care executive information systems will increasingly provide flexible leadership options, allowing top management to intervene more effectively in decentralized operations (27, 28).

To be effective in boosting profitability and market share, these interventions will have to penetrate deeply into the clinical settings where most of a provider's variable costs are generated, and where research on medical practice variations (discussed below) has revealed gross examples of waste and overutilization by physicians. Just as the corporate business sector has fostered a "computer literate" culture in other industries, large numbers of health care employees are now obtaining the requisite training and experience in advanced computer applications for medical records and medical decision-making. Sales of hospital patient care management information systems sales are expected to reach $5.6 billion by 1990 (up from only $900 million in 1979); the cost of installation of such systems in a single hospital runs between $1.5 and $9 million dollars (29). One New York hospital recently received Certificate of Need approval for a $25 million information system (30). The percentage of community hospitals that had a clinical care based MMIS rose from 10 percent in 1980 to 31 percent in 1986. Given that 25 percent of average hospital operating costs are related to information handling, MMIS expenditures are certain to rise above their current level of 1.6 percent of the average hospital's operating budget and 0.75 percent of the average hospital's capital budget (31). Hospitals are now being linked to physician offices as accounting firms, consultants, and software vendors establish industry-wide standards for "synergistically" linking cost accounting, patient care, and quality assurance modules into unified, upgradable systems (30).

Sophisticated MMIS software places an immensely powerful tool at the disposal of health care managers, purchasers, and third party payors who have previously been ill equipped to second-guess the clinical judgments of the health professionals to whom they send checks. Whereas a computerized medical record was formerly an economic luxury, at best useful for esoteric clinical research, now it can be used to monitor and regulate the clinical productivity of medical staff and allied health care employees. In order to grasp the potential power shift at the organizational and institutional levels made possible by impending advances in MMIS, it is useful to review the structural basis of traditional production relations in the health care industry.

## PHYSICIAN ACCOUNTABILITY FOR
## THE COST OF MEDICAL CARE

Physicians, comprising 0.5 percent of the U.S. population, have been the "traffic cops" of the health care system, directing the flow of hundreds of billions of dollars spent on personal health care services annually—now $600 billion, nearly 12 percent of gross national product (GNP) (32). Physicians' legal responsibility under tort (malpractice) law is limited to medical correctness and physical harm to the patient; physicians have not been generally liable for the financial consequences of their decisions, however inappropriate. Similarly, the doctrine of informed consent, established to protect dependent patients in an agency relationship with physicians, did not extend to the need to inform patients about their financial risk and liability for care provided. In the past, the financial structure of third-party hospital care reimbursement allowed physicians to opt out of direct contractual responsibility for the cost of care; consequently, they were not previously concerned with insurers' definitions of medical necessity. Physicians' largely fee-for-service status and their shared financial incentives with "not-for-profit" hospitals led to a dilution of physician liability for unnecessary costs incurred within the doctor-patient contractual relationship (33).

The medical profession has historically enjoyed exclusive authority over judgments about the quality and cost-effectiveness of diagnostic and therapeutic services initiated under physician orders. Until recently, there have been few epidemiological evaluations of common medical care services. The lack of coordinated research on the relationships between the structure, process, and outcomes of care has inhibited development of consistent methods of measuring costs and benefits, or of measuring the relationship of resource inputs and health outcomes. Freidson (34) has argued that the dominance of physicians in the medical division of labor is, in fact, largely based upon a tightly restricted flow of information to patients and the public. This lack of information on the relationship of medical process to patient outcome has restricted the development of a comprehensive system of needs-based health planning, under which the provision of selected services could be meaningfully weighed against the opportunity costs of foregone expenditures (35–37). Instead, physicians' financial incentives, training factors, subjective reactions to patient demands, and malpractice considerations have unduly influenced the practice of medicine. These aspects of physicians' judgments are now, for the first time, being scrutinized by corporate MMIS technology.

## THE COST CONTAINMENT ERA

Over the last several decades the medical profession helped convince the public that more medical care meant better health. This notion, translated into health care system dynamics, was symbolized by public subsidies for greater numbers of physician specialists, defined in large part by their ability to utilize new and complex hospital-based medical technologies. These technologies proliferated, in turn, through policies linking the National Institutes of Health, regional medical programs, and other biomedical research efforts to corporate suppliers. The enormous economic incentives for service intensive care, coupled with the "technological imperative" to achieve more precise diagnostic certainty through ever more biomedical instrumentation, were blindly assumed to improve quality of care (38, 39). Professional and institutional prestige became closely related to the acquisition of cost-increasing, equipment-embodied medical technologies, and the corresponding discouragement of cost-saving, coordinative, preventive, and cross-institutional technologies (40, 41). As Medicare and Medicaid fueled the growth of the old, physician-driven medical-industrial complex (composed of drug companies; medical equipment and supply firms; banks; accounting, insurance, and consulting companies; and real estate interests), health care became a magnet for increased private investment (42, 43). Meanwhile, the growth of third-party cost reimbursement undercut individual patients' resistance to mounting costs.

As health care expenditures absorbed a larger proportion of a more slowly growing GNP after the 1960s, a fundamental shift occurred in public policy. High levels of unemployment and inflation combined with increasing foreign competition to force a reevaluation of health care delivery systems. Large corporations became constrained in their ability to pass uncontrolled employee benefit costs to consumers as higher prices. The burden of financing a costly, ineffective system began to be realized by both government and business leadership (44, 45). In 1987 alone, employer-paid health insurance premiums to commercial insurers were scheduled to increase between 15 and 40 percent (46), with 10 to 30 percent increases to follow in 1988 (47). Difficulties in maintaining the regressive taxes used to fund health care programs, particularly shortfalls in the Part A Medicare Hospital Insurance Trust Fund and state-financed portions of the Medicaid program, led to a hardened stance on "waste and inefficiency." Despite evidence that underlying public opinion remains favorable toward increasing tax-supported access to high quality care, elite public policy institutions became almost exclusively concerned with efforts to restrain the growth of expenditures (48, 49).

Public policy has sought to reduce the flow of funds into the health care industry by reversing financial incentives. The Medicare prospective payment system based on diagnosis related groups (DRGs), combined with the growth of HMOs and preferred provider organizations, has yielded dramatic care-avoidance incentives for the hospital industry. New forms of competition in private health insurance, driven by the trend toward self-insurance by large employers, have stimulated a wide variety of selective contracting schemes designed to place providers at greater risk for the costs of care (50). Business health care coalitions have also produced ever more clearly delineated cost and quality standards to be enforced by private sector providers competing for "sponsored patients," i.e., patients with assured means for profitable reimbursement (51, 52).

Prospective payment has undercut the ability of providers to ignore clinical costs through cost shifting, increasing admissions or visits, or other forms of provider-induced revenue enhancement. Recent studies of the effects of prospective payment, state rate regulation, and selective contracting have found that hospitals are increasingly competing on cost. Whereas earlier studies found that nonprice competition drove up costs in highly competitive hospital markets, studies based on post-1983 data find that competing in highly competitive, regulated markets has forced hospitals to dramatically lower costs (53–55). Hospital management must now conserve resources used in clinical operations, which has spurred the purchase of MMIS software (and related consulting services) to systematically combine clinical and financial data. The resulting MMIS programs are part of the real hidden agenda of prospective payment: linking clinical decisions to the financial viability of hospitals and other prospectively financed provider enterprises (56). This linkage will propel managers to harness physician behavior to the increasingly constrained requirements of health industry price competition imposed by government and business purchasers.

## MEDICAL PRACTICE VARIATIONS AND MEDICAL EFFECTIVENESS

Automated claims data have been used to provide evidence of large geographical variations in the per capita consumption of medical services (57–59). Research on practice variations has highlighted the existence of apparently capricious notions of the efficacy (defined as the probability of benefit under ideal conditions of use) and effectiveness (defined as the benefits resulting from actual use under typical or average conditions) of many aspects of medical practice (60, 61). The resource use differentials found in practice variation studies raise serious questions about the range of acceptable clinical decisions made by physicians. These differences in practice style have been found to have major implications for the cost of medical care (62).

Until recently, judgments about medical effectiveness remained the exclusive preserve of local medical societies. Efforts to enforce public or institutional responsibility for medical standards, dating to Codman's effort to hold hospital trustees accountable for surgical outcomes, have been vociferously opposed by the medical profession (26). However, efforts to rationalize, standardize, monitor, or modify physician practice, once denounced as the imposition of "cookbook medicine," are now an outright cultural, legal, and economic challenge to long-preserved traditions of physician autonomy. Today, both popular and power elite opinion hold that it is not only legitimate but economically essential to review physician decisions about hospital admissions, lengths of stay, surgical procedures, and utilization of ancillary services.

MMIS technology allows advanced forms of monitoring and surveillance beyond previous, largely ineffective peer review. The latter has long been based on implicit judgments of local doctors (often the least knowledgeable, least distinguished, least busy) manually reviewing a small sample of medical records. As a harbinger of the "new era of assessment and accountability," the Health Care Financing Administration will spend $72 million over the next three years on an effectiveness initiative, including computerized collection of vast quantities of clinical data by professional review organizations (63, 64). The American Medical Association and various medical specialty societies have begun to develop their own practice "parameters" in a belated effort to head off the imposition of more restrictive government and insurance industry standards. The director of the RAND Health Sciences Program has summarized the need for research on explicit, public standards of medical practice (25, p. 81):

I am not nearly so concerned about the risks of "cookbook medicine" as I am about a small, troublesome group of practitioners who serve up too many untested dishes, or about the much larger number of practitioners who perceive incentives to provide care that contains needlessly rich gourmet ingredients. Finally, I think that patients will not think less of doctors who consult a definitive cookbook to determine standards of care. Just as most of us who eat out have little desire to go back and help the chef prepare the meal, most of us who go to the doctor are not interested in directing our medical care. Nonetheless, we may find it encouraging that expert chefs have specified a set of essential ingredients for a particular dish and reassuring that physicians who are acknowledged national experts have outlined standards of care.

## MEDICAL MANAGEMENT INFORMATION SYSTEMS AND THE CHANGING "HOSPITAL POWER EQUILIBRIUM"

The fact that physicians generate approximately 70 percent of all medical care costs has made examination of physicians' efficiency as resource managers a central concern of hospital cost containment. It is in this setting that MMIS technology can be the cutting edge for transforming the traditional relationship of physicians and managers, what Young and Saltman (65) have characterized as the "hospital power equilibrium." In analyzing the ability of New Jersey hospitals to avoid the financial implications of the initial prospective payment system based on DRGs, Weiner and associates have succinctly defined the old consensus (66, p. 466):

> Power within organizations is assumed by those who cope with the most serious uncertainties. In hospitals the most serious uncertainties are those of medical and surgical interventions, the domain of physicians. . . . The basic structure of hospitals separates financial management from clinical activities and gives priority to the latter. Traditionally, hospital administrators have seen themselves as facilitators, not managers in the corporate sense. The task of administrators is to maintain a stable, financially viable work place for physicians. An ability to temper external threats, and especially external financial threats, to this work environment is the expertise administrators claim.

They conclude (pp. 480–481):

> Because hospitals are not profit maximizers, the opportunities to accumulate surpluses that DRG rates may offer are not sufficient to induce a search for clinical savings. Only the threat of financial failure can precipitate action and, even then, administrators are likely to explore fully routine methods for regaining solvency before considering clinical changes. . . .Until either the state of medical knowledge becomes much more certain than it is or the financing of hospital care much less certain than can be expected, this division of labor is likely to persist, DRG incentives notwithstanding.

Intensified price and product line competition promises to dramatically alter tolerance of wide variations in resource use within provider firms. The internal administrative controls of "second generation" managed-care plans already rely heavily on MMIS-driven clinical interventions. Such interventions are inevitable in the wake of reduced opportunities for cost-shifting and more aggressive bargaining by business purchasers and third-party insurers (67). Given the role of physician-generated costs in determining market share and profitability, corporate providers will ultimately have to subject their physician employees to far more restrictive monitoring, surveillance, and disciplinary activities (68).

To date, hospital-physician conflicts have focused on traditional issues such as competition for outpatients and physician recruitment, rather than managed-care, hospital-physician group contracts, or the purchase of physician practices (69). As the authors of a study of the Hospital Corporation of America (HCA) note, for-profit chains have so far been particularly careful not to antagonize local physicians (70, p. 177):

> Physicians' sensitivity is so high throughout the company that it is unlikely that major innovations in hospital-physician relations of the kind so feared by Relman will be pioneered at HCA. In fact, the company, at least for the foreseeable future, is likely to consistently lag behind the "hotdogs" in the not-for-profit group, those hospitals already "restructuring" and forming for-profit subsidiaries. HCA, seen as the threatening behemoth by many in the medical establishment, is likely to walk softly around both new financial linkages with doctors and "big stick" utilization management.

Such surface tranquility will likely dissolve as vertically and horizontally integrated hospital systems evolve from what are now often defensively oriented networks, alliances, and partnerships. "Mature" hospital systems, with intensified linkages to their core medical staffs and regional physician groups, are likely to dominate the industry by the turn of the century (71). Hospital-physician linkages, whether through selective contracting, joint ventures, or outright purchase of physician practices, will necessarily assume the characteristics of managed-care plans. Thus, a managed-care hospital consultant, writing recently in *Modern Healthcare,* argues that hospitals will have to get tougher with physicians (72, p. 54):

> Sophisticated managed healthcare delivery systems will make such utilization review a prerequisite for physicians who want to join their systems. Physician membership in these health plans likely will become more competitive in the next few years. Those who can document efficient practice patterns will have an edge in being selected by and receiving favorable terms from "open access" HMOs and exclusive provider organizations. . . .To succeed as managed-care partners, hospitals need to take the courageous step of excluding physicians who provide poor-quality care from preferred networks. A less direct option is to use stringent utilization review procedures that eventually will drive them out. Hospitals can't continue to support heavy admitters to keep the census high and, at the same time, give them free rein to undermine managed-care plans.

Internal administrative controls will be spearheaded by external utilization management. Commonplace "level-of-care" length-of-stay criteria, preadmission screening, toll-free numbers to clear patient orders with insurance companies, and mandatory surgical second opinion programs are just the beginning of this effort. The *Wall Street Journal* in 1989 published two articles under the head-lines "Warm Bodies: Doctor-owned Labs Earn Lavish Profits in a Captive Market" and "Medical Tests Go Under the Microscope" (73, 74). The latter article details insurance companies' efforts to utilize advanced MMIS surveillance of frequencies of physician laboratory and radiology procedures with illness-specific appropriateness screens. As their sophistication grows, utilization management screens will play an ever larger role in clinical decision making.

Third-party insurers are already using computerized clinical criteria for precer-tification of up to 85 surgical and invasive diagnostic procedures. Many of these appropriateness protocols were recently developed by government-financed RAND Corporation studies; the software is marketed by a firm headed by RAND investigators. Physicians are required to satisfy highly specific, computer-guided telephone questioning by insurance intermediaries, resulting in initial precertifica-tion denial rates of 9 percent to 42 percent (75). Perhaps the most intensive monitoring and surveillance effort to date is being mounted against grossly in-flated rates of cesarean sections, which have grown from 5 percent of deliveries in 1970 to 24.4 percent in 1988 (76). Using MMIS claims and outcome data, Prudential, Aetna, CIGNA, Honeywell, and other insurers have contracted at discount prices with selected providers for organ transplants and other costly procedures. A highly publicized Rochester, New York, hospital payment system is even using MMIS patient outcome data to selectively adjust reimbursement rates (77).

As health care institutions (whether proprietary or "not-for-profit") adhere to an openly bottom-line orientation, top management will be offered greater com-petitive as well as personal financial incentives to challenge the clinical authority of physicians. Just as financial officers make up the bulk of U.S. corporate chief executive officers, the curricula of health management graduate programs increas-ingly emphasize finance. Hospitals now require huge administrative bureaucracies for marketing, strategic planing, and managed-care analysis. As executives of multihospital systems and large managed-care enterprises are required to mold physician practice habits to the cost-effectiveness criteria imposed by purchasers and insurers, physicians are likely to be subjected to far more administrative and bureaucratic controls than were conceivable even a few years ago (78). Major changes in traditional physician relationships are already being reported by numerous observers of the corporatization of U.S. health care (79–85).

## PHYSICIAN PRACTICE PROFILES: WHERE THE RUBBER MEETS THE ROAD

The measurement of productivity (i.e., output per hour of work) lies at the heart of the effort to monitor physician behavior. Attempts to continuously boost productivity are central to an individual firm's strategic plan and to the process of capital accumulation in health care industry generally. Productivity measures in health care are rendered all but meaningless in the absence of simultaneous measures of the quality of output. More expensive hospitals or physicians have always asserted they have better quality; their informational advantages and the difficulty in monitoring dependent, agency relationships with patients have historically produced a potentially gross "moral hazard" problem. As the cost of monitoring is reduced, traditional agency theory justifications for physician autonomy are undermined (86).

Since the advent of Medicare DRGs, MMIS profiles of physician resource use have frequently been employed by managers to identify what are deemed "efficient" practice patterns. Diagnosis-specific practice profiles summarize comparative physician-generated costs for treatment of essentially similar patients. In an era of intensified institutional competition and care-avoidance financial incentives, valid practice profiles will be essential for evaluating the contribution of individual practitioners and the medical staff as a whole to the efficiency, productivity, and financial viability of a hospital or group practice.

One estimate of the magnitude of physicians' direct impact on hospital costs was revealed in a study controlled for disease stage (87). It found that physicians accounted for an average of 17.5 percent of intra-DRG variation in length of stay in an outlier-trimmed sample of high volume DRGs from a teaching hospital, and an average of 29.4 percent of the intra-DRG variation in length of stay in three other nonteaching hospital samples. Another study of severity-adjusted and outcome-adjusted differences in practice style among 31 internists at a large Midwestern teaching hospital found a $2,000 per patient difference in total inpatient charges between high-cost and low-cost practitioners (88). In a study of six surgical procedures and three medical diagnoses at three New England teaching hospitals, physician panels defined "preferred practice patterns" for patients meeting specific severity-of-illness criteria. The study found between $800,000 and $2 million in potentially unnecessary annual hospital costs that resulted from deviations from the preferred patterns (89).

Horizontally and vertically integrated managed-care systems will now combine physicians' financial practice profiles with various quality of care and adverse occurrence measures (e.g., deaths and complications), most likely based on standardized measures of patient health status, satisfaction surveys, and process-of-care indicators. These patient-level data will be readily obtainable from automated medical records, with aggregate data also directly accessible by corporate purchasers. Using MMIS innovations, severity-adjusted and outcome-adjusted physician practices promise to differentiate between systematic patterns of wasteful, ineffective resource use, and the resource use variations related to presumably random (more or less equally distributed) differences inherent in the uncertainties and pitfalls of clinical observation and decision-making.

Practice profiles based on differences in resource use for similar patients will be used to alter physician behavior, whether through education, appeals to professional integrity, financial rewards or penalties, or direct administrative controls. A number of current research strategies involve dissemination and validation of "clinical prediction rules" and appropriateness criteria designed to standardize what are now highly variable physician practice habits (90). Large-scale capitated delivery systems, operated under care avoidance incentives, may use economic criteria to implement explicit test use criteria, and clinical protocols and algorithms (91).

Statistical process control of physician ordering requires major investments in MMIS research (e.g., on illness severity measures) as well as high labor costs associated with data entry, programming support, and statistical analysis. As the growth of MMIS spending already indicates, the current transformation of health finance and delivery is making such investments all but inevitable. MMIS physician profiling software is proliferating, with vendors searching for the pot of gold awaiting the most favored severity-of-illness or acuity adjustment (92).

The arrival of appropriateness standards is already producing a ripple effect, as the magnitude and scope of waste in acute care resources becomes more widely documented. Physicians will have a harder time ignoring sophisticated comparative MMIS feedback on average length of stay, ancillary charges, complications and infections, operating room minutes by procedure, readmissions, and mortality (93, 94). Presumably, feedback of variations data (such as the studies cited above) will stimulate discussions of appropriateness criteria among the medical staff of a given institution. Nevertheless, there is every indication that variations data will, at a minimum, justify an escalation of intrusive administrative and policy interventions.

## THE DECLINING AUTONOMY OF THE MEDICAL PROFESSION

The medical profession's control over the health care system has weakened in proportion to individual physicians' ability to recruit and maintain their patients (95). The personal loyalty, trust, and continuity that characterized individual patient-doctor relationships has increasingly given way to large corporate contracts, negotiated on a "prudent buyer" basis. These contracts usually involve various restrictions on physicians' clinical freedom as well as patients' choice of providers. This complex contractual process between hospitals, third-party insurers, and large physician groups is replacing hospitals' former dependency on the good will of individual physicians in their community, whose staff privileges were essential for maintaining hospital revenues.

The increasing supply of physicians is also serving to undermine physicians' market strength. The growth of the profession—from 142 professionally active physicians per 100,000 population in 1950 to 180 in 1975 and 228 in 1985, with

260 projected for the year 2000—has given hospitals (and other provider organizations seeking to recruit physician labor) more leverage over individual physicians competing for fewer positions. The number of physician group practices, in which physician-managers help to socialize their younger colleagues into acceptance of clinical limitations on clinical freedom, grew from 6,371 in 1969 to 10,762 in 1980 and 17,556 in 1986, with a growing average of over nine physicians per group. Of the nonfederal, nonresident physicians in practice today, over one-fourth are salaried employees, with an increase from 24.2 percent to 26.1 percent between 1983 and 1985. Excluding residents, 46.5 percent of physicians under the age of 36 are now salaried, compared with only 19 percent over the age of 55. About half of all female physicians are salaried employees. Physicians will likely continue to enjoy high incomes and some patient care flexibility, though considerably less in certain practice settings and specialties. As the average debt of medical school graduates (measured in constant dollars) climbed from $19,700 in 1981 to $28,000 in 1986, most graduates have found themselves with few options other than salaried slots (96, 97). These practitioners are more and more dependent upon the purpose and character of the employing provider organizations. These trends have led a few observers to declare an imminent "proletarianization" of physicians, comparable to the extinction of the handloom weavers during the industrial revolution in England (98). Others have referred to the "corporatization" or "deprofessionalization" of physicians, as the bureaucratization of health delivery systems imposes external controls and "formal" internal rationalization replaces the "substantive" rationality of professional ideology, such as the emphasis on altruism, authority over clients, and autonomy (99, 100).

The corporate restructuring of health care is definitely increasing the stratification of the medical profession. Hospitals, preferred provider organizations, and HMOs are attempting to incorporate respected clinical leaders into top administrative or policy posts, promoting a new class of physician MBA (Master in business administration) "product line managers" (82, 101–104). Within large independent physician practice associations, senior administrators utilize practice profiles to set salaries, distribute bonuses, and evaluate probationary physician employees. The underlying sociological basis for stratification has been the large number of medical school graduates (16,000 per year), the increased number of female physicians (and two physician families) seeking fewer, more regular hours of work, and the prohibitive cost of capitalizing independent private practices (105). Freidson has summarized the implications of this for professional autonomy (106, p. 31):

> Where once all practitioners could employ their own clinical judgment to decide how to handle their individual cases independently of whatever medical school professors asserted in textbooks and researchers in journal articles, now the professors and scientists who have no firsthand knowledge of those individual cases establish guidelines that administrators who also lack such

firsthand experience attempt to enforce. Where once all practitioners were fairly free to decide how to manage their relations with patients, now administrators attempt to control the pacing and scheduling of work in the interest of their organization's mission, which may regard the collective interests of all patients (or of investors or insurance funds) to be more important than the interests of individual practitioners and their relations with individual patients.

## THE ROLE OF THE FEDERAL GOVERNMENT

The decisive battles over the professional sovereignty of physicians are being increasingly fought at the level of federal executive branch agencies. It is here that legal efforts are reshaping the health industry environment (including invoking anti-trust litigation against physician fee fixing and using National Labor Relations Board rulings to impair physician unionization efforts). The federal government's financing of applied MMIS technology research is a direct assault on traditional physician practice habits.

The impetus for reorganizing medical production relations is part of the overall fiscal crisis of the state. The growth of federal budget expenditures on social welfare throughout the 1980s were paced by Medicare and Medicaid outlays. Between 1980 and 1987, the number of Medicare enrollees increased 7 percent, the GNP by 62 percent, Medicare Part A expenditures for hospital care increased by 100 percent, and Medicare outlays for physician services increased by 179 percent, from $7.9 billion in 1980 to $22 billion in 1987 (46). This has prompted the Health Care Financing Administration to initiate a physician preferred provider scheme, presumably to be based on Medicare physician practice profiles. In 1986, Congress passed the Health Care Quality Improvement Act, mandating the establishment of a national clearinghouse for physician data (107). Strongly opposed by the American Medical Association, this data base (which ostensibly would track disciplinary and malpractice actions against physicians) may greatly accelerate trends toward national MMIS oversight of the profession. Of equal significance, the law provides legal protection to physician peer review activities, protecting peer review administrators from lawsuits from disciplined physicians. Such changes take on increased importance as MMIS software vendors develop physician cost and quality hospital credentialling screens (30).

On a separate front, Congress is moving rapidly to brake escalating Medicare Part B costs, 75 percent of which represent payments to physicians. These payments have ballooned as DRG rates have compressed inpatient reimbursement. Between 1984 and 1986, Part B expenditures, which reached $35.1 billion in fiscal year 1988, increased at double the rate of GNP growth (despite a one year fee freeze) (46). The Physician Payment Review Commission is presently reviewing a time and complexity, resource-based relative value scale for physician reimbursement (107). Implementation of such a relative value scale, designed in part to increase payments for cognitive rather than technological services, will have far-reaching effects on physician practice habits (108). Nursing classification systems are also being used to quantify direct nursing care inputs for hospitals (109).

Measuring nurses' and physicians' work provides another example of the increasing role that MMIS systems can have in tracking resource input measures (110–112). Just as corporate managers were able to degrade the labor of skilled production workers when designing assembly line production techniques, these software technologies offer profound management engineering opportunities to "Taylorize" medical care production (113). This would entail dividing the work of health professionals into more discrete, less complex tasks to be automated or performed by less skilled employees, who will in turn be monitored by centralized clinical-administrative hierarchies. We may now be in the twilight of the physician role known since the historic Flexner Report.

## CONCLUSION

With an aging population and more severely ill patients in hospitals and nursing homes, information system technology offers many positive and overdue benefits: more cost-effective care, more appropriate care, less neglect, less risk of iatrogenic illness, more coordination among providers, and improved continuity of patient care. New medical decision analysis programs, employing sophisticated "criteria mapping" and branching logic "tree" programs, can overcome many of the obstacles to outcome assessment and quality measurement, which have eluded investigators using laborious manual chart audits (114, 115). Automated clinical data will increasingly be used in "sentinel" statistical screens to connect aspects of the structure and process of care to health outcome effects. Recent studies measuring variations in use rates and the appropriateness of controversial medical and surgical procedures have demonstrated the use of automated claims and MMIS data for assessing the relationship of clinical process and patient outcomes (116–118). Such findings are essential in providing patients with the necessary information on the utility of medical procedures; information on outcomes will increasingly be viewed as a legal requirement for "informed consent." Recent research on prostatectomy, leading to the production of an interactive videotape which patients can use to discern highly individualized utilities and the probability of complications, provides one outstanding example of how MMIS-based outcome research can enhance patient care (119). Above all, it is the potential empowerment of patients that makes MMIS investments worthwhile.

Yet, it is notable that MMIS technology is emerging as an organic part of the corporatization of the U.S. health care industry (120–122). The current changes in control of the delivery system are, in fact, associated with an explosion of unproductive administrative costs, the most rapidly growing component of health care expenditures in recent years (123). Managed-care costs have outstripped the growth of overall medical costs for the last two years (124). It is ironic that the industry expanded its administrative and managerial overhead by 20 percent from 1980 to 1985 (125) while new MMIS investments were eagerly sought to justify resource restrictions on the clinical level.

Applied technologies are always shaped by the political-economic climate in which they emerge. The contribution of a given technology to improved productivity is always constrained by the existing hierarchical division of labor, reflecting the often narrow goals of the organizations that invest in and diffuse technology. MMIS research, originally funded by corporate foundations and government agencies and developed by entrepreneurial consulting firms, is being tailored to maintain a health care system driven by private profit rather than the health needs of the entire population. Medical information technologies will be implemented by the rapidly proliferating ranks of managers (often physicians), supervisors, and statistical process control engineers employed by corporate multi-institutional health care firms. To the extent that the current technological and organizational upheaval in the industry mirrors antecedent changes in manufacturing, we can expect a "degradation" of skilled, highly interpersonal service work and its replacement by more regimented, repetitive, and fragmented labor. These changes will be justified as requirements for increased efficiency and improved productivity. For all their incredible promise in improving the coordination, continuity and cost-effectiveness of care, corporatized MMIS technologies nevertheless pose a serious threat to the traditional humanistic and charitable ethos of medical practice. In the past, professional-managerial groups have vacillated between "benign domination" of clients and consumers and the assertion of high ethical standards supposedly representing the interests of society at large (1). Today, physicians are being required to take sides in the debate over for-profit health care and the purpose of the health care endeavor. In the past, most organized expressions of physician interests have preferred to emphasize their commonality with business, rather than public interests. Most physician organizations and spokespersons have unfortunately continued beating a gradual retreat, defensively upholding the fading virtues of a past era before the consolidation of corporate health care.

Let us hope that more enlightened medical professionals will join with popular demands for reforming the U.S. health care system along more equitable and patient-oriented lines (126). Ensuring the use of MMIS technology for population-based health planning and patient empowerment, with appropriate safeguards for the sanctity of healing within the practitioner-patient relationship, should be our higher concern.

## REFERENCES

1. Ehrenreich, B., and Ehrenreich, J. The professional and managerial class. In *Between Labor and Capital*, edited by P. Walker. South End Press, Boston, 1979.

2. Salmon, J. W. Profit and health care: Trends in corporatization and proprietization. *Int. J. Health Serv.* 15(3): 395–418, 1985.
3. Cox, J. R., and Zeelenberg, C. Computer technology: State of the art and future trends. *J. Am. Coll. Cardiol.* 9(1): 204–214, 1987.
4. Kaplan, B. Development and acceptance of medical information systems: An historical overview. *J. Health Hum. Resources Admin.*, Summer 1988, pp. 9–29.
5. DeTore, A. W. Medical informatics: An introduction to computer technology in medicine. *Am. J. Med.* 85: 399–403, 1988.
6. Grams, S. The future of health care information systems. *J. Health Hum. Resources Admin.*, Fall 1988, pp. 194–217.
7. Tierney, W. M., Hui, S. L., and McDonald, C. J. Delayed feedback of physician performance versus immediate reminders to perform preventive care. *Med. Care* 24: 659–666, 1986.
8. Tierney, W. M., et al. Computer predictions of abnormal test results: Effects on outpatient testing. *JAMA* 259: 1194–1198, 1988.
9. McMullin, E. Diagnosis by computer. In *Logic of Discovery and Diagnosis in Medicine,* edited by K. E. Schaffner, pp. 199–222. University of California Press, Berkeley, 1985.
10. Simon, H. A. Artificial-intelligence approaches to problem solving and clinical diagnosis. In *Logic of Discovery and Diagnosis in Medicine*, edited by K. E. Schaffner, pp. 72–93. University of California Press, Berkeley, 1985.
11. Rennels, G. D., and Shortliffe, E. H. Advanced computing for medicine. *Sci. Am.* 257(4): 154–161, 1987.
12. Langlotz, C. P., Shorliffe, E. H., and Fagan, L. M. A methodology for generating computer-based explanation of decision-theoretic advice. *Med. Decis. Making* 8(4): 290–303, 1988.
13. Pryor, D. B., et al. Clinical data bases: Accomplishments and unrealized potential. *Med. Care* 23: 623–647, 1985.
14. Yen, V. C., and Boissoneau, R. Artificial intelligence and expert systems: Implications for health care delivery. *Hosp. Top.* 66(5): 16–19, 1988.
15. McDonald, C. J., and Tierney, W. M. Computer-stored medical records: Their future role in medical practice. *JAMA* 259: 3433–3440, 1988.
16. Blumberg, M. S. Risk adjusting health care outcomes: A methodological review. *Med. Care Rev.* 43: 351–393, 1986.
17. McMahon, L. F., and Billi, J. E. Measurement of severity of illness and the Medicare prospective payment system. *J. Gen. Intern. Med.* 3: 482–490, 1988.
18. Donabedian, A. Twenty years of research on the quality of medical care, 1964-1984. *Evaluation and the Health Professions* 8: 243–265, 1985.
19. Brook, R. H., and Lohr, K. N. Monitoring quality care in the Medicare program: Two proposed systems. *JAMA* 258: 3138–3141, 1987.
20. Webster, G. D. Computer simulations in assessing clinical competence: A fifteen-year perspective. In *Computer Applications in the Evaluation of Physician Competence,* edited by J. S. Lloyd, pp. 35–43. American Board of Medical Specialties, Chicago, 1984.
21. Weed, L. L. Coupling medical knowledge to patient problems via microcomputer. In *Computer Applications in the Evaluation of Physician Competence,* edited by J. S. Lloyd. American Board of Medical Specialties, Chicago, 1984.
22. McDonald, C. J., Tierney, W., and Blevins, L. The Benefits of Automated Medical Record Systems for Ambulatory Care. Proceedings of "Computer Applications in Medical Care 1986," Washington, D.C., October 25-26, 1986.

23. Gerbert, B., and Hargreaves, W. A. Measuring physician behavior. *Med. Care* 24: 838–847, 1986.
24. Escovitz, G. H., et al. The effects of mandatory quality assurance: A review of hospital medical audit processes. *Med. Care* 16: 941–949, 1978.
25. Williams, A. P. Malpractice, Outcomes, and Appropriateness of Care. U.S. Department of Health and Human Services, Proceedings of the research conference on "Health Care Improvement and Medical Liability," Washington, D.C., April 27, 1988.
26. Reverby, S. Stealing the golden eggs: Ernest Amory Codman and the science and management of medicine. *Bull. Hist. Med.* 55: 156–171, 1981.
27. Applegate, L. M., Cash, J. I., and Mills, D. Q. Information technology and tomorrow's manager. *Harvard Business Rev.* 88(6): 128–136, 1988.
28. Cerne, F. Executive systems give CEOs management tools. *Hospitals*, November 20, 1988, pp. 80–81.
29. Dornfest, S. *Business Opportunities in Hospital Computer Markets.* Sheldon Dornfest and Associates, Northbrook, Ill., 1987.
30. Gardner, E. Information system market changing: Hospitals increase information system purchases as software vendors more responsive to needs. *Mod. Healthcare,* February 3, 1989, pp. 34–60.
31. Glandon, G. L., and Shapiro, R. J. Benefit-cost analysis of hospital information systems: The state of the (non) art. *J. Health Hum. Resources Admin.*, Summer 1988, pp. 30–92.
32. Arnett, R. H., et al. Projections of health care spending to 1990. *Health Care Financing Rev.* 7: 1–36, 1986.
33. Eisenberg, J. M. *Doctors' Decisions and the Cost of Medical Care: The Reasons for Doctors' Practice Patterns and Ways to Change Them.* Health Administration Press Perspectives, Ann Arbor, Michigan, 1986.
34. Freidson, E. Professional dominance and the ordering of health services: Some consequences. In *The Sociology of Health and Illness,* edited by P. Conrad and R. Kern, pp. 184–197. St. Martin's Press, New York, 1981.
35. Tannen, L. Health planning as a regulatory strategy: a discussion of its history and current uses. *Int. J. Health Serv.* 10(1): 115–132, 1980.
36. Daniels, N. Why saying no to patients in the United States is so hard. *N. Engl. J. Med.* 314: 1380–1383, 1986.
37. Miller, F. H., and Miller, G. A. H. The painful prescription: A procrustean perspective? *N. Engl. J. Med.* 314: 1383–1385, 1986.
38. Reiser, S. J. *Medicine and the Reign of Technology.* Cambridge University Press, Cambridge, England, 1978.
39. Evans, R. W. Health care technology and the inevitability of resource allocation and rationing decisions, Part I. *JAMA* 249: 2047–2053, 1983.
40. Russell, L. *Technology in Hospitals: Medical Advances and their Diffusion.* The Brookings Institution, Washington, D.C., 1979.
41. Evans, R. W. Health care technology and the inevitability of resource allocation and rationing decisions, Part II. *JAMA* 249: 2208–2219, 1983.
42. Himmelstein, D. U., and Woolhandler, S. The corporate compromise: A marxist view of health maintenance organizations and prospective payment. *Ann. Intern. Med.* 15: 494–501, 1988.
43. Ehrenreich, B., and Ehrenreich, J. *The American Health Empire: Power, Profits, and Politics.* Random House, New York, 1970.
44. Thurow, L. C. Learning to say "no." *N. Engl. J. Med.* 311: 1569–1575, 1984.
45. Fuchs, V. R. The "rationing" of medical care. *N. Engl. J. Med.* 311: 1572–1573, 1984.

46. Forecast '88. *HealthWeek*, December 23, 1987, p. 7.
47. Page, L. New era in utilization review: Soaring 1989 insurance rates spur new scrutiny of MDs. *Am. Med. News*, December 9, 1988, pp. 1, 64.
48. Blendon, R. J., and Altman, D. E. Public attitudes about health-care costs: A lesson in national schizophrenia. *N. Engl. J. Med.* 311: 613–616, 1984.
49. Navarro, V. Federal health policies in the United States: An alternative explanation. *Milbank Mem. Fund Q.* 65: 81–111, 1987.
50. Goldsmith, J. Death of a paradigm: The challenge of competition. *Health Aff.* 3(3): 5–19, 1984.
51. Carter, M. F. Employers urged to overhaul benefits to promote use of alternate services. *Mod. Healthcare* 2: 58–62, 1984.
52. Meyerhoff, A. S., and Crozier, D. A. Health care coalitions: The evolution of a movement. *Health Aff.* 3(1): 120–127, 1984.
53. Robinson, J. C., and Luft, H. S. Competition, regulation, and hospital costs, 1972 to 1982. *JAMA* 257: 3241–3245, 1987.
54. Robinson, J. C., and Luft, H. S. Competition, regulation, and hospital costs, 1982 to 1986. *JAMA* 260: 2676–2681, 1988.
55. Melnick, G. A., and Jwanziger, J. Hospital behavior under competition and cost-containment policies: The California experience, 1980 to 1985. *JAMA* 260: 2669–2675, 1988.
56. Glandon, G. L., and Morrisey, M. A. Redefining the hospital-physician relationship under prospective payment. *Inquiry* 23: 166–175, 1986.
57. Wennberg, J., and Gittelsohn, A. Variations in medical care among small areas. *Sci. Am.* 246: 120–134, 1982.
58. Wennberg, J. Dealing with medical practice variations: A proposal for action. *Health Aff.* 3(2): 6–32, 1984.
59. Wennberg, J. E. On patient need, equity, supplier-induced demand and the need to assess the outcome of common medical practice. *Med. Care* 23: 512–520, 1985.
60. Paul Shaheen, P., Clark, J. D., and Williams, D. Small area analysis: A review and analysis of the North American literature. *J. Health Polit. Policy Law* 12: 741–809, 1987.
61. Wennberg, J. Which rate is right? *N. Engl. J. Med.* 314: 310–311, 1986.
62. Payne, S. M. C. Identifying and managing inappropriate hospital utilization: A policy synthesis. *Health Serv. Res.* 22: 709–769, 1987.
63. Relman, A. S. Assessment and accountability: The third revolution in medical care. *N. Engl. J. Med.* 319: 1220–1222, 1988.
64. Roper, W., et al. Effectiveness in health care: An initiative to evaluate and improve medical practice. *N. Engl. J. Med.* 319: 1197–1202, 1988.
65. Young, D. W., and Saltman, R. B. *The Hospital Power Equilibrium: Physician Behavior and Cost Control.* The John Hopkins University Press, Baltimore, 1985.
66. Weiner, S. L., et al. Economic incentives and organizational realities: Managing hospitals under DRGs. *Milbank Mem. Fund Q.* 65: 463–487, 1987.
67. Chernomas, R. An economic basis for the proletarianization of physicians. *Int. J. Health Serv.* 16: 669–674, 1986.
68. Levinsky, N. G. The doctor's master. *N. Engl. J. Med.* 311: 1573–1575, 1984.
69. Grayson, M. A. Breaking the medical gridlock. *Hospitals*, February 20, 1989, pp. 32–37.
70. Barrett, D., and Campbell, P. H. Walking softly: The role of management in altering physician practice patterns in the hospital corporations of America. *Adv. Health Economics Health Serv. Res.* 7: 157–178, 1987.

71. Shortell, S. M. The evolution of hospital systems: Unfulfilled promises and self-fulfilling prophesies. *Med. Care Rev.* 45(2): 177–214, 1988.

72. Boland, P. Hospitals must take lead in setting up utilization review. *Mod. Healthcare,* January 13, 1989, p. 54.

73. Waldholz, M., and Bogdanich, W. Warm bodies: Doctor-owned labs earn lavish profits in a captive market. *Wall Street J.*, March 1, 1989.

74. Ruffenach, G. Medical tests go under the microscope: Insurers refuse to pay for work judged needless. *Wall Street J.*, February 7, 1989.

75. Meyer, H. Payers to use protocols to assess treatment plans. *Am. Med. News,* December 9, 1988, pp. 1, 62–64.

76. Lutz, S. Providers forced to defend C-section rates. *Mod. Healthcare,* February 3, 1989, pp. 66–67.

77. Parrons, J. Program links hospital payment to clinical outcome. *Am. Med. News,* September 9, 1988, pp. 39–40.

78. Salmon, J. W. The medical profession and the corporatization of the health sector. *Theor. Med.* 8: 19–29, 1987.

79. Freedman, S. A. Megacorporate health care: Choice for the future. *N. Engl. J. Med.* 312: 579–582, 1985.

80. Alper, P. R. The new language of hospital management. *N. Engl. J. Med.* 311: 1249–1251, 1984.

81. Alper, P. R. Medical practice in the competitive market. *N. Engl. J. Med.* 316: 337–339, 1987.

82. Nash, D. B. Hospitals and their medical staffs: High anxiety. *Front. Health Serv. Manage.* 4(3): 24–25, 1988.

83. Bock, R. S. The pressure to keep prices high at a walk-in clinic. *N. Engl. J. Med.* 319: 785–787, 1988.

84. Scovern, H. Hired help: A physician's experiences in a for-profit staff-model HMO. *N. Engl. J. Med.* 319: 787–790, 1988.

85. Levey, S., and Hesse, D. D. Bottom-line health care? *N. Engl. J. Med.* 312: 644–646, 1985.

86. Dranove, D., and White, W. D. Agency and the organization of health care delivery. *Inquiry* 24: 405–415, 1987.

87. McMahon, L. F., and Newbold, R. Variation in resource use within diagnosis-related groups: The effect of severity of illness and physician practice. *Med. Care* 24: 388–397, 1986.

88. Feinglass, J., and Martin, G. J. The Financial Impact of Physician Practice Style on Hospital Resource Use. Working paper, Center for Health Services Policy and Research.

89. Robert Wood Johnson Foundation. Three Hospital Preferred Practice Pattern Study: Final Report. Project #80A-84, Part 1, 1986. [Brigham and Women's Hospital, Massachusetts General Hospital, and New England Medical Center.]

90. Wasson, J. H., et al. Clinical prediction rules: Applications and methodological standards. *N. Engl. J. Med.* 313: 793–799, 1985.

91. Goldberg, G., and Abbott, J. A. Explicit criteria for use of laboratory tests. *Ann. Intern. Med.* 81: 857, 1974.

92. Staver, S. Iameter program studies practice patterns. *Am. Med. News,* February 3, 1989, p. 17.

93. Gardner, E. Intermountain studying physicians' practice patterns. *Mod. Healthcare,* February 17, 1989, pp. 22, 24.

94. Burda, D. Changing physician practice patterns: Quality improves, and so do profits. *Mod. Healthcare* 19(7): 18–26, 1989.

95. Derber, C. Capitalism and the medical division of labor: The changing situation of physicians. In *Issues in the Political Economy of Health Care,* edited by J. B. McKinlay. Metheun, New York, 1984.

96. Kletke, P. R., Marder, W. D., and Silberger, A. B. *The Demographics of Physician Supply: Trends and Projections.* American Medical Association Center for Health Policy Research, Chicago, 1987.

97. Marder, W. D., et al. Physician employment patterns: Challenging conventional wisdom. *Health Aff.,* Winter 1988, pp. 137–145.

98. McKinlay, J. B., and Arches, J. Towards the proletarianization of physicians. *Int. J. Health Serv.* 15(2): 161–195, 1985.

99. McKinlay, J. B., and Stoeckle, J. D. Corporatization and the social transformation of doctoring. *Int. J. Health Serv.* 18(2): 191–205, 1988.

100. Ritzer, G., and Walczak, D. Rationalization and the deprofessionalization of physicians. *Social Forces* 67(1): 1–22, 1988.

101. Hillman, A. L., et al. Managing the medical-industrial complex. *N. Engl. J. Med.* 315: 511–513, 1986.

102. Shortell, S. M., Morrisey, M. A., and Conrad, D. A. Economic regulation and hospital behavior: The effects on medical staff organization and hospital-physician relationships. *Health Serv. Res.* 20(5): 597–628, 1985.

103. Burns, L. R., Anderson, R., and Shortell, S. M. Evidence on changing hospital-physician relationships. In *Cost Containment and Physician Autonomy: Implications for Quality of Care,* Proceeding of the Twenty-Eighth Annual George Bugbee Symposium on Hospital Affairs, May 1986.

104. Winkenwerder, W., and Ball, J. R. Transformation of American health care: The role of the medical profession. *N. Engl. J. Med.* 318: 317–319, 1988.

105. Kallenberg, G. A. H., Riegelman, R. K., and Hockey, L. J. K. Waiting for the doctor glut, or is the cavalry really coming? *J. Gen. Intern. Med.* 2: 251–255, 1987.

106. Freidson, E. The reorganization of the medical profession. *Med. Care Rev.* 42: 11–35, 1985.

107. Iglehart, J. K. Congress moves to bolster peer review: The health care quality improvement act of 1986. *N. Engl. J. Med.* 316: 960–964, 1987.

108. Christensen, C. Developing a relative value scale for physician payments. *Internist* 28(3): 6–9, 1987.

109. Jackson, B. S., and Resnick, J. Comparing classification systems. *Nurs. Manage.* 13: 13–19, 1982.

110. Roper, W. L. Perspectives on physician-payment reform: The resource-based relative-value scale in context. *N. Engl. J. Med.* 319: 865–867, 1988.

111. Hsiao, W. C., et al. Estimating physicians' work for a resource-based relative-value scale. *N. Engl. J. Med.* 319: 835–841, 1988.

112. Hsiao, W. C., et al. Results and policy implications of the resource-based relative-value study. *N. Engl. J. Med.* 319: 881–888, 1988.

113. Braverman, H. *Labor and Monopoly Capital.* Monthly Review Press, New York, 1974.

114. Schroeder, S. A. Outcome assessment 70 years later: Are we ready? *N. Engl. J. Med.* 316: 160–162, 1987.

115. Greenfield, S., et al. Comparison of a criteria map to a criteria list in quality-of-care assessment for patients with chest pain: The relation of each outcome. *Med. Care* 19: 255–272, 1981.

116. Chassin, M. R., et al. Does inappropriate use explain geographic variations in the use of health care services? A study of three procedures. *JAMA* 258: 2533–2537, 1987.

117. Luft, H. S., and Hunt, S. S. Evaluating individual hospital quality through outcome statistics. *JAMA* 255: 2780–2784, 1986.
118. DuBois, R. W., et al. Hospital inpatient mortality: Is it a predictor of quality? *N. Engl. J. Med.* 317: 1674–1680, 1987.
119. Wennberg, J. E., et al. An assessment of prostatectomy for benign urinary tract obstruction: Geographic variations and the evaluation of medical care outcomes. *JAMA* 259: 3027–3030, 1988.
120. Salmon, J. W. Organizing medical care for profit. In *Issues in the Political Economy of Medical Care*, edited by J. B. McKinlay. Methuen, New York, 1984.
121. Steinwachs, D. M. Management information systems: New challenges to meet changing needs. *Med. Care* 23: 607–622, 1985.
122. Berwick, D. M. Toward an applied technology for quality measurement in health care. *Med. Decis. Making* 8(4): 253–258, 1988.
123. Himmelstein, D. U., and Woolhandler, S. Cost without benefit: Administrative waste in U.S. health care. *N. Engl. J. Med.* 314: 441–445, 1986.
124. Kenkel, P. J., and Morrissey, J. Cost control: Still an uphill battle. *Mod. Healthcare* 19(2): 27–28, 1989.
125. Anderson, G. F. National medical care spending. *Health Aff.* 5(3): 123–130, 1986.
126. Himmelstein, D. U., Woolhandler, S., and the Writing Committee of the Working Group on Program Design. A national health program for the United States: A physicians' proposal. *N. Engl. J. Med.* 320: 1102–1108, 1989.

Originally publsihed in the International Journal of Health Services, Volume 20, Number 2, Pages 233–252, 1990.

# CHAPTER 8

## The Changing Character of the Medical Profession: A Theoretical Overview

### Donald Light and Sol Levine

At the very time when physicians can diagnose the inner reaches of the brain with magnets, disintegrate kidney stones using sound waves instead of scalpels, and command an increasingly impressive technology, the profession is feeling besieged (1). Although trust and respect are still in evidence, malpractice suits abound. The institutional and technical character of medical work has become so complex that it threatens to make physicians an appendage to rather than master of their technology (2).

Perhaps of even greater significance, the medical profession is no longer exempt from anti-trust law (3), a change implying that disinterestedness is no longer perceived as the distinguishing difference between doctors and businessmen, as Talcott Parsons maintained in 1939 (4). Health care corporations (which appear now to include most old-fashioned community hospitals) are openly concerned about profits or surpluses, and the front office monitors the financial performance of clinicians with increased stringency. Meanwhile, non-health corporations have rebelled against the escalating premiums for health insurance (5–7). Joined by Medicare, Medicaid, and other institutional buyers, they have initiated a wide range of programs to manage costs, utilization, quality and ultimately physicians.

This paradox of medical advances and professional decline calls for analysis. A prevailing concept since Freidson developed it in 1970 has been *professional dominance* (8, 9). Throughout the 1980s, Freidson has maintained that despite all the implicit and explicit assaults on the profession, physicians still dominate medicine either individually or collectively (10–13). Even when individual physicians find themselves in subordinate roles, other physicians will be managing them or shaping their management.

Three alternate and quite distinct concepts that challenge this perspective by reflecting recent social developments are: (a) *deprofessionalization,* with its connotation of consumer revolt and profound cultural change; (b) *proletarianization,* with its emphasis on the inevitable expansion of capitalist exploitation; and (c) *corporatization,* with its tragic sense of swallowing up professional work.

Finding concepts that characterize what is happening matters because good concepts capture essences, identify dominant forces, determine our focus, and suggest future direction. In the following, we provide a brief overview and assessment of Freidson's concept and the three alternatives. We then provide an historical overview that shows how the profession's long campaign for autonomy and dominance contributed, ironically, to a reversal in its fortunes.

## ALTERNATE CONCEPTS OF THE MEDICAL PROFESSION

### *Professional Dominance*

Theories and concepts about the professions tend to reflect the norms and outlook of their time (14, 15). In his essays, Talcott Parsons recast the medical profession's norms about how doctors and patients should behave into normative sociological theory purporting to describe how they do behave (4, 16, 17). Most of medical sociology followed his lead, working comfortably within the profession's construction of reality; but Freidson challenged the tenets of normative theory. He was one of the first to recognize conflict and complexities in doctor-patient relationships (18). At the macro level, his theory of professional dominance challenged the normative concepts of Parsons about the nature of the profession. For example, normative theory held that professional training differed from others in being prolonged, specialized and theoretical. Freidson provocatively asked how prolonged, how specialized, and how theoretical must it be to qualify as "professional"? Professions were said to be special in their service orientation, but how might one measure the difference between this orientation and that of a waiter or myriad other service "professionals"? What distinguished the professions, Freidson concluded, or at least the profession of medicine, was its dominance over its sphere of work.

In his original formulation, Freidson (8, 9, 19) discusses several vehicles for establishing professional autonomy. One is autonomy over work. This seems necessary but not sufficient for dominance; many occupations have autonomy over their work without having much power. A second is control over the work of others in one's domain. Such control provides power well beyond autonomy, but it implies bureaucratic structures (like hospitals), and bureaucracies have a way of generating their own sources of power through regulations and hierarchy. Yet another source of professional dominance lies in the cultural beliefs and deference that people exhibit towards doctors as healers. This credibility is reproduced in the class hierarchy, institutions and culture of medicine (20–22). We would argue, as did Barzun (23), that culture is the most fundamental source of professional power; but it is subtle, intangible, and may shift the ground from under the feet of the profession as deference is replaced by wariness.

A final source of professional dominance is institutional power. Perhaps the most coherent formulation of the theory of professional dominance would center on Weber's analysis of social authority: a profession parlays its claim of valuable and complex knowledge into cultural and legal authority and thence into institutional authority (19, 24, 25). Each advance in authority provides new resources for further extensions of its dominance (26).

Freidson pointed out the problems produced by medical dominance. Because of it, physicians tended to practice where they wanted, resulting in maldistribution and the underservice of millions. Taking on the mantle of individual autonomy, physicians frustrated any effort by the profession to monitor the quality of their work as expected by society in granting the profession collective autonomy. These and other dimensions of Freidson's wide-ranging critique were backed by research, some of it by Freidson himself, and conveyed a sense of inevitable hegemony (27). Ironically, just as Parsons' "universal" theory of the medical profession captured the uncritical admiration of doctors in the prewar and postwar era, so Freidson's theory of professional dominance captured that mixed sense of awe and resentment that people felt towards the medical profession (and other large institutions) during the Vietnam years (14). Freidson's theory outlined a dynamic of ever-increasing dominance that almost precluded decline.

By 1985, Freidson had narrowed the original multi-faceted concept of professional dominance to the control over subordinate health workers and the power of licensure. Despite the assault from the women's health movement, the consumer health movement, the emergence of for-profit corporations, the pressures of cost containment, the changing patterns of medical work, the rise of HMOs, the growing supply of physicians, and the growth of competition, Freidson maintained that the profession remains dominant because it is still legally empowered to make decisions and oversee the medical work of others. Whatever may be the case, the situation begs for a reformulation that encompasses some of the most profound changes in half a century.

There is a great opportunity to investigate the changing nature of autonomy, of doctor-patient relations, of institutional power, and of control over the medical division of labor. Each of these needs to be researched by speciality and by institutional setting; for the profession is far more differentiated than before. Of particular interest are physicians who design and/or carry out systems that review physicians' practices, or computer systems that make diagnoses more accurately than the average specialist (28–31). Equally important would be research on how much nonphysicians and non-medical institutions affect the management, monitoring and clinical work of physicians (32–36).

## Deprofessionalization

At about the same time that Freidson perceived the growing excesses and imbalances of professional dominance, Haug (37) described the beginnings of deprofessionalization. Reacting against the fashionable idea among intellectuals that soon nearly all of post-industrial society would be professionalized (38), Haug argued that deprofessionalization would be the trend of the future. Specifically, she defined it as the professions losing "their monopoly over knowledge, public belief in their service ethos, and expectations of work autonomy and authority over the client" (37, p. 197). Her wide-ranging and suggestive essay discussed new aggregations of professional specialization such as family medicine and new configurations of work manifested in the proliferation of paraprofessionals such as physicians' assistants.

Other forces weakening the dominance of professions, she noted, were the diffusion of knowledge through computers, increased literacy, and the rising dissatisfaction among laymen with professionals who were self-serving rather than client-serving. Haug predicted, "The tension between the public demand for accountability and the professional's insistence on final authority has not yet erupted into general warfare. . . .But there have been skirmishes." As the ideology grows worldwide that professionals' decisions are subject to lay questioning, as the professional charisma dims, such challenges to expert authority and autonomy can be expected to occur with increasing frequency. In this sense the bureaucratization of professional practice carries with it the seeds of its own destruction (37, pp. 306–307). Since her initial essay, Haug has explored this theme in greater depth (39, 40). Her 1976 survey with Lavin (41) showed that sizable minorities of citizens said they were willing to challenge physicians' authority and participate in decision-making.

Freidson (11) dismisses much of the deprofessionalization argument. He believes that most if not all of the consumer health movement affects physicians little and that the public confidence in doctors has declined no more than for other prestigious groups. He is unimpressed with the alleged closing of the knowledge gap as patients become more educated, because the growth of complex knowledge accumulates at an even faster pace. The pre-eminent legal and institutional dominance of the profession remains intact.

Although Haug has identified several profound changes that no future assessment of the medical profession can ignore, we need systematic analysis of existing evidence and carefully designed studies to examine the ways in which the medical profession is being affected by the forces she described. The women's health movement and the consumer health movement initiated a significant cultural shift that has changed health habits in the United States, fostered new lines of business to manage risk factors or promote health, and even altered the practice of medicine in some quarters. Computerization is breaking down strongholds of professional dominance. Freidson may be correct for that small group of physicians that helps to develop these programs, but in so doing they contribute to deprofessionalization by rationalizing the core of professional skills so that the performance of physicians can be subjected to external evaluation. Computerized systems that compare medical practices serve to define the norms of acceptable practice at the same time as they identify deviant practitioners (42, 43). A systematic review could probably make a good case for deprofessionalization since 1970, and even the profession's legal and institutional prerogatives no longer remain intact.

## Proletarianization

A provocative effort to understand the institutional changes affecting physicians centers on the debate between some Marxists, Weberians, and liberal intellectuals about the nature of professional work in advanced economies. Bell's (38, 44) description of the post-industrial society, in which knowledge replaces capital as the central factor of production, has been dismissed as naive by proletarianization theorists. They emphasize the role and relations of professionals to capital and to other classes. They see parallels between the deskilling and routinization of craftsmen in the nineteenth century and what is beginning to happen to professionals since the mid twentieth century (45–50). Technological developments have increased requirements for capital, forcing professionals to depend on capitalists for supplies and equipment. As this dependency grows, so does the power of capitalists to shape "production." Will professionals experience the final step of having their craft knowledge subsumed into new industrial technology so that their craftmanship is no longer needed, or will they retain a fair degree of control over the technical aspects of their professional work?

There is no question that many doctors feel imposed upon, compromised and controlled from all sides. As McKinlay (51) outlined in a provocative review of Freidson's work, there is a logic to capitalism that drives it to find new markets and expand, then plow the profits into further expansion and into creating through advertising a demand or a craving for more commodities. Implanting unnecessary pacemakers, the boom in plastic surgery, and persuading patients with terminal lung cancer to undergo surgery for profit are some recent examples of a long-standing trend (23, 52–54). McKinlay went on to fault Freidson for not addressing the relations between the medical profession and capitalism, the class interests behind professionalism, the political-economic consequences of medicalization when medicine has only a modest impact on health, and the relation between the medical profession and capitalism. By 1985, McKinlay and his colleague Arches (55) sharpened part of this larger argument in an article on the proletarianization of physicians that has generated controversy (56–59). The expansion of capitalism, they argue, has brought more bureaucracy as its principal form of social control. Increasingly, physicians take salaried positions in bureaucratic organizations where regulatory norms and administrative hierarchy shape the delivery of medical care. McKinlay and Arches add that the rapidly growing number of physicians weakens their market power and strengthens the bureaucrat's power to set terms. The recent emphasis on technological training makes graduates dependent on large organizations. The emphasis on "value neutrality" or "detached concern" in professional training fits well into the dehumanized approach of bureaucratic medicine. Specialization and sub-specialization carry the seeds of deskilling, a key capitalist technique for paying workers less, making them more replaceable, and extracting more surplus value out of their labor.

This formulation has been valuable in focusing attention on important developments, but it must also be remembered that physicians have been energetically pursuing specialization since the turn of the century in order to realize more income, greater prestige, and more interesting work (60). There seems to be no evidence that physician specialization has been the basis for deskilling or lower income. In fact, many physicians have ardently pursued technological advances and ordered the latest medical devices so as to advance their clinical skills, meet the demands of patients, and increase their income. The growth of bureaucracy owes much to the professional emphasis on specialization and technology. The proletarianization perspective does not explain the millions of unnecessary procedures, prescriptions, operations and hospitalizations ordered by physicians that led the U.S. Congress and major corporations to seek the controls over medical expenses (58, 61).

It is important to distinguish three major changes encompassed in the proletarianization argument: the increasing technical and organizational complexity of modern medicine which is found in socialist countries as well as in capitalist societies (62, 63); the rise of investor-owned health care corporations, particularly hospital chains (64) which tend to attract physicians with more amenities and institutional support or risk losing them to nonprofit competitors (65, 66); and the revolt of institutional buyers who seek to control the rising bill for services. Besides the need to keep these institutional and economic changes distinct, there is the question of how apt the concept of proletarianization may be (46, 67, 68). Navarro (68) holds that the concept "proletariat" refers to supervised manual workers who do not have control over the means or organization of production. Even if this strict definition among Marxist scholars were somewhat broadened, one doubts that it would apply to physicians because their powers remain substantial.

Other writers concerned about these issues have moved beyond proletarianization in their effort to understand the place of professionals and other middle-level groups in modern society (46, 48, 67, 69–74). They view "proletariat" as inappropriate and have been searching for a new concept that depicts the role of professionals and managers employed by corporations.[1] Although physicians and students of health care do not generally read this literature on social class, it addresses more thoughtfully than any other the basic questions of professional identity in an age of corporate (i.e., capitalist) health care.

One such concept is the "professional-managerial class" (PMC) introduced over a decade ago by the Ehrenreichs (71). It consists of "salaried mental workers who do not own the means of production and whose major function in the social division of labor may be described broadly as the reproduction of capitalist culture and capitalist class relations" (71, p. 13). The fundamental differences between the PMC and classic petty bourgeoisie reflect the underlying change experienced by physicians who have gone from being self-employed professionals to professionals in corporations. As petty bourgeoisie, self-employed physicians have been structurally outside and therefore "irrelevant to the process of capital accumulation and to the process of reproducing capitalist social relations" (71, p. 18). But once in the corporation, they are involved in both.

The Ehrenreichs hold that the PMC is essentially "nonproductive" and paid from the surplus value gained from the exploitation of workers elsewhere in the corporation. This may be true of the company doctor but not of physicians working for health care corporations. They are high-class workers who may be exploited but still retain considerable control over the means of production, like craftsmen in the first stage of proletarianization when capitalists bankrolled their financial needs but left them alone to turn out valued products. From a theoretical perspective, whether or not professional services produce surplus value depends on ownership and the structuring of pricing that frames the services (58, 75, and other articles in the *International Journal of Health Services*).

Another insightful line of analysis beyond proletarianization is found in Wright's ideas about professionals in "contradictory class locations" (76). As applied to doctors, examples would include employed physicians as located between the working class and the petty bourgeoisie, and physicians running group practices as located between the petty bourgeoisie and capitalists. More recently, Wright (74) has explored the ways in which class position depends on exploiting the rights to other kinds of property involved in production such as skills, special knowledge, and the organization of work. Thus, while a much more differentiated analysis remains to be done of how different types of medical careers relate to capital, surplus value, and the means of production, this body of

---

[1] Most of these authors share the problem of treating managers and professionals together, when their relations to the mode of production and to capital are quite different. They are not focused on highly paid professionals who can be exploited to produce significant surplus value for the owners of a corporation. Nor do they distinguish front-line physicians on salary, who supervise only their nurse and a couple of staff as they treat patients, from a medical director who supervises a large staff with an eye to the bottom line. A third group, physician-entrepreneurs are also not discussed, but they pose little problem: they are budding capitalists.

work goes well beyond the proletarianization perspective to identify the structural relations between physicians, workers, and owners of corporations.

## Corporatization

To a significant degree, corporatization encompasses the proletarianization thesis without the same Marxist assumptions (57). It refers to the experience of being subjected to forms of corporate control such as utilization and quality review, incentive pay structures, restrictions on practice patterns and the organization of practice, and the restructuring of the marketplace from solo or small-group providers to multi-institutional complexes (1, 77). These are the experiences not just of the working class but of managers as well (75). Corporatization also refers to the paradox of physicians relying on complex organizations and financial arrangements to carry out their sophisticated work, yet realizing that these institutions intrude on their work, mediate their relations with patients, and potentially injure their credibility with society as a whole. Legitimacy is both extended and threatened.

Again, a sorting out is in order. To what extent are the long-standing complaints about rationalization and bureaucracy being attributed to "corporatization"? The traditional emphasis on autonomy and independence make American physicians ill-prepared coming in to the organizational structures of the modern industrial world (78). Yet even though corporatization may be rationalization and bureaucracy in contemporary garb, it does bring with it what Derber calls "ideological proletarianization" (46, pp. 169–187). By this he means losing control over the product or ends of one's work while maintaining control over the means or techniques of work.

Derber believes that most professionals accommodate to ideological proletarianization. They will desensitize themselves to the issue by disassociating themselves from the goals of the institution and/or by denying that control over the product of their work is all that important. What matters is that one does one's work well. Physicians, like other professionals, are trained to make an end out of means as a way of resolving troublesome sources of uncertainty (25). They then may take the second step of identifying with the goals of the institution. At the same time, the professionals provide a valuable source of legitimation for the organization.

Logically, the term corporatization should also encompass the development of the corporate impulse within the profession (79, 80). Professional corporatization has become widespread as physicians unbundle services from hospitals and turn their offices into capital-intensive ambulatory centers for diagnosis and treatment. Thus, corporatization is a concept worth pursuing, but in a way that recognizes its two-sided nature.

In conclusion, each of the four concepts discussed illuminates important developments in modern medical practice; yet each reflects a theoretical and political perspective that captures only part of a larger whole. We show how developments characterized by deprofessionalization, proletarianization and corporatization are not entirely exogenous to, but were facilitated by, unanticipated consequences of the professional dominance which the medical profession attained.

## PROFESSIONAL DOMINANCE AND CORPORATIZATION

The rise to professional dominance of the "regular" or allopathic sect has been well documented by a number of scholars (60, 75, 81–86). A coherent autonomous profession, or what Larson (47) calls "the professional project," was in part aimed at preventing medical work from being controlled by corporations near the turn of the century. Already, the railroads, the lumber industry, mining companies, and some textile mill towns employed or retained thousands of "company doctors" (86, Ch. 6). Less well known were a growing number of companies as well as governmental departments and fraternal societies that put out medical service contracts for bids, often on a capitated basis (87–89). Reports from various cities estimated that a quarter to a third of the population obtained services under competitive contracts. To put the matter more abstractly, institutional buyers were structuring wholesale markets before 1910.

The profession's drive for autonomy and control involved wresting control from institutional (i.e. corporate and governmental) buyers, minimizing competition, and eliminating forms of cost containment. Besides reinstating medical licensing boards, using their examinations to institutionalize the new scientific curriculum, and using the new curriculum to drive many medical schools out of business with the demands of the new curriculum, leaders of medicine campaigned intensively against "contract medicine." State and county societies urged members not to bid against each other for the contracts and threatened expulsion if they did. The profession succeeded in getting employers and other contractors to stop providing direct services and instead to help pay the bills of autonomous doctors. The profession also inveighed against the free care provided by dispensaries and by the leading public health departments (82). At the same time, physicians were extraordinarily successful in obtaining capital for their own professional purposes. They professionalized hospitals and used them both to develop their skills further and to increase their fees (90, 91).

What the profession sought was a precapitalist guild in the middle of a capitalist society. Leaders understood that if they could get physicians to unite against competition, everyone would win. As Weber wrote, guilds are a form of closed order which pursues quality, prestige, and profit to the mutual benefit of its members (92, pp. 46, 342–346). Weber's description captures essential elements of professionalization (93, pp. 298–364; 94). As Larson put it, the profession gained autonomy, created ideology, which it presented as the most valid definition of reality, and monopolized competence. Professionalization, she writes, is "the process by which producers of special services sought to constitute and control a market for their expertise" (47, p. xvi). It is neither inevitable nor "natural" (95).

By the 1920s, the medical profession had gained control of its markets, mode of practice, training, and institutions (82, 84, 86, 96). The rapid growth of hospitals, built by doctors, religious orders, charitable organizations and community donations, not only gave physicians a technical workshop but also provided a way of disciplining errant colleagues by not granting privileges unless they were in "good standing" with the local medical society. The sponsors who provided immense amounts of capital, however, did not control the profession (67). Although forms of contract medicine continued, they now existed only at the periphery and faced fierce opposition from local societies. Complete control by the guild seemed possible until the Depression perpetrated a crisis in how to pay for services. New forms of prepaid contracts arose among companies, hospitals, medical societies, volunteer associations and governments. They sought through various types of subscription and payment mechanisms to cover the high costs of those few who became ill (96–98).

The AMA remained adamantly opposed to any arrangement that put a middleman between doctor and patient, but the hospitals were more desperate (100). The American Hospital Association selected one from the wide range of plans in operation that met their requirements: no profit, no middlemen, no interferences with the practice of medicine, non-competitive, and confined only to hospital bills so opposition from medical societies could be avoided (101). It is commonly believed that Justin Kimball at Baylor Hospital came up with just the right plan that would solve the fiscal crisis of American hospitals (102, p. 10); but we must remember that other hospitals created prepaid plans. More important, comprehensive forms of prepaid health insurance were passed over and later vigorously opposed (86, 96).

There followed a sustained and difficult campaign to forge competing hospital prepaid plans into area-wide noncompetitive plans, to foster the creation of such plans where they did not exist, and to create a legal basis for provider-controlled, nonprofit, noncompetitive, community health insurance for those who could afford the premiums. Named Blue Cross, this partial form of social insurance was designed to minimize any middleman role by giving control of the plans to physicians and hospital administrators or trustees. Some years later the physicians decided to follow suit with Blue Shield along similar but not exactly parallel lines.

Instituting health insurance along professional lines and defeating prior efforts to legislate national forms of social insurance completed "the professional project" (75). The results are captured by Freidson's term, professional dominance, a health care system whose organization, laws, and financing reflect the priorities of the medical profession to provide the best clinical medicine to every sick patient, to enhance the prestige and income of the profession, and to protect the autonomy of physicians (63, pp. 14–17). The profession has both used state powers to pursue its goals and feared state intervention as a threat to professional autonomy. In fact, the American case is distinguished from many other countries by the reluctance of government to intervene (62, 103–105).

## PROFESSIONALISM IN A CORPORATE SOCIETY

The influence of corporations on the medical guild occurred in more subtle and indirect ways. Through licensure and guild rules, the profession inadvertently created protected markets and allowed in health-related corporations. Although today we tend to think of this happening with corporations involved in direct services, the earliest and perhaps most important instance involved the profession creating an "ethical" (i.e., in conformity with AMA ethics about professional control) drug industry (81, 106, 107). As early as 1906, the AMA mounted a vigorous campaign against nostrums and patent medicine. The profession, joined by druggists who were also feeling the competition from patent medicine manufacturers, sought to cordon off and control the sale of only those drugs whose recipes were revealed, tested, and approved by the AMA. Aside from many other facets of the story, this created a protected professional market. Since the profession opposed any state participation, and capitalism constituted the "natural" economic environment of the nation, it was inevitable that "ethical" drug companies experienced tremendous growth and profits. What the profession did not anticipate is that these same corporations would come to influence professional judgment and make many facets of professional life dependent on them (108–110).

Over subsequent decades, corporations have flourished in every other sector of the protected medical market—hospital supply, hospital construction, medical devices, laboratories, and insurance—until the only large sector left untouched was medical services itself. Physicians somehow thought that they could allow corporations to dominate all these other sectors without being touched themselves. Yet ironically their judgments and decisions were being commercialized in numerous ways by how insurance policies were written, by what medical devices were promoted, by how supplies were packaged, by what new lab tests were made available, by which company sponsored professional presentations, and by which salesmen they saw. Thus the rise of corporate providers, however much the profession regarded it as a shocking radical departure (97), was very much an organic part of the profession's long-term relation with capitalism.

The other aspects of corporatization that result from bureaucratic complexity also evolved in part as a natural consequence of professional dominance. The profession's emphasis on elaborated techniques and specialization led to more complex organizations of work and finance, with a given physician only part of a larger complex. In order to manage large hospitals and health centers, administrators became more professionally qualified and powerful. Thus administrative control and bureaucratic rules grew steadily after World War II, well before the current era of large health care corporations. These new corporations have further extended bureaucratic tendencies, but they have also catered to physicians (66).

The proletarian perspective alludes to similar features and developments which ironically accompanied the profession's drive for autonomy and dominance. In addition, the relentless rise of medical expenditures for every test and procedure ordered to provide the best clinical care regardless of cost has led institutional buyers to impose new mechanisms for accountability. Recent developments include physician practice profiles, utilization reviews, norms for treatment, and systems for allocating resources (111, 112). Putting contracts out for bid once again, institutional buyers have prompted doctors, clinics, and hospitals to assume new corporate forms and restructure services. The center of power in American health care is now shifting from the profession to buyers.

Aspects of deprofessionalization have also evolved in part from the excesses and deficiencies of a professionally driven health care system. We have already described the bureaucratic and corporate dimensions. From a patient's point of view, the professional emphasis on ever more specialization results in fragmented care and a dehumanizing emphasis on technology. More than ever before, consumers are wary of overmedicalization, keen on reading about medicine, and determined to control what is done to their bodies. Meantime, the profession has displayed little interest in prevention and chronic care until recently. The first does not involve sick patients, and the second consists of sick patients who do not respond well to treatment. Such excesses and deficiencies have contributed to the consumer health movement with its emphasis on empowerment and staying well.

Thus viewed historically, the four principal concepts about the medical profession are interconnected in ways that provide a new perspective distinct from that of Freidson. To remember wistfully the Golden Era of doctoring in the fifties and sixties is to forget how its features contributed to the current era. The very notion of what it means to be professional is undergoing basic change. We must go beyond concepts of professionalism that emphasize autonomy (8, 9, 93), or the loss of autonomy. A new framework is needed, one that incorporates historical trends and current features of the complex organizations and networks in which medical care is taking place (111, 113).

## REFERENCES

1. Stoeckle, J. D. Reflections on modern doctoring. *Milbank Mem. Fund Q.* 66, Suppl. 2, 1988.
2. Arney, W. R. *Power and the Profession of Obstetrics,* Part Two. University of Chicago Press, Chicago, 1982.
3. Rosoff, A. J. Antitrust laws and the health care industry: New warriors into an old battle. *St. Louis University Law J.* 446: 458–489, 1979.

4. Parsons, T. The professions and social structure. In *Essays in Sociological Theory*, revised, pp. 34–49. The Free Press, Glencoe, Ill., 1954.
5. Goldsmith, J. C. Death of paradigm: The challenge of competition. *Health Aff.* 3: 5–19, 1984.
6. Fruen, M. A. *Health Care in the Future.* John Hancock Mutual Life Insurance Company, Boston, 1986.
7. Gabel, J., et al. The commercial health insurance industry in transition. *Health Aff.* 6: 46–60, 1987.
8. Freidson, E. *Professional Dominance: The Social Structure of Medicine.* Atherton, New York, 1970.
9. Freidson, E. *Profession of Medicine.* Dodd, Mead, New York, 1970.
10. Freidson, E. The changing nature of professional control. *Annu. Rev. Sociol.* 10: 1–20, 1984.
11. Freidson, E. The reorganization of the medical profession. *Med. Care Rev.* 42: 11–35, 1985.
12. Freidson, E. The medical profession in transition. In *Applications of Social Science to Clinical Medicine and Health Policy*, edited by L. Aiken and D. Mechanic, pp. 63–79. Rutgers University Press, New Brunswick, N.J., 1986.
13. Freidson, E. *Professional Power: A Study of the Institutionalization of Formal Knowledge.* Rutgers University Press, New Brunswick, N.J., 1986.
14. Light, D. W. Social control and the American health care system. In *Handbook of Medical Sociology*, edited by H. E. Freeman and S. Levine. Prentice-Hall, Englewood Cliffs, N.J., 1988.
15. Light, D. W. Turf Battles and the theory of professional dominance. In *Research in the Sociology of Health Care*, Vol. 7. JAI Press, Greenwich, Conn., 1988.
16. Parsons, T. The motivation of economic activities. In *Essays in Sociological Theory*, revised, pp. 50–68. The Free Press, Glencoe, Ill., 1954.
17. Parsons, T. Social structure and dynamic process: The case of modern medical practice. In *The Social System*, pp. 428–479. The Free Press, Glencoe, Ill., 1951.
18. Freidson, E. *Patients' Views of Medical Practice.* Russell Sage Foundation, New York, 1961.
19. Freidson, E. The impurity of professional authority. In *Institutions and the Person*, edited by H. S. Becker, et al., pp. 25–34. Aldine, Chicago, 1968.
20. Navarro, V. *Medicine Under Capitalism.* Prodist, New York, 1976.
21. Navarro, V. *Crisis, Health and Medicine.* Tavistock, New York, 1986.
22. Waitzkin, H. *The Second Sickness: Contradictions of Capitalist Health Care.* The Free Press, New York, 1983.
23. Barzun, J. The professions under siege. *Harper's*, October 1978, pp. 61–68.
24. Light, D. W. Professional Superiority. Paper read at the American Sociological Association, Montreal, August 27, 1974.
25. Light, D. W. Uncertainty and control in professional training. *J. Health Soc. Behav.* 20: 310–322, 1979.
26. Lieberman, J. K. *The Tyranny of Experts.* Walker, New York, 1970.
27. Waitzkin, H., and Waterman, B. Social theory and medicine. *Int. J. Health Serv.* 6: 9–23, 1976.
28. Barnett, G. O., et al., DXplain: An evolving diagnostic decision-support system. *JAMA* 258: 67–74, 1987.
29. Rennels, G. D., and Shortliffe, E. H. Advanced computing for medicine. *Sci. Am.* 257 (4): 154–161, 1987
30. Shortliffe, E. H. Computer programs to support clinical decision making. *JAMA* 258: 61–66, 1987.

31. Goldman, L., et al. A computer protocol to predict myocardial infarction in emergency department patients with chest pain. *N. Engl. J. Med.* 318: 797–803, 1988.
32. King, S., and Skinner, C. Evaluating utilization review. *Business and Health* 1(9): 40–42, 1984.
33. Ricks, T. E. New corporate program lets employees compare local doctors' fees and training. *Wall Street J.*, August 4, 1987, p. 37.
34. Inlander, C. B. Consumers can put health care data to good use. *Business and Health* 4(7): 26-27, 1987.
35. Ollier, C. The data connection. *Health Week* 1(8): 22ff, 1987.
36. Aquilina, D., Daley, J., and Coburn, J. Using hospital data to spot utilization problems. *Business and Health* 4(7): 28–33, 1987.
37. Haug, M. R. Deprofessionalization: An alternate hypothesis for the future. *Sociol. Rev. Monograph* 20: 195–211, 1973.
38. Bell, D. *The Coming of Post-Industrial Society.* Basic Books, New York, 1973.
39. Haug, M. R. The erosion of professional authority: A cross-cultural inquiry in the case of the physician. *Milbank Mem. Fund Q.* 54: 83–106, 1976.
40. Haug, M. R., and Lavin, B. Practitioner or patient—Who's in charge? *J. Health Soc. Behav.* 22: 212–229, 1983.
41. Haug, M. R., and Lavin, B. *Consumerism in Medicine Challenging Physician Authority.* Sage Publications, Beverly Hills, 1983.
42. O'Donnell, P. S. Managing health costs under a fee-for-service plan. *Business and Health* 4(5): 23–29, 1987.
43. Feldstein, P. J., Wickizer, T. M., and Wheeler, J. R. C. Private cost containment: The effects of utilization review programs on health care use and expenditures. *N. Engl. J. Med.* 318: 1310–1314, 1988.
44. Bell, D. *The Cultural Contradictions of Capital.* Basic, New York, 1976.
45. Aronowitz, S. *False Promises: The Shaping of American Working Class Consciousness.* McGraw-Hill, New York, 1973.
46. Derber, C. *Professionals as Workers: Mental Labor in Advanced Capitalism.* G.K. Hall, Boston, 1982.
47. Larson, M. S. *The Rise of Professionalism: A Sociological Analysis.* University of California Press, Berkeley, 1977.
48. Oppenheimer, M. White collar revisited: The making of a new working class. *Social Policy,* July/August 1970, p. 1.
49. Oppenheimer, M. The unionization of the professional. *Social Policy* 5: 34–40, January/February 1975.
50. Oppenheimer, M. *White Collar Politics.* Monthly Review Press, New York, 1985.
51. McKinlay, J. B. The business of good doctoring or doctoring as good business: Reflections on Freidson's view of the medical game. *Int. J. Health Serv.* 7: 459–487, 1977.
52. Greenberg, E. R., et al. Social and economic factors in the choice of lung cancer treatment. *N. Engl. J. Med.* 318: 612–617, 1988.
53. Greenspan, A. M., Kay, et al. Incidence of unwarranted implantation of permanent cardiac pacemakers in a large medical population. *N. Engl. J. Med.* 318: 158–163, 1988.
54. McCleery, R. S., et al., One *Life—One Physician: An Inquiry into the Medical Profession's Performance in Self-Regulation.* Public Affairs Press, Washington, D.C., 1971.
55. McKinlay, J. B., and Arches, J. Toward the proletarianization of physicians. *Int. J. Health Serv.* 15: 161–195, 1985.

56. McKinlay, J. B., and Arches, J. Historical changes in doctoring: A reply to Milton Roemer. *Int. J. Health Serv.* 16: 473–477, 1986.
57. McKinlay, J. B., and Stoeckle. J. D. Corporatization and the social transformation of doctoring. *Int. J. Health Serv.* 18(2):191–205, 1988.
58. Chernomas, R. An economic basis for the proletarianization of physicians. *Int. J. Health Serv.* 16: 669–674, 1986.
59. Roemer, M. I. Proletarianization of physicians or organization of health services? *Int. J. Health Serv.* 16: 469–472, 1986.
60. Stevens, R. *American Medicine and the Public Interest.* Yale University Press, New Haven, 1971.
61. Rensberger, B. Thousands a year killed by prescriptions. *The New York Times,* Jan. 28, 1988, p. 1.
62. Larkin, G. *Occupational Monopoly and Modern Medicine.* Tavistock, London, 1983.
63. Light, D. W., and Schuller, A. (eds.). *Political Values and Health Care: The German Experience.* M.I.T. Press, Cambridge, Mass., 1986.
64. Light, D. W. Corporate medicine for profit. *Sci. Am.* 255(6): 38–45, 1986.
65. Alexander, J. A., Morrisey, M. A., and Shortell, S. M. The effects of competition, regulation, and corporatization on hospital-physician relationships. *J. Health Soc. Behav.* 27: 220–235, 1986.
66. Shortell, S. M., Morrisey, M. A., and Conrad, D. A. Economic regulation and hospital behavior: The effects on medical staff organization and hospital-physician relationships. *Health Serv. Res.* 20: 597–628, 1985.
67. Derber, C. Sponsorship and the control of physicians. *Theory and Society,* 12: 561–601, 1983.
68. Navarro, V. Professional dominance or proletarianization? Neither. *Milbank Mem. Fund Q.,* 66, Suppl. 2, 1988.
69. Burris, V. Class structure and political ideology. *The Insurgent Sociologist* 14(2): 7–47, 1987.
70. Carchedi, G. *On the Economic Identification of Social Classes.* Routledge and Kegan Paul, London, 1977.
71. Ehrenreich, B., and Ehrenreich, J. The professional-managerial class. *Radical America* 11(2): 7–32, 1977.
72. Poulantzas, M. *Classes in Contemporary Capitalism.* New Left Books, London, 1975.
73. Wright, E. O. *Class, Crisis and the State.* New Left Books, London, 1978.
74. Wright, E. O. *Classes.* New Left Books, London, 1985.
75. Larson, M. S. Proletarianization and educated labor. *Theory and Society* 9: 131–175, 1980.
76. Wright, E. O. Varieties of Marxist conceptions of class structure. *Politics and Society* 9: 323–370, 1980.
77. Burnham, J. F. The unfortunate care of Dr. Z: How to succeed in medical practice in 1984. *N. Engl. J. Med.* 310: 729–730, 1984.
78. Rueschemeyer, D. *Power and the Division of Labor.* Stanford University Press, Stanford, 1986.
79. Goldstein, M. S. Abortion as a medical career choice: Entrepreneurs, community physicians, and others. *J. Health Soc. Behav.* 25: 211–229, 1984.
80. Relman, A. S. Dealing with conflicts of interest. *N. Engl. J. Med.* 313: 749–751, 1985.
81. Burrow, J. G. *AMA: Voice of American Medicine.* Johns Hopkins University Press, Baltimore, 1963.

82. Burrow, J. G. *Organized Medicine in the Progressive Era: The Move Toward Monopoly.* Johns Hopkins University Press, Baltimore, 1977.
83. Berlant, J. L. *Profession and Monopoly: A Study of Medicine in the United States and Great Britain.* University of California Press, Berkeley, 1975.
84. Rothstein, W. G. *American Physicians in the Nineteenth Century.* Johns Hopkins University Press, Baltimore, 1972.
85. Rothstein, W. G. *American Medical Schools and the Practice of Medicine: A History.* Oxford University Press, New York, 1987.
86. Starr, P. *The Social Transformation of American Medicine.* Basic Books, New York, 1982.
87. Henderson, C. R. *Industrial Insurance in the United States.* University of Chicago Press, Chicago, 1909.
88. Ferguson, C. W. *Fifty Million Brothers: A Panorama of American Lodges and Clubs.* Farrar & Rinehart, New York, 1937.
89. National Industrial Conference Board. *Experience with Mutual Benefit Associations in the United States.* NICB, New York, 1923.
90. Rosner, D. A. *A Once Charitable Enterprise: Hospitals & Health Care in Brooklyn and New York 1855-1915.* Cambridge University Press, New York, 1982.
91. Vogel, M. *The Invention of the Modern Hospital, Boston, 1870-1930.* University of Chicago Press, Chicago, 1980.
92. Weber, M. *Economy and Society: An Outline of Interpretive Sociology,* edited by G. Roth and C. Wittich. Bedminster Press, New York, 1968.
93. Carr-Saunders, A. M. and Wilson, P. A. *The Professions.* Clarendon Press, Oxford, 1933.
94. Scull, A. T. *Museums of Madness: The Social Organization of Insanity in Nineteenth-Century England.* St. Martin Press, New York, 1979.
95. Kennedy, F. R. The American Medical Association: Power, purpose, and politics in organized medicine. *The Yale Law J.* 63: 938–1022, 1954.
96. Rayack, E. *Professional Power and American Medicine: The Economics of the American Medical Association.* World Publications, Cleveland, 1967.
97. Relman, A. S. The new medical-industrial complex. *N. Engl. J. Med.* 303: 963–970, 1980.
98. Williams, P. *The Purchase of Medicinal Care Through Fixed Periodic Payments.* National Bureau of Economic Research, New York, 1932.
99. Avnet, H. H. *Voluntary Insurance in the United States: Major Trends and Current Problems.* Medical Administration Service, New York, 1944.
100. Leland, R. G. *Contract Practice.* American Medical Association, Chicago, 1932.
101. Rorem, C. R. *Non-Profit Hospital Service Plans.* Commission on Hospital Service, American Hospital Association, Chicago, 1940.
102. Fein, R. *Medical Care, Medical Costs: The Search for a Health Insurance Policy.* Harvard University Press, Cambridge, Mass., 1986.
103. Coburn, D., Torrance, G. M., and Kaufert, J. Medical dominance in Canada in historical perspective: Rise and fall of medicine? *Int. J. Health Serv.* 13: 407–432, 1983.
104. Willis, E. *Medical Dominance: The Division of Labour in Australian Health Care.* Allen and Unwin, Sydney, 1983.
105. Wilsford, D. The cohesion and fragmentation of organized medicine in France and the United States. *J. Health Polit. Policy Law* 12: 481–503, 1987.
106. Rorem, C. R., and Fischelis, R. P. *The Costs of Medicine.* University of Chicago Press, Chicago, 1932.

107. Caplan, R. L. Pasteurized Patients and Profits: The Changing Nature of Self-care in American Medicine. Ph.D. Dissertation, Department of Economics, University of Massachusetts, 1981.
108. Goldfinger, S. E. A matter of influence. *N. Engl. J. Med.* 316: 1408–1409, 1987.
109. Lexchin, J. Pharmaceutical promotion in Canada: Convince them or confuse them. *Int. J. Health Serv.* 17: 77–89, 1987.
110. Mintz, M. *By Prescription Only,* 2nd edition, revised. Houghton Mifflin, Boston, 1967.
111. Ellwood, P. M. Shattuck lecture—Outcomes management. *N. Engl. J. Med.* 318: 1549–1556, 1988.
112. Caper, P. Defining quality in medical care. *Health Aff.* 7(1): 49–61, 1988.
113. Schulz, R., and Harrison, S. Physician autonomy in the Federal Republic of Germany, Great Britain and the United States. *Int. J. Health Plann. Manage.* 2:336–355, 1986.

Reprinted with permission from The Milbank Quarterly, Volume 66, Supplement 2, Pages 10–32, 1988.

# CHAPTER 9

# Professional Dominance or Proletarianization? Neither

## Vicente Navarro

This chapter questions some of the basic assumptions of the theoretical position that considers the medical profession the dominant force in medicine. It argues that the medical profession is not only losing the power it once had in medicine, but that it was never the dominant force shaping the production of medical knowledge or the practice and organization of medicine. The medical profession has always been submerged in a social, economic, and political context that determines the realm of the possible and probable in medicine. Thus, the evolution of medicine has responded to many different, competitive, and conflicting sets of forces, of which professional forces are not the only or even the most important ones. This reality has become increasingly evident as a result of the process referred to as the corporatization of U.S. medicine. The chapter cautions, however, against identifying the medical profession's loss of autonomy with the process of proletarianization; physicians are not becoming proletarians. The political consequences and risks of this misidentification are also discussed.

### THE PROFESSIONAL DOMINANCE POSITION

One of the most important theoretical positions put forward to explain the nature of medical knowledge and practice and the organization of U.S. medicine has been the *professional dominance* position, articulated primarily by Freidson (1–4); among others are Berland (5), Illich (6), and Arney (7). In this position, the medical profession dominates the medical care system in the production of medical knowledge, in the division of labor in medicine, in the provision of health services, and in the organization of medicine. This dominance comes from the monopolistic control of the medical profession over the production of medical knowledge and the provision of medical services, and is reproduced by cultural, economic, and legal means. Culturally, the medical profession has been able to convince the dominant elites in our society of the value of its trade. As Freidson (2, pp. 72–73) indicates, "it is essential that the dominant elite remain persuaded of the positive value or at least the harmlessness of the profession's work, so that it continues to protect it from encroachment."

While the dominant elites are those that need to be persuaded, the state is the main guarantor of the monopolistic control of physicians' trade since it gives the medical profession its exclusive right to practice (Freidson does not touch on the relationship between the dominant elite and the state. Thus, the source of state power is not analyzed in the professional dominance position) (2, pp. 23–24):

> The foundation of medicine's control over work is thus clearly political in character, involving the aid of the state in establishing and maintaining the profession's preeminence. . . .The most strategic and treasured characteristic of the profession—its autonomy—is therefore owed to its relationship to the sovereign state from which it is not ultimately autonomous.

Another requirement for the reproduction of professional dominance is that the profession convince the general public of the value of its work (2, p. 188):

> I suggested that scholarly or scientific professions may obtain and maintain a fairly secure status by virtue of winning solidly the support of a political, economic and social elite, but that such a consulting profession of medicine must, in order to win a secure status, make itself attractive to the general public which must support its members by consulting them. The contingency of the lay public was thus critical to the development of medicine as a profession.

It is important to stress that Freidson's position has remained remarkably unchanged during a time when we have witnessed enormous changes not only in the production of knowledge but in the individual and collective practice of medicine. In his most recent article on this topic, in which he predicts the further evolution of medicine, Freidson (8, p. 32) restates that "there is no reason to believe that [in the future] medicine's position of dominance, its key position in the health care system, will change."

In this theoretical scenario, physicians and the medical profession are the dominant force that shapes the nature of U.S. medicine. This position does not deny, of course, that other forces are competing with the medical profession for the power to determine the present and future course of medicine, but it does claim that the *medical profession has been, is, and will continue to be the dominant force in medicine.*

## DO DOCTORS CONTROL MEDICINE?

Let us focus on the basic assumptions that sustain the professional dominance position and see the degree to which current and historical experience supports them. First, even in the lay press, the perception that doctors are in charge in the institutions of medicine is changing very rapidly. As a *New York Times* article put it recently: "Doctors have lost some of their authority and independence to government officials, insurers, corporate managers and hospital administrators and they are alarmed at the trend" (9, p. 1). In the same article, the head of a government regulatory agency is quoted as saying that "this loss of autonomy is extremely frustrating to doctors; doctors are pulling their hair out when bureaucrats like me tell them how to practice medicine" (9, p. 1). The article documents how government, insurance companies, and hospital administrators are increasingly dictating what is medically acceptable or appropriate in the treatment of patients. On the receiving end, the physicians increasingly feel that their autonomy is being forcefully challenged by non-doctors. The article concludes with the following statement from an orthopedic surgeon: "The judgement of physicians has been usurped by cookbook criteria created by people who are not doctors" (9, p. 1). Physicians themselves seem to feel that they are indeed losing control over their practice of medicine. According to a survey by the Association of American Medical Colleges of 500 students who scored well on admissions tests but did not apply to medical schools, 29 percent said that they had been discouraged from attending by physicians. In the middle 1970s, there were 28 applicants for every 10 places in U.S. medical schools; in 1987, there were only 17 applicants for every 10 places. This finding is in accord with the trend in recent years: while the number of people graduating from college has not changed significantly in the last three years, the number applying to medical school has declined 22 percent in that period, from 35,944 to 28,123. Needless to say, this decline is a result of many different forces. But, it is important to note that doctors seem to be advising the young to look for other careers. This advice further illustrates doctors' frustrations.

I am, of course, aware of the argument that these data reflect mere popular and professional perceptions and may not correspond to reality. But, in the realm of power relations, perceptions are indeed important and part of reality. And in this case, they are also indicators of a trend in which physicians are losing power to shape the practice of medicine (10).

Other trends also question some of Freidson's assumptions, such as high public trust in the medical profession and the subservience of other health care occupations to the medical profession. In support of the first position, Freidson quotes several polls indicating the high esteem that physicians enjoy among the U.S. population (8). But it is important to separate how people feel about their own doctors from how they feel about the collectivity of doctors as an organization, and how they feel about the medical system that doctors presumably dominate. Unpublished data from Louis Harris and Associates reveal that the public's confidence in medicine has fallen dramatically since the middle 1960s, from 73 percent to 39 percent (in 1985) (cited in 11). And the degree of dissatisfaction with the system of U.S. medicine is very high. A recent survey shows that the majority of the U.S. population is dissatisfied with the medical system in this country, and is calling for major changes (12).

Similarly, in the last 15 years we have witnessed an increasing number of health occupations that can practice without having their patients referred from physicians, as used to be the case. Physical therapists, for example, are able to receive patients directly in 16 states, and this number is growing.

## DID THE DOCTORS ONCE DOMINATE MEDICINE? THE HISTORICAL ROOTS OF THE PROFESSION

My thesis, however, is not that the medical profession has lost dominance in medicine, but rather that it never had such dominance. Indeed, I believe it would be wrong to conclude from these observations, polls, and studies that once upon a time there was a medical profession that dominated medicine, but that this profession has been losing dominance with time. The lessening of power of the medical profession in the house of medicine does not necessarily mean that doctors were the most powerful force—the meaning of dominance—in that house to start with.

Indeed, a historical survey of how the professions came about does not show, as the professional dominance position postulates, that professions were able to convince the elite of the merits of their work. Rather, the elites were the ones who selected, reproduced, and established the professions. Actually, these elites were fractions of a dominant class that played a central role in defining the social, political, and economic context of the professions. Medicine as we know it—Flexnerian medicine—was established in a context of great social unrest in Germany in the nineteenth century.

Capitalism was being established, changing society from a mercantile to an industrial system. As I have shown elsewhere, these changes had an overwhelming impact on the definition of health and disease and on medicine (13). A conflict of ideologies took place, corresponding to different class interests. One version of medicine, advanced by the working class and revolutionary elements of the nascent bourgeoisie such as is described by Virchow, saw disease as a result of the oppressive nature of extant relationships of society, and thus saw the necessity for socio-political and economic interventions aimed at altering those power relationships. Epitomized by the dictum that medicine is a social science and politics is medicine on a large scale, its best representative was Engels, whose work on the living and health conditions of the English working class had an enormous influence on Virchow and on the leadership of the labor movement. Engels' study was a dramatic document showing the political nature of the definition and distribution of disease. Engels' solution, reproduced by Virchow and the leadership of large sectors of the labor movement, was to call for profound change in the power relationships of society (14). This version of medicine did not prevail, however. The bourgeoisie, once it won its hegemony, felt threatened by the calls for structural change, and supported another version of medicine that did not threaten it.

From that time, the dominant social order, in which the bourgeoisie prevailed, was considered the natural order in which its class rules could be veiled and presented as rules of nature. Consequently, disease was seen not as an outcome of specific power relationships, but rather as a biological-individual phenomenon in which the cause of the disease was a microagent, the bacteria. In this redefinition, clinical medicine became the branch of medicine to study the biological-individual phenomenon, and social medicine and public health became the branch of medicine that studied the distribution of disease as the aggregate of individual phenomena. Both branches of medicine shared the same understanding of disease as a pathological alteration or change in the human body (perceived as a machine) caused by an outside agent (unicausality) or several agents (multicausality). This mechanistic view of disease and health is still the predominant interpretation of medicine. *Dorland's Medical Dictionary* (15) defines health as "a normal condition of body and mind, i.e., with all the parts functioning normally"; and disease as "a definite morbid process having a characteristic strain of symptoms—it may affect the whole body or any of its parts, and its etiology, pathology, and prognosis may be known or unknown." This mechanistic understanding of health and disease explains the division of labor (specialization) in medical knowledge and practice that has evolved around specific pieces of the body machine, i.e., cardiology, neurology, etc.

This mechanistic interpretation of medicine was built upon knowledge that had been produced earlier (discovery of blood circulation by Harvey in 1928; invention of the microscope by Van Leeuwenhoek in 1683, etc.). But it would be wrong to assume that mechanistic medicine was the result of a linear evolution of scientific discoveries. The establishment and development of the edifice of mechanistic medicine was not the result of the piling up of scientific discoveries like bricks in that construction. Science and technology are not the motors of history. Nor is the medical profession the shaper of the history of medicine. This point must be stressed in the light of the dominant historiography of medicine that sees the history of medicine as divided into stages determined by the discovery of new medical advances that shape the nature of medicine, advances that are led and reproduced by the medical professions. Scientists and medical professionals are seen as the leaders of change. They convince society, or the dominant elites and/or the receptive populace, of the merit of their projects.

What this interpretation ignores is the socio-political context in which these scientific and professional events take place. There is a continuous struggle and competition between different views and positions whose resolution does not depend primarily on the intellectual potency of the successful position. Rather, success depends on the articulation of these positions with the dominant power relationships in that society, of which class relationships are the determinants. Thus, mechanistic medicine was not the result of a linear growth of scientific discoveries that imposed themselves by the strength of its discourse or the power of its agents. To use a Kuhnian term, a shift of paradigms took place in which a new paradigm was established, supported and directed by the bourgeoisie who established a new scientific and professional order. Consequently, mechanistic medicine was established because it reproduced the ideology and the material interests of the newly established bourgeoisie. Alternative positions were repressed and not allowed to flourish.

For the same reason, this version of medicine—mechanistic medicine—was supported and reproduced by the U.S. bourgeoisie at the beginning of this century by the implementation of the recommendations of the Flexner Report. The establishment of the medical profession in the U.S. was not just the result of medical reformers convincing the elite—the Rockefeller Foundation—of the merits of its reforms. Not only the medical profession was established then; most of the professions were established at that time, and not only by the Rockefeller Foundation.

Those professions were to represent the cadre of experts supposed to carry out the rationalization of the social order under the hegemony of the capitalist class or bourgeoisie. As Kirschner (16), a historian of professions in the U.S., shows, there was a kinship between the calls for expertise as the leverage for change and the containment of social unrest, fear of revolt from below, and contempt for the working class with its strong immigrant component. Experts, rather than the populace, were supposed to guide the change. But that guidance took place within a context in which the capitalist called the shots, both outside and within the professional terrain. As Kirschner (16) indicates, there was (and continues to be) a structural tension between democracy (popular desire to rule) and the experts, supported by the dominant establishment, as to how to direct change and society and for whose purposes.

This historical detour on the origins of the medical profession is essential to an understanding of the socio-political context in which the power of the professions was established and continues to be reproduced. Professional power was and is submerged in other forms of power such as class, race, gender, and other forces that shape the production of the knowledge, practice, and institutions of medicine. The power of the professions is subservient to more powerful forces such as the dominant classes that have an overwhelming influence in medicine. Needless to say, dominated classes and other dominated forces such as minorities and women can also influence the development of medicine. But the dominance of a class and the hegemony of its ideology determine the parameters within which this set of influences takes place and the realization of these influences.

## HOW OTHER SOCIAL FORCES SHAPED
## WHAT DOCTORS BELIEVE, HOW THEY PRACTICE,
## AND HOW THEY ARE PAID AND ORGANIZED

In summary, whatever happens in medicine is an outcome of the resolution of internal conflicts and contradictions that occur within a matrix of class, gender, race, and other power relationships—of which the professional views and interests are important but not dominant in the production of knowledge and in the practice and organization of medicine. Let me briefly outline how these sets of ideological, political, and economic influences occur in the understanding of health and disease, in the production of medical knowledge, in medical practice, and in the organization of medicine.

1. *Health and disease* are collective phenomena realized individually; they have a material base. Disease, for example, is also a biological process with a relative autonomy. For example, although social conditions shape the nature and distribution of epidemics such as plague, the biological base of these epidemics gives them a certain autonomy in their development. The process we call disease is also perceived and interpreted by scientists according to a certain set of understandings and assumptions held not only by the scientific community but by the dominant ideology in that society. I have already indicated how the individual biological and mechanistic understanding of health and disease that dominates medical thought was based on a specific class ideology that was and continues to be hegemonic in our society. This understanding of disease continues to be reproduced today, even when non-physicians form the majority of producers of medical knowledge. Most of the scientific breakthroughs of medicine are produced by non-physicians: the overwhelming number of Nobel Prizes in Medicine are awarded to non-physicians, and most basic and laboratory research in medicine is done by non-physicians. But the understanding of health and medicine and the priorities derived from it have not changed.

2. *Medical knowledge* is part of the social thought, the collective set of beliefs, ideas, and knowledge in which the social thoughts of some classes, races, and gender are more dominant than those of others. It has a scientific element, due in part to the relative autonomy of science, and an ideological element reproduced by the values, beliefs, and experiences of the scientists who work and operate in universities and social settings subject to a whole set of class, gender, race and other forms of influences. Both elements—the scientific and the ideological—are not related in conditions of exteriority, i.e., scientific knowledge is not outside its ideological dimension. Rather, one is in the other. The history of medicine is crowded with examples of variations in the occurrence of scientific discoveries and their interpretations. Smith (17), for example, has shown how black lung was "discovered" far earlier in the U.K. than in the U.S., and how the interpretation of causality and symptomatology of that disease was different in both countries. As

Smith indicates, the existence of a stronger labor movement in the U.K. explains these differences.

In brief, how these two elements—the scientific and the ideological—have intermixed depends on the power relationships in society that continuously redefine the production of knowledge, i.e., what is and is not happening in medical knowledge and how it is happening.

3. *Medical practice* is part of the social practice and as such has a *technical division* of labor as well as a *social division* of labor. The former, the technical distribution of tasks in medical practice, is determined by the latter, which occurs within a well-defined set of power relationships. Thus, the different tasks carried out by the medical team (physicians, nurses, auxiliaries, and others)—the technical division of labor—are determined by the class, gender, and race relations in society—the social division of labor. None other than Florence Nightingale, the founder of nursing, spoke about the role of the nurse as one of: (*a*) supporting the physician, equivalent to the supportive role of the wife in the family; (*b*) mothering the patient; and (*c*) mastering the auxiliaries. In essence, in medicine we witness the reproduction of the Victorian family. Today, just as the family is being redefined, the health team relationships are also being redefined. Nurses and wives are rebelling against their subordination. The increased independence of formerly dependent professions, such as physical therapists, from their past bosses is just part of that trend, which is continuing in spite of the resistance of the assumed dominant profession.

4. *Medical organization* has been changed in the same way that the dynamics of capitalism led to the change from petty commodity production to capitalist manufacture: petty cottage medicine has been transformed into capitalist or corporate medicine. This development has been occurring in U.S. medicine for several decades. It is important to make this observation in the light of the frequently heard remark that the corporatization of medicine and its commodification are recent phenomena due to the involvement in medicine of the "for-profit hospitals." This reductionist view of capitalist medicine ignores the dynamics in which medicine and medical services have been commodities and sources of profits for quite a long time. Indeed, the existence of the medical-industrial complex is not a reality discovered by Relman (18) and Starr (19); nor is this reality determined by the "for-profit hospitals." Several years before these authors, Kelman (20), Navarro (21), Salmon (22), and McKinlay (23) described the existence of this phenomenon and predicted its further expansion. The frequent practice of mainstream authors of ignoring "unorthodox" views of realities leaves them stuck in their own terrain. Starr, for example, refers to the corporatization of medicine as an unexpected phenomenon. It was not unexpected; it was very predictable, and those other authors did predict it. Indeed, the penetration of capitalism into the social services, including medical care, is a logical outcome of the overwhelming influence of corporate America in all areas of economic and

social life. This class is the most powerful class in the Western world because of its centrality in the Western system of power. Moreover, its power is unhindered by a working class movement—such as a mass-based labor, social democratic or socialist party—that could restrain some of its excesses. Consequently, we have an underdeveloped welfare state. The U.S. is the only industrialized country except South Africa that does not offer comprehensive and universal health coverage. To attribute this absence to the power of the medical profession is to overrate the power of that profession. Other countries with equally powerful medical associations have a national health program. To repeat: we do not have a national health program because we do not have a mass-based labor movement.

The primary focus on the medical profession in much of medical historiography leads to an overrepresentation of the role of the medical profession in the process of medical change. The limitation of this approach is frequently compounded by seeing history as being made by individuals rather than by social forces. Fox (24), for example, denies that the labor movement was the main force behind the establishment of a National Health Service in the U.K., arguing that prominent physicians and surgeons were in favor of such a service, while some socialist leaders were against it. Fox seems to be unaware that the fact that some medical leaders were in favor and some labor leaders against such a project did not mean that the medical profession was the main or even a minor force behind such a program or that the labor movement did not play a major role in the establishment of such a program. The history of medicine is more than what the great medical men (and occasionally great women) do and say. Without denying the importance of personalities in the unraveling of events, one needs to see the forces that these individuals represent and the ideologies and interests that they reproduce. Another limitation of Fox's work is that he indicates that "in both practical and philosophical sense there is no past—nor correct description of an earlier time. There is only evidence, which history must reinterpret continuously. The study of history is a source of experience" (24, p. 212). This position assumes that the historian only builds his or her vision of reality and ideology after neutrally examining the evidence. Reality, however, is different from this idealized version of historical inquiry. The historian has a personal ideology prior to selecting his or her sources of information. What evidence to look for, how to look at it, and the social construction of how the evidence appears to the historian are submerged in ideology. Fox's reading of how the National Health Service was established in Great Britain, for example, was fed by an ideology different from—and in clear conflict with—mine (24, 25). This difference explains his remarks that he finds "astonishing" my statement that "the nationalization of the main components of the health sector was a victory for the British working class" (26). A reading of history different from Fox's shows that the labor movements have been the major force behind the establishment of national health programs (27).

Indeed, our lack of a national health program is not due primarily to opposition from the medical profession. Without minimizing the power of organized medicine, we must see that its power is limited compared with the enormous power of corporate America, unhindered by a counterbalancing force, the power of a mass-based labor movement. The power of corporate America is such that even when government responds to popular pressure and provides health benefits coverage, the way these programs are designed and operated benefits not only the population but many corporate groups—such as the insurance companies—and professional interests. And these latter benefits subtract from the benefits received by the population.

Needless to say, corporate America is not uniform, nor is its power omnipotent. It needs to compromise with other forces such as the medical profession. The power relationships that underlie such arrangements are changing, however, with corporate interests gaining over the professional interests. Witness, for example, the growth of the private insurance companies—the main source of financial capital in the U.S.—taking over the dominance that Blue Cross/Blue Shield once held in the medical premium market (21).

## PROLETARIANIZATION OF PHYSICIANS?

Thus, while the medical profession has never been the dominant force in medicine, it has nevertheless been a major force. Its power, however, has been declining for some time now. But this loss of power cannot be equated with the "proletarianization" of the medical profession. This understanding is rooted in Marx and Engels' initial understanding that with capitalist development we would witness an increased polarization of classes. According to this thesis, an increasing number of strata, including the professions, would be drawn into one of the two opposing classes: the capitalist class or owners of the means of production, and the working class, which owns only its labor power and sells it to capital. As Marx and Engels (28, p. 120) wrote: "Society as a whole is more and more splitting into two great hostile camps, into two great classes directly facing each other—bourgeoisie and proletariat." The invasion of capitalist relationships in all spheres of life would mean the continuous expansion of the working class. Thus, "the bourgeoisie has stripped of its halo every occupation hitherto honored and looked up to with reverent awe. It has converted the physician, the lawyer, the priest, the poet, the man of science, into its paid wage laborers" (28, p. 123). While Marx and Engels did not use the term proletarian in this sentence, it seems clear from the previous quotation that they meant proletarian when they used the term "wage laborers."

Following this position, usually attributed to the young period of Marx, several contemporary authors have defined the process of declining control of professionals over their working conditions as a process of proletarianization (29). In the medical field, McKinlay and Arches (10) are the most articulate authors of this thesis when they write that "as a result of bureaucratization being forced on medical practice as a consequence of the logic of the capitalist expansion, physicians are being reduced to a proletarian function."

The intellectual contribution of these authors to dismantling the theoretical position of professional dominance has been considerable. But we must differentiate the well-documented process of losing professional autonomy from the process of proletarianization. Indeed, one of the predictions of Marx and Engels that has been proven wrong concerned the increasing polarization of our societies into two major classes. The structural class maps of our society show a growing professional-technical stratum with material interests different from those of the polar classes. Needless to say, members of this professional-technical stratum— creatures of the need for rationalizing the system—have increasingly become wage earners and have seen their autonomy decline. The perception of that trend has been the great merit of the proletarianization school. But, it may not be accurate to say that proletarianization is "the process by which an occupational category is divested of control over certain prerogatives relating to the location, content and essentiality of its task activities and is thereby subordinated to the broader requirements of production under advanced capitalism" (10, p. 161).

Indeed, the process of proletarianization—of establishing the proletariat or working class—has included such a process, but it has also included many other activities, including the transformation of an intellectual activity into a manual one. An enormous and productive debate is now underway about the nature and boundaries of the working class, both within and outside the Marxist tradition. There is a certain agreement, however, at least among large numbers of Marxist scholars, that the working class or proletariat is composed of supervised, manual wage earners. These laborers do not have control over the means of production or over the organization of production; nor do they have skills that need to be credentialed. Proletarians do not have supervision over others, do not have space for some form of decision-making, do not realize mental rather than manual work, and do not have skills that need to be credentialed by the state. Moreover, by their structural position, proletarians cannot exploit others, at least in class terms.

In spite of losing professional power over the material means of producing medical services (such as hospitals, medical equipment, and other resources), over the organizational forms (such as the systems of funding and organization of medical care), and even over the credentialing of their skills, physicians still retain considerable influence over these production assets, far superior to the influence that proletarians have over theirs. Moreover, professionals will not become uncredentialed skilled workers. This impossibility is a result not only of the different nature of work and the different relationships with the production assets for professionals and workers, but of the different functions that professionals and workers have in capitalist society.

As I have indicated elsewhere, medicine has a function—curing and caring— that is needed in any society. But how that needed function occurs depends on the power relationships in that society as reproduced in the knowledge, practice, and organization of medicine. As the social movements in the 1960s and 1970s showed, medicine reproduces the dominant classism, sexism, and racism in society, not only in the uses of medicine (i.e., allocation of resources), but also in the production of medicine (i.e., knowledge and practice of medicine). In other words, medicine has a needed as well as a dominating function. And the two functions are not related in conditions of exteriority; rather, one function is realized through the other. How the needed function takes place is determined by the controlling or dominating functions.

This point is important in the light of the overabundance of authors who see medicine *primarily* as an agency of control and dominance (6). To believe this is tantamount to believing that the popular demand for a national health program is a result of a masochistic desire for being more controlled and/or a response to an enormous false consciousness that the dominant class and the medical profession have imposed on the majority of the population. This school of thought ignores the needed function proven by the effectiveness of medical care (frequently over- stated) in alleviating the damage created by disease.

On the other hand, there is the equal danger of seeing medicine as a *neutral set* of organizations, institutions, practices, and knowledge whose growth needs to be stimulated as part of "progress." This version of medicine focuses only on the needed and useful function without understanding that this function has been structured in such a way that it reproduces patterns of class, gender, and race discrimination. This "neutral" understanding of science and medicine is respon- sible for the unchanged professionalization of medicine in some post-capitalist societies (30), with the reproduction of class, gender, and race power relationships in medicine. This reproduction of dominant relationships conflicts with the democratic force in those countries. The linkage of dominant sectors of society with the "expert" profession can lead to a new dominant force that inhibits the full expression of the dominated forces.

Medicine has not only a needed but also a dominating function; the need to reproduce these dominant-dominated relationships, both in society and in medicine, by the state credentialing of skills and the associated allocation of privileges explains the impossibility of the profession becoming uncredentialed. The credentialing of skills is important not only to the recipients of the credentials but to the grantors of the credentials.

The term "proletarianization of physicians," however, seems to indicate that physicians can and will become proletarians after all. This is not likely to be the case. The process whereby professionals are losing autonomy is indeed a very real one, and the challenge made by "proletarianization" theorists to the professional dominance school remains unanswered, but the term and concept of "proletarianization" used by these authors does not accurately define and explain what happens in the house of medicine.

## REFERENCES

1. Freidson, E. *Professional Dominance*. Atherton Press, New York, 1970.
2. Freidson, E. *Profession of Medicine*. Harper and Row, New York, 1970.
3. Freidson, E. *Doctoring Together*. University of Chicago Press, Chicago, 1980.
4. Freidson, E. *Professional Powers: A Study of the Institutionalization of Formal Knowledge*. University of Chicago Press, Chicago, 1986.
5. Berland, J. C. *Profession and Monopoly*. University of California Press, Berkeley, 1975.
6. Illich, I. *Medical Nemesis*. Pantheon Books, New York, 1976.
7. Arney, W. R. *Power and the Profession of Obstetrics*. University of Chicago Press, Chicago, 1982.
8. Freidson, E. The reorganization of the medical profession. *Medical Case Rev.* 42(1): 32, 1985.
9. Pear, R. Physicians contend systems of payment have eroded status. *New York Times,* December 26, 1987, p. 1.
10. McKinlay, J. B., and Arches, J. Towards the proletarianization of physicians. *Int. J. Health Serv.* 15(2): 161–195, 1985.
11. Blendon, R. J., and Altman, D. E. Public opinion and health care costs. In *Health Care and Its Costs*, edited by C. J. Schramm, p. 54. W.W. Norton, New York, 1987.
12. Schneider, W. Public ready for real change in health care. *National J.* 3(23): 664–665, 1985.
13. Navarro, V. Work, ideology and science: The case of medicine. *Soc. Sci. Med.* 14C: 191–205, 1980.
14. Taylor, R., and Rieger, A. Medicine as a social science: Rudolf Virchow on the typhus epidemic in Upper Silesia. *Int. J. Health Serv.* 15(4): 547–559, 1985.
15. *Dorland's Medical Dictionary*. W.B. Saunders, Philadelphia, 1968.
16. Kirschner, D. S. *The Paradox of Professionalism: Reform and Public Service in Urban America 1900-1940*. Greenwood Press, Westport, Conn., 1986.
17. Smith, B. E. Black lung: The social production of disease. *Int. J. Health Serv.* 11(3): 343–359, 1981.
18. Relman, A. S. The new medical-industrial complex. *N. Engl. J. Med.* 303: 963–970, 1980.
19. Starr, P. *The Social Transformation of American Medicine*. Basic Books, New York, 1983.
20. Kelman, S. Toward the political economy of medical care. *Inquiry* 8: 130–138, 1971.
21. Navarro, V. *Medicine Under Capitalism*. Neal Watson, New York, 1976.
22. Salmon, J. Monopoly capital and the reorganization of the health sector. *Rev. Radical Politi. Econ.* 9: 125–133, 1977.
23. McKinlay, J. On the medical-industrial complex. *Monthly Review* 30(5): 38–42, 1978.
24. Fox, D. *Health Policies, Health Politics: The British and American Experience 1911-1965*. Princeton University Press, Princeton, N.J., 1986.
25. Navarro, V. *Class Struggle, the State and Medicine: An Historical and Contemporary Analysis of the Medical Sector in Great Britain*. Martin Robertson, Oxford, 1978.
26. Fox, D. Review of Navarro, V., "Crisis, Health and Medicine." *Bull. Hist. Med.* 61(2): 302–303, 1987.

27. Navarro, V. Why some countries have national health insurance, others have national health services, and the U.S. has neither. *Soc. Sci. Med.* 28(9): 887–898, 1989.
28. Marx, K., and Engels, F. The Communist Manifesto. In *Communist Manifesto: Socialist Landmark. An Appreciation Written for the Labour Party*, edited by H. Laski. George Allen and Unwin, London, 1948.
29. Oppenheimer, M. *White Collar Politics*. Monthly Review Press, New York, 1985.
30. Navarro, V. *Social Security and Medicine in the USSR: A Marxist Critique*. Lexington Books, Lexington, Mass., 1978.

Reprinted with permission from The Milbank Quarterly, Volume 66, Supplement 2, Pages 57–75, 1988.

# CHAPTER 10

# The Changing Doctor-Patient Relationship and Performance Monitoring: An Agency Perspective

## William D. White, J. Warren Salmon and Joe Feinglass

Doctors do not simply provide medical services to patients. They manage their care. Traditionally, this managerial function has been vested in autonomous physicians acting as independent agents and employed directly by patients. External supervision has been limited. At most physicians have been subject to occasional peer review. The primary methods of quality control have been credentialing of physician qualifications and market decisions by patients. Socialization of physicians through formal educational programs has also played a role. So too has socialization through informal professional contacts and decisions by peers regarding referrals and hospital staff privileges. But historically, routinized external monitoring of physicians' clinical or financial performance has been conspicuously absent.

In recent years, marked changes have begun to take place in the traditional physician-patient relationship. The locus of managerial responsibility has shifted dramatically away from individual physicians towards organizations. Under the banner of what has come to be known as managed care, payors and providers have become increasingly involved in monitoring both doctors' clinical decision making and their financial performance. A growing number of physicians are (essentially) salaried employees of health care providers such as Health Maintenance Organizations (HMOs), academic medical centers and other forms of group practice. And as such, they are directly subject to internal reviews by these organizations. (The share of non-federal physicians who were employees in 1986 was over 26 percent, including almost half of all physicians under age 36 (1).) Even physicians who remain in fee-for-service practice are increasingly subject to reviews by hospitals and third party payors, including Preferred Provider Organizations (PPOs). Medicare claims are reviewed by Professional Review Organizations (PROs), while many private insurance plans now require preadmission certification, second opinions and/or case review as conditions for reimbursement. Finally, the context in which physicians' work is being altered by the penetration of large national for-profit corporations into the health care field and by a greater emphasis on financial performance even by "not-for-profit" providers. These alterations in medical practice partly reflect issues related to the internal organization of the health care industry. But they also reflect a public policy directed at diminishing the welfare state while restructuring the overall organization of production (2).

Such unprecedented changes have raised questions about the traditional doctor-patient relationship. Among those exploring the future of physicians, the prognoses range considerably. Some, such as Freidson (3, 4), argue that doctors will retain control over medical decision making, albeit under modified circumstances. McKinlay and Arches (5) and McKinlay and Stoeckle (6) see an imminent "proletarianization" or "corporatization" of the profession. Still others believe a process of "deprofessionalization" is underway (7, 8).

Premises on which these analyses are based vary as much as their conclusions. However, most of this literature shares several common features. First, it tends to emphasize the role of social and political conflicts between a historically "dominant" medical profession and other major players in the health sector in determining relationships of physicians vis-à-vis patients. Second, discussion focuses primarily on distributional aspects of conflicts and issues of professional control.

Drawing on a broader political economic framework, Navarro (9) argues that neither the notions of "professional dominance" nor "proletarianization" are adequate to examine recent developments. Navarro maintains physicians have never truly dominated the house of medicine. Corporate interests, far from being a new force in the evolution of the health care system, played a key role in the emergence of modern "scientific" medicine at the turn of the century in the face of alternative and potentially threatening paradigms (e.g. a social conception of disease). However, he sees a true "proletarianization" of physicians as unlikely because of a continuing need for a high level of technical skill to perform the curing and caring functions of medicine. In this context, he stresses that from a functional perspective, it is important to recognize that the organization of medicine reflects concerns not only about social control and the distribution of resources, but also about the efficacy with which health care is produced. However, neither Navarro (9) nor other participants in the current debate attempt to examine factors affecting efficacy in detail.

In this chapter, we examine in depth the implications of recent developments in monitoring for the doctor-patient relationship from an efficacy perspective. In doing so, our objective is to complement existing analyses focusing on broad issues of distribution and control. Our starting point is the economic theory of agency. Agency theory examines the efficiency implications of problems with monitoring for the organization of work. Within the structure of the present market driven system in the U.S., economists have frequently argued that difficulties by patients, payors and providers with monitoring physicians' performance have played a central role in shaping the traditional doctor-patient relationship (10, 11). One need not accept monitoring problems as the primary determinant of the existing system of health care delivery. But to the extent they are important, it is clear that changes in the ability to monitor will have a major impact, where agency models provide a useful framework for considering the possible effects.

This chapter has two basic goals. The first is to introduce the unfamiliar reader to the central features of agency theory. The second is to draw on an agency framework to examine: (*a*) recent trends leading to increased payor and provider monitoring of physicians; and (*b*) the implications of increased monitoring for the doctor-patient relationship within the context of the growing corporatization of medicine (12).

Before embarking on this analysis, it is important to note some of the limitations of agency theory as well as its strengths. In common with much of economic theory, the approach in agency models is basically deductive. Not only do deductive models tend to be inherently ahistorical, but there is a serious risk in applying them of mistaking rationalizations for changes for their causes. Even where issues of efficacy figure prominently in public debates about health care, the true genesis of change may in fact lie in the outcomes of political conflicts over the distribution of income and services (13).

On the other hand, it is also possible to err in the other direction. Efficacy issues addressed in agency models may be a key factor in determining the underlying balance of power and the political viability of vested interest groups, physicians being no exception. Unfortunately, agency models do not always lend themselves well to capturing the kinds of historical interactions that may occur between efficiency and distributional considerations. Consequently, our analysis is stylized at times. Nevertheless, drawing on evidence of the impact of increasing monitoring on physicians, we believe our analysis serves to illuminate important directions that might otherwise be overlooked in the current vigorous debate over the changing character of the medical profession (14, 15).

## THE THEORY OF AGENCY

In economics, virtually anyone who acts on behalf of another at their direction (i.e., implicitly or explicitly contracts to perform a task) may be described as an "agent." Large gains may be realized from delegating tasks to agents. For example, employing a physician as one's agent may be far more economical than attempting to acquire the knowledge and expertise needed to treat oneself (16). Physicians have not only technical expertise in providing specific medical services, but also the knowledge and skill important in determining what care is needed. In addition, they have expertise in coordinating the actual delivery of care and in acting as what Harris (17) describes as a patient's "paladin" in negotiating the complexities of the modern health care delivery systems to assure that the services desired are actually provided.

However, delegation is not without problems. Communication may not be perfect. And agents may not always perform as agreed. Physicians may misunderstand what a patient wants. They may also deliberately provide care below (or above) an agreed standard for their own benefit at the expense of a patient (or at the expense of whoever foots the bill for the patient's care). The central question addressed in agency models is how employers or clients can best structure relationships with agents to control deliberate abuses of trust (i.e., efforts by individual agents to use their position to extract gains for themselves at the expense of their employers or clients).

### The Agency Problem

Opportunities to "cheat" exist in virtually any agency relationship. In agency models, whether an agent does so will depend on whether the expected benefits exceed the expected costs. Thus, physicians presumably will not provide substandard services if they always expect to end up worse off as a result. The magnitude of the benefits and costs from cheating will depend both on an agent's opportunities for gain (e.g., a physician's opportunities for increasing his or her welfare through under- or over-providing care), and the losses which may occur if the agent is apprehended (e.g., the sanctions which may be imposed on a physician found abusing his or her trust). An individual hiring an agent may try to control abuses of trust either by reducing an agent's expected gains from cheating or by increasing the losses the agent may incur if caught (or both).

Not only may abuses of trust be costly to an employer or client, but so may their deterrence. From the perspective of a purchaser of an agent's services, the basic agency "problem" is to select an optimal control system given: (a) the potential benefits of controlling abuses; and (b) the costs of doing so. This leads to an obvious, but nevertheless important insight, namely that the structure of agency relationships themselves may change for functional reasons because of changes in either of these two dimensions of the agency "problem." Thus, a change may occur in the doctor-patient relationship because patients' (or payor's) anticipated gains from controlling abuses by physicians increase or decrease. Or a change may occur because of an increase or decrease in the costs of operating control systems (or for both reasons simultaneously).

## Methods of Control

If an agent is absolutely honest and always does his or her best to adhere to any agreement made, deliberate abuses of the agency relationship should never occur. One solution to agency problems is to seek agents who internalize values such as honesty and concern for the welfare of clients (19). The sociology literature suggests one important function of formal training for the professions may be to socialize individuals, or at least to screen them; in addition, of course, socialization may also occur in informal settings as well (20). Purchasers may then require evidence of socialization, for example an educational degree, as a condition for buying services, or at least offer a premium for it.

A second solution is to alter the external environment an agent faces through the manipulation of incentive systems. For example, incentive systems may be devised which place physicians at risk for a loss of income, prestige, or even the right to practice, if they are found providing substandard or unnecessary services.

Economic models of agency focus on the manipulation of external incentives. Internalized values are taken as given. An agency "problem" arises if such values alone are insufficient to eliminate abuses of trust. This approach is followed here. However, possible interactions between the structure of external incentive systems and systems of control based on internalized values will be considered briefly later in the chapter.

## Standard Agency Models

In standard agency models, the purchaser's "problem" reduces to the selection of an optimal incentive system given: (a) the costs associated with abuses of trust; and (b) the costs of operating incentives systems to control them (11). Losses associated with abuses of trust are usually taken as given. The primary focus is on the costs of operating incentive systems. These costs can be analyzed in terms of two components: a system for monitoring an agent's performance and a payment scheme for rewarding (or punishing) the agent on the basis of this monitoring. Both components are clearly necessary for an incentive system to function. For instance, suppose a third party payor monitors the quality of care a physician provides. If the physician paid the same amount regardless of the results of this monitoring and there are no other adverse effects for her or him, there will be no external incentive for the physician to alter her or his behavior. (The physician may find providing substandard care distasteful, but this is a separate issue.) Conversely, establishing severe penalties for poor quality care without linking these penalties to a system for evaluating quality is equally unlikely to have much impact.

To be effective in obtaining a desired level of performance, a "contract" must satisfy two conditions. First, it must make providing the desired level of performance sufficiently attractive that an agent will be willing to provide this level of performance. (If a contract fails to satisfy this condition, only individuals who plan to cheat will accept it.) Second, the contract must make it unattractive for an agent to provide less than this level of performance if she or he accepts it. (Cheating must not pay.)

A very simple scheme satisfying both of these conditions is to monitor an agent, for instance a physician, 100 percent of the time and then pay him or her a wage sufficient to make carrying out the desired tasks worth his or her while if performed as agreed and nothing otherwise (i.e., impose an implicit fine equal to the wage if he or she does not perform as agreed). In this case, if willing to accept a contract to provide care at all, the physician will always perform as agreed, since there is no gain (at least financially) to be had from cheating.

The difficulty with this type of contract in the context of medical care is that monitoring can be expensive. When standardized tasks are involved with predictable outcomes, for example on an assembly line, monitoring costs may be trivial. Casual observation of a worker's level of effort or output may be sufficient to detect abuses. But in medical care, as Arrow (10) and others have observed, the very features which make employing a physician as an agent attractive to manage care also make it difficult to monitor performance. Patients hire physicians as agents to manage care precisely because they do not know what care is good for them and accordingly, are in a poor position to evaluate their treatments—even "routine" cases tend to have at least some non-routine aspects. If it were possible to perfectly predict the outcome of care, patients (or their family or friends) could still easily monitor performance by observing what happens to the patient. However, the outcomes of medical treatments are notoriously difficult to predict. If it is feasible at all, the cost of 100 percent monitoring based on observing either the process by which care is produced, or its outcome, is likely to exceed the benefits of controlling abuses. Full monitoring is not, however, the only option.

*Trade-offs between Monitoring and*
*Rewards and Punishments*

A basic insight of standard agency models is that trade-offs may exist between the level of monitoring and the magnitudes of rewards and punishments. The larger the loss imposed on an agent who is apprehended failing to perform as agreed, the less monitoring may be necessary. Hence, it may be possible to economize by monitoring the performance of physicians only infrequently, but imposing a large sanction if they are caught providing low quality care, for instance loss of the right to practice.

There are, however, a variety of factors which may limit the extent of this trade-off between monitoring and penalties. Two are of particular interest here: (*a*) limitations on the magnitudes of penalties; and (*b*) problems with writing complete contracts which can realistically be enforced. The maximum financial penalty which can be imposed on agents will be limited by their wealth, present and future. Non-pecuniary penalties may also be imposed (e.g. imprisonment). But social limits on penalties exist, where there is often a sense that the punishment should fit the crime. Stripping a physician of the right to practice simply because he or she suggested a return visit of doubtful medical value for a sore throat is likely to be deemed excessive. In addition, agents may be risk averse and much more concerned about incurring large losses than small ones. If there is any possibility of large losses occurring independently of an agent's level of performance, the agent may demand a risk premium in order to accept a contract. The larger the risks, the larger this premium is likely to be, helping to explain why prepayment contracts for medical care with individual physicians with no provisions for shifting financial risks are rare.

Several other types of considerations may also limit the types of contracts which are feasible. One is "dual agency" problems. A second, related problem is with writing complete contracts. Dual agency problems arise when an employer or client cannot be trusted to truthfully represent the results of monitoring, especially if hard to verify, subjective measures of performance are involved. For instance, as White and Dranove (11) note, one reason "pay only when cured" contracts are not generally offered by physicians may be that "cure" is often defined in terms of subjective evaluations by patients (e.g., "I say my back still hurts and you can't prove it doesn't"). As a result, patients may be able to avoid payment by misrepresenting their condition.

A "pay only when cured" contract also illustrates problems with writing complete contracts. Suppose only objectively verifiable symptoms are at issue. Defining "cure" in a way which is not unduly simplistic and yet can realistically be implemented can be very difficult because of the extreme heterogeneity and complexity of medical services and problems in predicting their outcomes. Even if ex post, a consensus can be reached on an ad hoc basis that a "cure" was achieved under a particular set of circumstances, describing the set of all such "cures" ex ante may be impractical (e.g. what constitutes a "successful" course of treatment of a stroke victim with massive complications?).

These problems are likely to be particularly severe when a purchaser buys services from an agent only once. An important related insight in agency theory is that the existence of ongoing relationships between agents and purchasers may significantly extend the basis for control. Where repeat purchases are involved, an agent must not only consider the present transaction, but the possible effects of her or his actions on future demand. Even if it is not possible to economically work out an explicit agreement regarding a physician's performance in a given period, what is known as the "repeat purchase mechanism" can serve as a powerful disciplinary device. Consider traditional fee-for-service practice. Typically, barring extreme problems, patients agree to pay for services received even if they have questions about their quality or cost. Accordingly, a physician may easily gain in the current period by providing unnecessary or substandard care. But if the physician knows that by displeasing patients she or he will lose their future business, and also perhaps that of the patients' friends and relatives (i.e. there are reputation effects), this may be sufficient to restrain her or him. At the same time, if a patient must pay for services received even if dissatisfied, there will be no direct advantage from terminating a relationship with a physician. The patient will only change physicians if he or she feels better services can be obtained elsewhere. As a result, through the repeat purchase mechanism, this type of arrangement avoids dual agency problems and the need for elaborate contracts specifying acceptable care while, at least in theory, creating powerful economic incentives for physicians to maintain acceptable levels of performance.

## MEDICAL CARE

As suggested by some of the examples above, the case of medical care is significantly more complex than the simple type of case considered in standard agency models. Abuses of trust can take a variety of forms. A wide range of alternative monitoring and payment arrangements exist. Responsibility for paying for services frequently lies with private insurers and public agencies acting as third party payors, rather than with the patients actually using services.

The most frequently discussed types of abuses by physicians are those involving excessive costs and substandard quality. Alternative methods for evaluating physician performance include: (a) peer review; (b) monitoring by patients; and (c) monitoring of physicians by hospitals, HMOs, PPOs and insurance carriers. Alternative methods of payment include fee-for-service, where physicians are paid on the basis of services rendered, either out-of-pocket by patients or by third party payors, and prepayment.

Because more than one type of abuse may occur in the doctor-patient relationship and several types of monitoring arrangements are available, trade-offs may exist between different types of incentive systems regarding the types of abuses they encourage (or discourage). In addition, trade-offs may exist between different types of monitoring methods in their ability to efficiently collect and utilize information. Finally, where third party payors are involved, their interests may diverge from those of both patients and doctors. This may potentially lead to dual agency problems involving all three groups simultaneously.

### Fee-for-service Payment versus Prepaid Group Practices

Only a decade ago, fee-for-service payment with minimal review of physician performance was the norm. Today, there is a rapidly growing range of compensation schemes and monitoring methods in use. A useful way of highlighting underlying trade-offs involved in these different types of systems is to compare traditional fee-for-service with prepayment (HMOs or the type of prepaid group practice plans long advocated as alternatives to fee-for-service medicine, for example by the Committee on the Costs of Medical Care in the late 1920s (21)).

Under traditional fee-for-service payment, individual physicians, acting as patients' autonomous agents, were paid directly on the basis of services rendered either by patients themselves or third parties. Until the late 1970s, as long as charges for individual services were judged "reasonable," third party payment for covered services was usually automatic. There was little attempt by public or private payors to evaluate the quality or appropriateness of care; essentially they served as passive conduits for funds. The primary methods of monitoring performance were loose peer review and patient satisfaction.

Under prepaid group practice plans and HMOs, the provision of care and the provision of insurance are united within a single institution. Typically the contractual unit involves a large group of physicians, rather than a single practitioner, pooling risks across a large population of patients. In return for a fixed annual fee paid in advance, a plan is placed at risk for all the care specified in a benefit package that a patient may need during the year. At the same time, the plan assumes the right to determine both which physicians a patient can see and how much care is acceptable for a patient to receive given the nature of any occurring illness. A patient is thus not free to change physicians at will. And physicians' compensation depends on contractual agreements established between them and plans, rather than being directly tied to services rendered to patients. Patient satisfaction may still be a basis for determining compensation, along with formal monitoring of physicians by the plan. But the direct link between patient satisfaction and repeat visits is broken. If a patient quits the plan because of dissatisfaction with a physician, any impact on the physician must come through the plan's internal performance evaluation and compensation systems, and these systems may vary significantly between plans, for example between a group practice HMO and an independent practice association (IPA).

### Trade-offs between Cost and Quality

Abuses of trust under both kinds of systems may occur at several levels. Individual services may be provided inefficiently, increasing costs. They may also be of substandard quality. Beyond this, even if individual services are efficiently produced at an acceptable level of quality, physicians, in their capacity as managers, may provide too few (or too many) services given the standard of care contracted for by a patient (or payor). That is, there may be abuses involving under- (or over-) provision of care overall, as well as problems with the cost and quality of specific services.

Holding the quality and cost of individual services fixed, fee-for-service payment and prepayment clearly create opposite incentives. In the fee-for-service case, a physician's income will increase with the quantity of services provided. There will be an incentive to provide more services than necessary to achieve a given standard of care, inflating costs at the expense of the patient or third party payor. In the case of an HMO, the less care provided, the lower will be a plan's current costs and the higher its current net income. Substandard care today may risk higher demands tomorrow. But to the extent current gains outweigh the risk of future costs, there is an obvious incentive to under-provide care.

### Trade-offs between Control Systems

Any choice between fee-for-service payment and prepayment must weigh not only the types of incentives they create, but the costs of operating the control systems associated with them. These costs will depend not only on the costs of alternative methods of monitoring, but also on the efficiency with which information from monitoring is utilized. Setting aside the issue of peer review, which may potentially occur under either payment system, fee-for-service basically relies on patient evaluations. This has two central disadvantages. The first is difficulties by patients in realizing economies of scale in monitoring physician performance, especially where episodic illnesses are involved which are complex in nature. The second disadvantage arises when fee-for-service payment is combined with cost-based insurance reimbursement. If patients bear costs directly, the provision of services whose costs exceed their benefits risks patient dissatisfaction. However, if services are paid for by insurance, the impact of providing additional services to an individual patient on his or her insurance costs will be minuscule (22). Consequently, it will be in the interest of a physician seeking to build or maintain a practice to provide additional services as long as they add to patient satisfaction. Indeed, trying to hold down costs may create patient dissatisfaction as the benefits from reduced insurance costs at the individual level will be small. On the other hand, at least in theory, fee-for-service offers an efficient way of utilizing private patient information through the repeat purchase mechanism without the need for specifying elaborate (and difficult to enforce) contracts, although the actual efficacy of patient monitoring is controversial (23).

In prepaid arrangements, any information from monitoring must be filtered through some sort of administrative mechanism. If its compensation scheme simply replicates fee-for-service practice, there are unlikely to be any efficiency gains; the primary effect will be to add a layer of bureaucracy. In order to achieve a superior level of performance, a plan must utilize information on patient satisfaction more efficiently than the fee-for-service system and/or engage in other types of surveillance, such as directly monitoring physicians' clinical and financial performance. In both cases, plans may realize economies of scale in monitoring. For example, they may be able to collect and analyze patient satisfaction data more systematically than individual physicians. More significantly, they may be able to achieve large economies of scale in directly monitoring and analyzing aggregate data on physicians' clinical and financial performance.

But gains from economies of scale have to be weighed against problems in utilizing information once it is obtained. Compensating physicians on the basis of information collected by a plan either on patient satisfaction or their clinical or financial performance can create dual agency problems because it is in a plan's financial interest to hold down its costs. This is likely to generate pressures to base contracts between plans and physicians on objectively verifiable criteria, which may severely limit the use of qualitative information. Suppose, for instance, a patient concludes (correctly) that a physician is unduly cavalier in dismissing diagnostic information reported by the patient, but there is no specific "hard" evidence of error. Under fee-for-service, the patient is free to terminate his or her relationship with this physician immediately. In the case of an HMO, contracts are likely to be structured to protect physicians from arbitrary sanctions or dismissal and such "soft" information may be considerably harder to use. A patient can still quit the HMO, at least when the next enrollment opening occurs. But this choice to leave will only impact the individual physician involved to the extent the patient's departure figures into compensation criteria. (Of course, if each HMO consisted of a single physician, this problem would be eliminated. But so would any risk pooling, where, logistical issues aside, the necessary risk premium to induce physicians to accept such contracts is likely to be prohibitive.)

Because a great deal of the information obtained through patient monitoring and peer review may be idiosyncratic in nature, this discussion suggests a second trade-off between fee-for-service and prepayment. Not only do they differ with respect to the incentives they create, but they may also differ with respect to the efficiency of control mechanisms. Efficiency gains may be achieved in collecting information by shifting monitoring to third parties. But these gains may be offset by a reduction in the scope of information which can actually be used in implementing incentives.

While the preceding theoretical exposition may appear abstract, the issues at hand are currently being vigorously debated in policy circles. For instance, *The New England Journal of Medicine* published commentaries from physicians, one in an HMO and the other employed in a fee-for-service walk-in clinic, that explored the ethics of physicians under- and over-providing care given alternative payment mechanisms (24, 25). And there is growing dispute over the efficacy of both the traditional patient/peer group oriented system of monitoring and new payor and provider systems (26, 27). The next section explores recent developments from an agency perspective.

## THE RISING CHALLENGE TO PHYSICIAN AUTONOMY

### Doctor, Patient, Bureaucrat

A whole range of new institutional forms have emerged in recent years in response to concerns about the cost and quality of health care. Innovations have occurred in the organization of prepaid schemes. Public and private third party payors have introduced "risk-based" payment, the prime example being the Medicare Prospective Payment System (PPS), which combines prospective rate setting with fixed payments for treatment of patients by diagnosis related group (DRG), making individual hospitals accountable for their costs. Preferred Provider Organizations offering discounts to large purchasers and payors, have also grown rapidly. Finally, direct payor and provider review of fee-for-service physicians' clinical and financial performance has become common. Not only are Medicare inpatient services subject to review by Professional Review Organizations, but as of 1987, some 56 percent of all privately insured patients were enrolled in plans involving some sort of managed care (28).

The incentives created for physicians by these various forms of institutional innovation are complex, especially in the face of increased penetration of the health sector by for-profit firms. (For instance, both the HMO and the fee-for-service practice discussed in *The New England Journal of Medicine* commentaries cited above were operated by for-profit firms (24, 25).) But all share a common feature: They challenge the traditional autonomy of physicians and their role as the patient's "paladin" by inserting new actors linked to hierarchical organizations into the doctor-patient relationship. With remarkable speed, the traditional bilateral relationship between doctor and patient has been transformed into one of "doctor, patient, bureaucrat," as one practitioner described it in an Op-Ed in *The New York Times* (29).

Today, almost all physicians serve more than one master. In the case of physicians working as employees, this is explicit. The flow of patients to a doctor employed by an HMO or hospital is determined by management. It can be terminated at will; patients are a physician's because the HMO or hospital permits them to be. In the case of physicians remaining in private practice, control is indirect through the payment mechanism. But it is nevertheless omnipresent. Under the Medicare PPS, for instance, PROs may deny payment for hospital services deemed inappropriate, with obvious potential repercussions for the physicians involved (30).

Relman (31) and others have argued that these changes mark the dawn of a new era of assessment and accountability for physicians. The discussion of agency models in the previous section suggests that from an efficacy perspective, it may be useful to explore both the forces behind this emerging "revolution" and its implications for the future in terms of: (*a*) changes in underlying cost/quality trade-offs; and (*b*) changes in the ability to evaluate performance through utilization review.

Looking at cost/quality tradeoffs and the ability to monitor performance is suggestive of both why the traditional fee-for-service system may have persisted for so long and why changes are now occurring. Through the early 1970s, it seems fair to characterize the general attitude towards medical technology as "more is better." At the same time, utilization review methods based on the use of paper patient-records were both costly to operate and of questionable effectiveness (30). In this context, it may be argued that delegating managerial responsibility to autonomous fee-for-service physicians had significant attractions, at least for patients whose financial access to the system was sufficient to permit them a choice of providers. If the system erred on the level of services provided, it tended to be on the high side. And it provided a mechanism for directly utilizing private patient information in the face of limited alternatives. Conversely, recent changes may be seen as the combined result of a reassessment of the costs and benefits of under- versus over-provision of care and advances in the ability to monitor by providers and payors. Viewed from this perspective, the question becomes one of exploring the relative importance of these factors in explaining recent developments in doctor-patient relationships, although political forces clearly have also played a role as well.

Somewhat paradoxically, the unprecedented expansion of payor and provider surveillance of physician activities in recent years has its origins in cost containment policies implemented during the heyday of "pro-competitive" reforms in the early 1980s. Currently, this process of expansion appears to be accelerating as a result of the development of a feedback loop. The growth of utilization review activities has led to refinements in monitoring techniques. These refinements have increased the promise of performance monitoring not only as a cost containment strategy, but also as a means for upgrading underlying standards of care. The combined effect has been to create growing demand for yet further monitoring. Briefly examining historical linkages between monitoring and cost containment efforts provides a useful starting point for exploring the forces behind the development of this feedback loop and its implications for the future of the doctor-patient relationship.

### Cost Containment and Monitoring

Since World War II the U.S. health care sector has been in an expansionary mode. Expenditures on care have risen from 4 percent of GNP in 1950 to nearly 12 percent (32). This process of rapid growth has been accompanied by a dramatic shift in health care policy. Until the late 1960s, equity and access were the watchwords. Financial access expanded through the growth of private insurance coverage as an employee benefit in the 1950s and 1960s and, after 1965, through the passage of Medicare and Medicaid. Since the end of the 1960s, however, the focus has shifted. As medical care costs have continued to mount, their containment has emerged as the preeminent concern.

Cost containment efforts have passed through two major phases since this shift in policy emphasis began. In the 1970s, containment efforts were limited mainly to public payors, who followed a strategy of trying to control expenditures through retrospective, cost-based rate regulation and controls on capital investments by hospitals through Certificate of Need (CON) regulation. Then in the early 1980s, the focus of containment efforts shifted towards "pro-competitive" policies and risk-based payment. At the same time, the scope of containment activities expanded in several ways. Private payors began to become actively involved in containment efforts. And in conjunction with the growth of risk-based payment, utilization review activities expanded and the shift to "doctor-patient-bureaucrat" mentioned above began on a large scale. Now, a little less than a decade later, utilization management has emerged as a primary cost containment strategy in its own right to complement rate regulation, suggesting we have entered a third phase.

Against this history of rapid change, it is important to note several elements of continuity. As Evans (33) observes, there has been consistent resistance to budgetary caps on overall spending as a containment strategy. In contrast to budget driven systems in countries such as England or Canada, expenditures in the American health care system remain purchase-driven. Under the Medicare PPS, for instance, payments are now set prospectively on the basis of patient DRG. But it still remains the case that the more patients seen, the more providers are paid.

Also as Evans (33) observes, American regulators historically have consistently been more willing to embrace utilization review as a cost containment strategy than their counterparts in Canada or England. While, at least until recently, the primary emphasis has been on rate review, provisions for performance monitoring have routinely been incorporated. Thus the original legislation enacting Medicare in 1965 included provisions requiring hospitals to set up internal utilization review committees. The first efforts to initiate large scale external surveillance of providers, albeit on a modest scale, date from 1972, when Professional Service Review Organizations (PSROs) were established to review utilization of inpatient services under Medicare. And despite a blaze of free-market rhetoric, the origins of the current expansion of monitoring activities lie in "pro-competitive" policies introduced in the early 1980s.

*Risk-based Payment*

Risk-based public and private cost containment policies implemented in the early 1980s have served to promote an expansion of large scale performance monitoring in two basic ways: (*a*) indirectly through the creation of incentives for providers to hold down their costs; and (b) directly through the expansion of public and private third party surveillance of providers.

Looking first at the indirect impact of risk-based payment, one obvious provider response to incentives to hold down costs is to begin monitoring physicians' managerial decisions regarding utilization of provider resources. Major changes have occurred in utilization patterns since the early 1980s. Hospital occupancy rates have dipped, while outpatient utilization has surged (32). However, the extent to which these trends are explicitly related to changes in provider surveillance of physicians is not clear. Studies of early experiments with prospective payment systems for hospitals, for example in New Jersey, suggest that hospitals have been slow to introduce controls over physicians (34). On the other hand, there is now a thriving market for computerized programs to evaluate physicians' performance. This suggests that routine scrutiny is becoming the norm (35, 36).

In addition to creating incentives for hospitals to monitor physicians, the introduction of large scale risk-based systems, particularly the Medicare PPS, has also contributed to an expansion of monitoring activities internally (and also externally) at a mechanical level. Medicare PPS reporting requirements provide a standardized framework for linking financial and clinical data and have encouraged the computerization of medical records. Diagnosis related groups allow hospitals, albeit rather crudely, to identify "product lines." Large standardized data sets generated from Medicare records offer a ready starting point for developing guidelines for physician practice.

The expansion of direct governmental monitoring of providers actually began slightly before the much heralded introduction of the Medicare PPS in 1983. In 1982, with relatively little fanfare, Congress enacted legislation replacing PSROs with a new, considerably strengthened entity to carry out area-wide monitoring, the Professional Review Organization. PROs, which became operational in 1984, enjoyed not only expanded powers and responsibilities, but also expanded budgets (30, 37, 38). They provided a laboratory for the large scale implementation of monitoring. They also set a precedent for third party monitoring in the private sector, helping to spur a wide range of experiments with managed care.

*Forces for Expansion*

In the early 1980s regulatory precedents clearly existed for utilization review as a cost containment strategy. But the historical experience with it was hardly encouraging. By the late 1970s, the general verdict was that neither internal utilization review committees nor PSROs had any significant impact on utilization patterns (30). In the face of this less than promising record, an obvious question is why adopt any policies involving expanded monitoring? For if utilization review by providers didn't work, what hope was there that even if providers wanted to improve performance, they would be able to successfully respond to the economic incentives created by risk-based payment? And if external reviews were ineffective, why bother expanding governmental surveillance?

Looking at reasons for the failure of early surveillance efforts is instructive in examining subsequent events from an agency perspective, particularly with respect to changes in the ability to monitor cost/quality trade-offs. Problems with monitoring techniques probably were a factor in this failure. Both utilization review committees and PSROs lacked a uniform set of standards for evaluating performance. Conducting reviews on an ad hoc basis using paper records made them expensive. It also limited their credibility, since findings hinged largely on the judgment of the individual reviewers.

But far more important than mechanical problems, there never appears to have been any commitment to effectively implement either program. As a result, neither represented a real test of the potential efficacy of monitoring. In the case of utilization review committees, given cost based reimbursement, there was no economic incentive for hospitals to make them work. For why limit lengths of stay (except possibly as a rationing device when operating at capacity) when longer stays meant more revenue? In the case of PSROs, these organizations were never provided with either the budgets or the regulatory authority to implement effective controls in the face of broad opposition from the medical profession (30, 37, 38). In terms of both structure of incentives and the level of direct support, policies introduced in the 1980s mark a decisive break with past precedents.

*Falling Surveillance Costs*

In the late 1970s and early 1980s, the efficacy of monitoring was clearly improving, while its costs were falling. Advances in computer technology sharply reduced information processing costs, as they continue to do today. (Statistical analyses which not long ago required sophisticated programming skills and a mainframe computer can now be carried out using simple, user friendly software and a desk top microcomputer.) Falling processing costs made it increasingly feasible to apply computerized analytical techniques to the large scale payor and provider data sets being created in conjunction with rate review efforts. The result was to set in motion the development of increasingly sophisticated techniques for generating standardized criteria for evaluating financial, and, to a lesser degree, clinical performance.

These trends certainly facilitated the expansion of surveillance activities in the early 1980s. However, they are not sufficient to explain the shift to risk-based payment which underlay this expansion. There is a risk of over emphasizing the problems of techniques based on reviews of paper records, given the lack of an all-out effort to apply them during the half-hearted experiments with utilization review in the 1970s. Had the advances in computerized techniques not occurred, or at least had they only occurred on a smaller scale, it is not clear that this would have been a major hindrance. Debates over "pro-competitive" risk-based policies were far ranging. But they focused primarily on cost/quality trade-offs and issues of equity and access and the financial and clinical performance of the existing cost based, fee-for-service system, rather than questions about the degree of progress in monitoring.

## Changing Trade-offs

It comes dangerously close to trivializing the vast changes taking place in health care delivery and finance during the last decade to ascribe them to what may be labeled within an agency framework as a "reassessment" of cost/quality trade-offs. Changes in cost containment policies have been not simply a matter of changing individual patient preferences. Indeed, it is controversial whether any real change in underlying preferences has occurred (2). What is clearer is that a basic restructuring of power relationships has taken place. Who is doing the "assessing" has been altered. Public and private payors have assumed an increasingly dominant role in purchasing decisions. In the wake of this shift, there has been a much greater willingness to experiment with new cost containment methods at the possible expense of quality and to attempt to regulate not only what providers are paid, but what services they provide and how.

At least two immediate developments within the health sector help to explain there shifts from a functional perspective. The first was a growing recognition, supported by a series of economic studies at the end of the 1970s (39), that traditional forms of rate regulation and Certificate of Need laws were failing to stem rising costs. The second was growing recognition of serious problems with the clinical as well as the financial performance of the existing system of health care delivery, as evidenced for example by studies by Wennberg (40) and others indicating large variations in physician practice patterns independent of patient characteristics.

The first set of findings, raising the prospect of a continued explosion in costs, provided advocates of change with a powerful stick with which to goad opponents. The second set of findings served to undermine the traditional defense of the existing system of fee-for-service medicine that it was providing a high standard of care and that tampering with it risked a serious decline in quality. In addition, albeit largely as an aside at the time, these findings held out the possibility of potential quality improvements as a carrot.

Echoing earlier caveats, while changing perceptions about financial and clinical performance served as a motivation for change, it is important to point out that other types of factors were at work as well. Support in the late 1970s and early 1980s for stepped up cost containment efforts, and particularly "pro-competitive" risk-based strategies, also reflected the outcomes of broad political and ideological conflicts extending well beyond the boundaries of the health industry. Other types of social services besides health care came under heavy pressure where comparable cost increases were not occurring. And especially under the Reagan administration, there was little enthusiasm for alternative approaches to cost containment, for example establishing a comprehensive, budget driven national health insurance system.

In any case, in the context of risk-based payment, expanded provider monitoring may be seen as a natural (and much desired) consequence arising from shifting financial risk to providers. Expanded external payor monitoring may be seen as both a cost containment strategy in its own right and a response to the undesired consequences of shifting risk. Initially, the second motivation appears to have been the most important.

There are strong economic incentives to "game" the system in several ways under the Medicare PPS and other risk-based systems in which payments are determined independently of individual provider's costs. Net revenues may be increased by increasing efficiency. But the usual problem with prepayment exists that they may also be increased by avoiding costly patients and lowering standards of care. In addition, there are potential gains from manipulating the payment system, for example through DRG "creep"—reclassifying patients from low paying DRGs into higher paying ones—and keeping patients longer than necessary to qualify for outlier payments.

All of these problems generate a demand for outside surveillance as a by-product of the payment system. The issue of under-provision of care, particularly the arbitrary discharge of Medicare patients to hold down costs, has received considerable attention (30). But not surprisingly, early on the focus of PRO activities, and also of private third party monitoring, appears to have been primarily on controlling abuses likely to increase reimbursement costs. More recently, however, this situation has begun to change.

*A Feedback Loop*

In many respects, the health care system currently appears poised in the middle of a feedback loop with respect to monitoring. The initial growth of surveillance activities in the early 1980s may be explained essentially as a byproduct of cost containment policies. But now monitoring activities are generating a momentum of their own and creating independent pressure for their further, and fuller, implementation.

Several factors help to explain increasing pressures for expanding monitoring. The rapid growth of public and private surveillance activities has been accompanied by growing evidence that utilization management can be an effective cost containment strategy (30). For example, Feldstein and coworkers (41) found that utilization review activities by selected private insurance programs reduced costs during the period 1984–86. In the public sector, Sloan, Morrisey and Valvona (42) argue that PROs played a major role in reductions in patient admission patterns under the Medicare PPS in the period 1984–85, although they do not provide any direct evidence.

Also adding to the attractiveness of monitoring are recent improvements in techniques. Advances in physician "profiling" and the development of standardized treatment protocols, which will both be discussed in more detail below, are providing increasingly powerful tools for identifying deviations from desired standards of care. In addition, there has been a growing acceptance of the notion put forward by Wennberg (40, 43) and others that protocols based on large scale assessments of alternative treatments offer promising opportunities for improving the underlying standard of care (44–46).

The combined result has been to create growing demand for expanded monitoring both as a containment technique and as a means of enhancing the quality of care. In particular, advocates ranging from HMO champion Paul Ellwood (45) to William Roper (46), former presidential health advisor and head of the Health Care Financing Administration (HCFA), have begun to make what amounts to a "have your cake and eat it too" argument. The thrust of this argument is that, drawing on recent refinements in utilization monitoring techniques, expanded payor and provider surveillance can deliver both less costly and higher quality care. The balance of this section explores recent refinements in more detail before considering their possible implications for the doctor-patient relationship.

### Recent Advances in Monitoring

Payor and provider monitoring systems have developed along rather lopsided lines. Minutely detailed information on cost variations for Medicare patients are available on a DRG by DRG basis. But comparable indicators of the quality of services are largely lacking, HCFA's efforts to use death rates as a quality measure being more illustrative of the problems involved than the solutions (47, 48). However, while measuring clinical performance remains problematic, important advances have taken place. Since the late 1970s there has been a rapid shift away from ad hoc reviews of paper patient-records. Quality assessments based on the judgment of individual reviewers have given way to large scale computerized monitoring based on standardized criteria. Two major developments have occurred in computerized techniques during the last decade. The first has been refinements in "profiling" physician practice patterns. The second, more recent development, has been the emergence of standardized treatment protocols.

*Physician Profiling.* The notion in physician profiling is that individual physicians' clinical and financial performance can be evaluated through comparison with their peers. Computerized data on practice patterns are examined to identify doctors who are "outliers" with respect to resource utilization and/or patient outcomes. The results of such analyses can be used as a basis for initiating further, ad hoc review and/or determining compensation, as described by Feinglass and Salmon (49).

Profiling techniques have the attraction that they are relatively mechanical to implement. Given a data base, a group profile can be readily used to screen individual physician performance without developing an underlying objective model of what constitutes "appropriate" medical practice. However, the absence of any formal model of practice limits the extent to which this type of monitoring can be used to affect behavior, especially for the medical profession as a whole. While profiling provides a powerful tool for challenging the decisions of individual physicians when their practice patterns deviate sharply from the norm, it does not provide any basis for challenging their collective judgment. What physicians should be doing is basically defined in terms of what a chosen group is doing. Administrators may attempt to use profiling to nudge clinical decision making in a desired direction. Thus, as Feinglass and Salmon (49) observe, incentives may be designed to reward those physicians who are more parsimonious in rendering a given standard of care. But attempts to move too far from group norms will evoke conflict and may undermine the legitimacy of the monitoring system. Significant "gray areas" are also likely to exist, giving physicians considerable latitude. As a result, a good deal of monitoring activities may involve what one commentator describes as "nurses haggling with doctors over the need for admissions" (50, p. 62). Moreover, while administrators may tinker with what groups are selected for comparison and how norms are used, the process of determining group norms under profiling ultimately remains a "black box," based on physician judgment.

*Standardized Treatment Protocols.* The underlying notion behind treatment protocols is that objective criteria can be established to guide physician behavior. In essence, what is being advocated with protocols is the standardization of the care production process itself through the development of models of what explicitly constitutes appropriate care. This approach is very much in the spirit of calls for "scientific management" advocated by Frederick Taylor and his followers at the turn of the century. Rejecting the use of group norms, (the profiling approach), Taylor called for the systematic analysis of job content as a basis for setting performance standards (51).

Two types of methods have been combined to develop protocols in health care. One is consensus standards reached through a "Delphic" approach—bringing together recognized experts to agree on appropriate treatments for specific conditions. The other is to empirically assess the performance of alternative treatments, comparing patient outcomes and resource utilization using large scale data bases (26). In both cases, important differences exist compared to profiling at not only the individual physician level, but the medical profession as a whole.

Under profiling, the "average" physician, practicing according to established standards, has no reason to expect to significantly improve his or her performance. In contrast, protocols offer the individual physician potential access to superior expertise and state of the art information. As Ellwood (45) and others have noted, this may imbue protocols with an important additional element of legitimacy absent in profiling. But protocols may significantly reduce the individual physician's scope for exercising independent judgment and make adherence to set routines a primary criterion for evaluating performance. In addition, they may serve to shift control over standards away from physicians as a group. Because protocol standards depend on the opinion of elite "experts" and the work of academic and government researchers, neither the implicit nor explicit approval of the rank and file of the profession is required to alter them. This last point has not been lost on medicine. Calls are multiplying for the profession (or at least specialty segments) to take the initiative and to develop protocols before others do so (45, 50, 52). Already the American College of Surgeons has embarked on such a program, with other groups following. At the same time, dire prognostications are not lacking. For instance, in response to *The New England Journal of Medicine* article by former HCFA head Roper and colleagues (46) calling for a major increase in government involvement in monitoring health outcomes, one commentator observes "Unless I am greatly mistaken, this article announces that work has begun on what physicians have long feared, the Great American Medical Cookbook, intended ultimately to prescribe what physicians may and should do in every case posed by their patients" (53, p. 21).

Currently, protocols are far from providing the basis for such comprehensive regulation. However, while their implementation is still in its infancy, one can expect a short childhood. Recent work by the Rand Corporation gives an indication of the intended direction. Building on 36 protocols developed by Rand under federal funding, 85 protocols have recently been developed by a private company and are now being implemented by large payors such as Aetna and the national Blue Cross and Blue Shield Association (50).

Most of these protocols deal with specific technical procedures, such as coronary angiography and artery bypass surgery, hysterectomies, and knee arthroscopy. The primary focus is on identifying their inappropriate use. Physicians whose practice decisions are deemed not to conform to protocols risk not being reimbursed. But beyond this, these protocols are being presented as a means of upgrading standards of care. As the president of one of the companies involved in developing these protocols puts it "managed care needs to go beyond somewhat ham handed financial risk allocation techniques to helping providers make better judgments" (50, p. 62).

How close to realizing this goal protocols will actually come remains an open question. The pioneer protocols mentioned above involve mostly narrow, technical procedures and focus largely on gate keeping functions (i.e., evaluating whether a procedure is "appropriate"). Significantly, the issue of under-utilization is not addressed (50). However, the Agency for Health Care Policy and Research (formerly the National Center for Health Services Research) is funding more general studies of patient care (54). And work is underway by Rand researchers to assess treatment outcomes in diabetes and hypertension (55). These studies should help in gauging the general applicability of protocols to patient care.

Returning to analogies with manufacturing in this context, it is clear that if protocols are to be successfully employed on a large scale, they have to go beyond the type of rigid standardization typical of turn-of-the-century mass production. Assembly line techniques in the mode of Henry Ford's manufacturing system for model T's in which every patient always receives an identical treatment for a given illness are unlikely to achieve anything remotely approaching an acceptable level of quality. Not only is there far too much variation in treatment requirements from patient to patient, but patient needs often necessitate frequent reassessment in the course of providing care. The 85 proprietary protocols described earlier alone involve analysis of a total of some 10,000 "indicators" (50).

In many ways, however, efforts to develop standardized medical protocols dovetail with recent trends in manufacturing towards the use of more flexible techniques. As described by Piore and Sabel (56), the essence of these techniques is to adapt mass production to respond to individual customer needs by minimizing set up costs. In the future it seems possible that such techniques could be a powerful tool for helping to develop protocols permitting successful "customization" of treatments to patient needs.

## LOOKING TO THE FUTURE

### Standardization and the Production Process

While monitoring activities seem almost certain to increase in the future, it is too soon to evaluate either at what pace they will proceed or how far they will go. Much is dependent upon the outcome of political conflicts pitting professional self-interest against those seeking to rationalize the health care system. Broad social decisions regarding access to care and the willingness to accept growing inequity in its distribution will also play an important (and perhaps overriding) role. Finally, the pace of change may be significantly affected by the availability and rate of diffusion of management information technologies and may well not be uniform across different areas of medicine.

Even strong advocates of managed care such as Ellwood (45) suggest the process may be a slow one, taking perhaps ten to fifteen years. Particularly in the context of standardized treatment protocols and the twin goals of cost containment and quality enhancement, it is also important to note that utilization review is a two edged sword.

More intensive surveillance may identify over-utilization of costly techniques, reducing expenditures. But it may also identify under-utilization, increasing them. This lack of predictability may confound hopes that standards of care can be raised and costs contained simultaneously. Indeed, Evans (33, 57) suggests that precisely because of the unpredictability of the impact utilization review, payors and providers by mutual consent have shied away from it in the past in countries with budget driven systems such as England and Canada. The promise of expanded monitoring now seems too great to abandon it outright. But it is quite possible that conflicts may soon arise between quality and cost goals that force a reassessment of policies based on current optimistic assessments of their compatibility.

Assuming that monitoring does continue to expand, there is a variety of current trends which have broad implications for the doctor-patient relationship. One is a continued advance in the level of managerial oversight over physician decision making and greater routinization of treatment activities. A second is the emergence of an expanding bureaucracy to carry out oversight functions. Finally, the increasing specificity of monitoring criteria seems likely to make some standardization of standards necessary within the context of the current highly fragmented system in which one provider is often subject to several sets of different public and private standards.

To the extent standardization of tasks increases through the use of profiling and protocols, the level of autonomy of individual physicians will almost certainly be diminished. At a minimum, statements such as "they won't let me do that" will become common, as will allegations that physicians are putting the interests of providers or payors ahead of patient care. However, if profiling remains a primary form of monitoring, a significant element of autonomy could remain for physicians. An "outlier" approach is more appropriate for identifying extreme behavior than "fine tuning." Within the "gray area" that constitutes "acceptable" performance, individual physicians are likely to enjoy considerable latitude in decision making, while the profession at large would probably continue to play a major role in determining standards. The large scale implementation of standardized protocols could have a much more profound effect. If protocols succeed in truly standardizing treatment tasks, the traditional rationale for physician autonomy would be largely eliminated. For not only would the physician's exercise of independent judgment be reduced, lessening opportunities for abuse of the agency relationship, but monitoring would be greatly simplified in so much as performance could be defined in terms of adherence to protocols. There would be little reason on agency grounds in this case not to integrate physicians into centralized hierarchical systems of control and the stage would be set for the practice of medicine to be largely reduced to the performance of routinized technical tasks under large corporate structures.

In the past, routinization of technical tasks in medicine has usually led to the substitution of subordinate technical personnel for physicians. Thus, a wide range of tasks have been delegated to nurses (58) and to specialized support personnel in areas like radiology (59) and clinical pathology (60). In the long run, a similar process seems likely to occur again. The potential substitution of technical personnel in the basic treatment process raises the question, however, of what is to become of the physician?

From an efficacy perspective, much depends on just how far the standardization processes goes, although the final outcome may reflect political and economic considerations as much as technical ones. If by and large, protocols simply continue to be limited to the use of particular technical procedures, leaving physicians to still manage the bulk of the overall treatment process, then their impact could be modest. But if routine care does in fact become truly standardized, then the effects could be far reaching.

In the short run, a rapid standardization of treatment processes could result in considerable dislocation in the physician labor market. Even within the ten to fifteen year horizon discussed by Ellwood (45), unless there is an offsetting increase in employment opportunities for physicians elsewhere, many could find themselves in the position of choosing between essentially working as subordinate technicians or leaving the profession. The result could be a period of sharply diminishing expectations with overtones of the type of "proletarianization" which McKinlay and Arches (5) and McKinlay and Stoeckle (6) discuss in the case of skilled workers displaced during the industrial revolution. While it is easy to discount such predictions and argue that politically the medical profession would never permit this to happen, it is perhaps instructive to recall that not so very long ago, it was popular wisdom that for hospitals, a built bed was a filled bed (61). On the other hand, as Navarro (9) observes, significant changes may take place in the role of physicians without anything as dire occurring as a true "proletarianization."

### The Doctor-Patient Relationship

In the longer run, if large scale standardization does occur, three types of futures seem likely to lie ahead for physicians. One is a continued role as a care manager, but now primarily in cases too complex to be dealt with by lower level technical personnel within a protocol framework. A second role is as the provider of technical services which require a high level of skill combined with a significant amount of general background knowledge, essentially already the role of a growing number of medical specialists. A final and rapidly growing role is as a manager not of patient care, but of those who provide it—the physician administrator.

If this forecast is correct, for most patients the physician would become an increasingly remote figure. Rather than the patients' primary contact with the system, encounters with physicians would be the exception. The main reasons for seeing a physician would be either an unusual medical problem, the need for a particularly complex service, or an administrative matter. And especially in the last case, the relationship would likely become one simply of patient-bureaucrat.

The success of standardized protocols could also have broad implications for the type of organizational setting in which doctors work as well as the doctor-patient relationship per se. To the extent standardization of production diminishes agency problems, opportunities may increase for the expansion of for-profit tendencies even within so-called "not-for-profit" organizational structures. This would surely accelerate trends towards the corporatization of medicine and further alter the tone of doctor-patient relationships, while issues also exist regarding the scale of health care enterprises (62).

## CONCLUDING REMARKS

The ongoing debate over the future role of physicians within a corporatized health care system has addressed primarily broad issues of medical autonomy and professional control. In this chapter we have attempted to complement these analyses by drawing on an agency framework to examine changing patterns of physician practice and the dynamics of monitoring. Our thrust has been to suggest that while the cost containment efforts of the 1980s have been the dominant factor triggering recent changes in the doctor-patient relationship, new abilities to monitor physician performance are now taking on a powerful momentum of their own.

Although agency models are helpful in identifying important forces for change at a functional level, there are many aspects of the implementation of new types of monitoring systems (or the expansion of old ones) which standard models do not address. One question which is frequently raised is whether doctors will dominate the new administrative hierarchies emerging in the wake of expanding efforts to manage care. Another important issue is the extent to which changing patterns of monitoring and payment may impact on systems for controlling agency abuses based on internalized values. We close by briefly commenting on these issues, where our comments are suggestive both of possible extensions of the agency framework and some of its limitations.

There is clearly a need for ongoing physician input in implementing monitoring under managed care systems and in developing and employing protocols. The key issue is at what level. Will physician practitioners simply provide medical input into the evaluation process, for example helping to design specific protocols and supervising their use? Or will they dominate the entire process? Currently, physicians lack any special claim to administrative expertise in running large organizations. But growing numbers are seeking to acquire it, for instance through MBA programs, and a specialty board in "administrative medicine" has been proposed (63, 64).

From an agency perspective (as opposed to a political one), the question of whether or not to employ physicians as administrators is primarily one of relative costs. Here at least two types of issues are involved. One is the direct costs of employing highly trained physicians as opposed to less educated personnel, where, however, the growing supply of physicians may have a significant impact in forcing down wage levels in the occupation. The other is that of professional socialization. Even if physician administrators are more costly to hire, they may pay for themselves because they are more successful in dealing with other physicians. On the other hand, they may also be more likely to identify their interests with the medical profession, rather than the institutions that employ them, and this seems particularly likely to be a source of conflict in the type of large for-profit organizations associated with the process of corporatization of the industry.

In exploring these issues, patterns in the use of professional experts in manufacturing, such as scientists and engineers, may be instructive. Comparing the United States and England, Lazonick (65) identifies two quite different models. In the United States he observes that professional experts have tended to be integrated into the managerial structure, rising through the ranks to top management positions while acquiring skills as generalists in the process. In contrast, in England, they have been far more compartmentalized, remaining isolated from upper level decision making. The American model would seem the natural one for U.S. health care. But it is worth noting that scientists and engineers have historically been much less involved in their own governance and do not seem typically to have the same type of strong collective professional identity as physicians. To the extent that these characteristics set physicians apart, this could produce pressures to move in the direction of the British model.

This last observation, however, begs the question of whether professional values and self-governance will continue to be as important in the future as they have in the past. The discussion in this chapter has been predicated on the assumption that internalized values can be taken as a given and that additional controls can be added in an incremental fashion. On the surface, this assumption seems reasonable. However, it is important to recognize that growing external intervention by providers and payors into the doctor-patient relationship may ultimately be antithetical to systems for nurturing internalized values. Freidson (20) and many others have questioned the importance of such values in shaping behavior. However, the existence of a strong professional identity among physicians suggests that a powerful socialization process is at work, although not necessarily primarily for the benefit of either patients or the general public. In any case, to the extent that internalized values play a role, greater external control could lead to erosion of these values.

If physicians come increasingly to see themselves as employees subject to administrative controls over which they have little influence either as individuals or as an occupation, they may become increasingly alienated, especially in the face of the growing emphasis on market performance and profitability associated with the corporatization of health care. This raises the possibility that increasing centralized surveillance may set off a downward spiral. Thus, expanded payor and provider monitoring diminishes the efficacy of complementary professional systems of quality assurance by eroding values. This may create growing agency problems. Growing agency problems may, in turn, generate a demand for further surveillance of performance.

Increased surveillance requirements could significantly increase costs. These costs could offset some or even all of the anticipated gains from utilization management efforts. Moreover, there could be significant discontinuities in the way in which an erosion of values affects surveillance needs. Most of the current physician population were trained under traditional fee-for-service and are habituated to its values. While subject to increasing external controls, they are likely to continue to provide a critical mass of support for professional organizations and exert peer pressure on their fellows. Consequently, it may appear on the surface as if no major changes are taking place, only adjustments at the margin.

But as the share of physicians trained under current conditions increases, a "tipping" phenomenon could occur. Thus, when the older generation begins to retire, there could be a rapid collapse of many of the traditions taken for granted in medicine, and indeed the entire system of internalized values associated with them. Once gone, these traditions and values could prove very difficult to rebuild and a quantum leap in monitoring could be required simply to assure existing levels of performance. This suggests that expanded efforts to manage utilization could initially be accompanied by an illusion of large gains, only to be shattered later by an explosion in monitoring costs.

## REFERENCES

1. Marder, W. D., et al. Physician employment patterns: Challenging conventional wisdom. *Health Aff.* 7(4): 137–145, 1988.
2. Navarro, V. *Crisis, Health, and Medicine.* Routledge and Kegan Paul, New York, 1986.
3. Freidson, E. The reorganization of the medical profession. *Med. Care* 42: 11–35, 1985.
4. Freidson, E. Professional dominance and the ordering of health services: Some consequences. In *The Sociology of Health and Illness,* edited by P. Conrad and R. Kern, pp. 184–197. St. Martin's Press, New York, 1981.
5. McKinlay, J. B., and Arches, J. Towards the proletarianization of physicians. *Int. J. Health Serv.* 15: 161–195, 1985.
6. McKinlay, J. B., and Stoeckle, J. D. Corporatization and the social transformation of doctoring. *Int. J. Health Serv.* 18: 191–205, 1988.
7. Ritzer, G., and Walczak, D. Rationalization and the deprofessionalization of physicians. *Social Forces* 67(1): 1–22, 1988.
8. Haug, M. R. A re-examination of the hypothesis of physician deprofessionalization. *Milbank Mem. Fund Q.* 66 (Suppl. 2): 48–56, 1988.
9. Navarro, V. Professional Dominance or Proletarianization?: Neither. *Milbank Mem. Fund Q.* 66 (Suppl. 2): 57–75, 1988.
10. Arrow, K. Uncertainty and the welfare economics of medical care. *Am. Econ. Rev.* 53(3): 941–973, 1963.
11. Dranove, D., and White, W. Agency and the organization of health care. *Inquiry* 24: 405–415, 1987.
12. Salmon, J. W. Special section on the corporatization of medicine.: Introduction. *Int. J. Health Serv.* 17(1): 1–6, 1987.

13. Navarro, V. Medical history as justification rather than explanation: A critique of Starr's The Social Transformation of American Medicine. *Int. J. Health Serv.* 14(4): 511–528, 1984.

14. McKinlay, J. B. The changing character of the medical profession. *Milbank Mem. Fund Q.* 66 (Suppl. 2), 1988.

15. Salmon, J. W. (ed.). *The Corporate Transformation of Health Care, Part I: Issues and Directions.* Baywood Publishing Co., Amityville N.Y., 1990.

16. Arrow, K. The economics of agency. In *Principals and Agents: The Structure of Business,* edited by J. Pratt and R. Zeckhauser. Harvard Business School, Cambridge Mass., 1985.

17. Harris, J. The internal organization of hospitals: Some economic implications. *Bell J. Econ.* 10(1): 74–91, 1979.

18. White, W. D. Why is regulation introduced in the health sector? A look at occupational licensure. *J. Health Polit. Policy Law* 4(3): 536–553, 1979.

19. Ackerloff, G. Gift exchange and efficiency wage theory, four views. *Am. Econ. Rev.* 74(2): 79–83, 1984.

20. Freidson, E. The futures of professionalism. In *Health and the Division of Labour,* edited by M. Stacey, et al., pp. 14–40. Prodist, New York, 1977.

21. Starr, P. *The Social Transformation of American Medicine.* Basic Books, New York, 1982.

22. Pauly, M. The economics of moral hazard: Comment. *Am. Econ. Rev.* 58(3): 531–537, 1963.

23. Cleary, P. D., and NcNeil, B. J. Patient satisfaction as an indicator of quality of care. *Inquiry* 25: 25–36, 1988.

24. Scovern, H. Hired help: A physician's experiences in a for-profit staff-model HMO. *N. Engl. J. Med.* 319: 787–790, 1988.

25. Bock, R. S. The pressure to keep prices high at a walk-in clinic. *N. Engl. J. Med.* 319: 785–787, 1988.

26. Chassin, M. R. Standards of care in medicine. *Inquiry* 25: 437–453, 1988.

27. James, F. E. Controversy mounts over efforts to measure quality of health care. *Wall Street J.,* December 17, 1987.

28. Kenkel, P. J. Managed care will dominate within a decade—experts. *Mod. Healthcare,* July 29, 1988, p. 31.

29. Lazar, H. P. Doctor, patient, bureaucrat. *The New York Times,* December 20, 1986, p. 19.

30. Ermann, D. Hospital utilization review: Past experience, future directions. *J. Health Polit. Policy Law* 13(4): 683–704, 1988.

31. Relman, A. Assessment and accountability: The third revolution in medical care. *N. Engl. J. Med.* 319(18): 1220–1222, 1988.

32. National Center for Health Statistics. *Health, United States: 1988.* Public Health Service, U.S. Government Printing Office, Washington, D.C., 1989.

33. Evans, R. Finding the levers, finding the courage: Lessons from North America. *J. Health Polit. Policy Law* 11(4): 585–616, 1987.

34. Hsaio, W., et al. Lessons of the New Jersey DRG payment system. *Health Aff.* 5(2): 32–43, 1986.

35. Dornfest, S. *Business Opportunities in the Hospital Computer Market.* Sheldon Dornfest & Associates, Northbrook Ill., 1987.

36. Gardner, E. Information system market changing: Hospitals increase information systems purchases as software vendors more responsive to need. *Mod. Health Care,* February 3, 1989, pp. 34–60.

37. Smits, H. The PRSO in perspective. *N. Engl. J. Med.* 305: 253–259, 1981.

38. Dans, P. E., Weiner, J. P., and Otter, S. E. Peer review organizations: Promises and pitfalls. *N. Engl. J. Med.* 313: 1131–1137, 1985.
39. Steinwald, B., and Sloan, F. Regulatory approaches to hospital cost containment: A synthesis of the empirical evidence. In *A New Approach to the Economics of Health Care,* edited by M. Olsen, pp. 273–307. American Enterprise Institute, Washington, D.C., 1981.
40. Wennberg, J. Dealing with medical practice variations: A proposal for action. *Health Aff.* 3(2): 6–32, 1984.
41. Feldstein, P., Wickizer, T., and Wheeler, J. The effects of utilization review programs on health care use and expenditures. *N. Engl. J. Med.* 318(1), 1988.
42. Sloan, F., Morrisey, M., and Valvona, J. Effects of the Medicare prospective payment system on hospital cost containment: An early appraisal. *Milbank Mem. Fund Q.* 66(2): 191–220, 1988.
43. Wennberg, J. On patient need, equity, supplier-induced demand and the need to assess the outcomes of common medical practices. *Med. Care* 23(5): 512–520, 1985.
44. Faltermayer, E. Medical care's next revolution. *Fortune* 118(8): 126–133, 1988.
45. Ellwood, P. M. A technology of patient experience. *N. Engl. J. Med.* 318:1549–1556, 1988.
46. Roper, W., et al. Effectiveness in health care: An initiative to evaluate and improve medical practice. *N. Engl. J. Med.* 319: 1197–1202, 1988.
47. Blumberg, M. S. Comments on HCFA hospital death rate statistical outliers. *Health Serv. Res.* 21: 715–739, 1987.
48. Rosen, H. M., and Green, B. A. The HCFA excess mortality lists: A methodological critique. *Hosp. Health Serv. Admin.,* February 1987.
49. Feinglass, J., and Salmon, J. W. Corporatization of medicine: The use of medical management information systems to increase the clinical productivity of physicians. *Int. J. Health Serv.* 20(2): 233–252, 1990.
50. Meyer, H. Payers to use protocols to assess treatment plans. *Am. Med. News,* December 9, 1988, pp. 1, 62–64.
51. Chandler, A. *The Visible Hand: The Managerial Revolution in American Business.* Belknap, Harvard University Press, Cambridge, Mass., 1977.
52. Saltman, R. Designing standardized clinical protocols: Some organizational and behavioral issues. *Int. J. Health Plann. and Manage.* 1(2): 129–140, 1986.
53. Schwartz, H. A critical look at initiative to evaluate practice. *Am. Med. News,* December 2, 1988, p. 21.
54. Agency for Health Care Policy and Research. *Program Note: Medical Treatment Effectiveness Research.* Rockville, Md., March 1990.
55. National Center for Health Services Research. Patient outcome study NCHSR-supported projects in FY 1988. *NCHSR Research Activities,* No. 113, January 1989, pp. 1–2.
56. Piore, M. J., and Sabel, C. F. *The Second Industrial Divide: Possibilities for Prosperity.* Basic Books, New York, 1984.
57. Evans, R. G. The Dog in the Night Time: Medical Practice Variations and Health Policy. Discussion Paper HPRU 89:7, University of British Columbia, June 1989.
58. Kalisch, P., and Kalisch, B. *The Advances of American Nursing.* Little Brown, Boston, 1978.
59. Brecher, R., and Brecher, E. *The Rays: A History of Radiology in the United States and Canada.* Williams & Wilkins, Baltimore, 1969.
60. White, W. D. *Public Health and Private Gain: The Economics of Licensing Clinical Laboratory Personnel.* Maaroufa Press/Metheun, New York, 1979.
61. Feldstein, P. *Health Care Economics,* Ed. 2. Wiley Medical, New York, 1983.

62. White, W. D. The "corporatization" of U.S. hospitals: What can we learn from the nineteenth century experience? In *The Corporate Transformation of Health Care, Part II: Perspectives and Implications* edited by J. W. Salmon. Baywood Publishing Company, Amityville, N.Y., 1993.
63. Carlsen, A. The doctor's new clothes—some doctors are trading their lab coats for business suits as they take on roles in health care management. *Health Week*, October 3, 1988, p. 17.
64. Ross, A. Building physician-administrator teams. *MGM Journal*, November/December 1988, p. 19.
65. Lazonick, W. Strategy, structure, and management development in the United States and Britain. In *The Development of Managerial Enterprise,* edited by K. Kobayashi and H. Morikawa. University of Tokyo Press, Tokyo, 1985.

# CHAPTER 11

# Canadian Medicine: Dominance or Proletarianization?

## David Coburn

Health care systems all over the world are being transformed. However, just as we know that health care systems have changed over time, we also know that they vary spatially, across nation states. Changes in health care systems are occurring differently in various social formations, though there are international similarities as well as differences. Medicine, a central health care occupation, can be expected to reflect these changes and differences. Certainly, the Canadian medical profession has vastly changed over the past century, and even over the past two decades, and the Canadian experience is different even from developments in those two nations with which it has been, and is, most closely related, Britain and the United States. In this chapter we concentrate on the historical development of the medical profession in Canada as a national case study.

There are both substantive and conceptual disagreements regarding the changing social position of medicine over time. Substantively, some authors claim that medicine is declining in dominance (1), is deprofessionalizing (2, 3) or is being proletarianized (4), others feel that medicine is either stable (5, 6) or actually increasing in power. Those who have written in detail on the historical development of the profession in Britain, the United States, and Australia are equivocal about the current role of medicine although perhaps leaning towards decline (7–9). Yet, while we now commonly speak of "world-systems" few analysts have as yet examined the "world-system" of medicine and the manner in which broader international relationships, and the nature of medicine as a transnational activity itself, constrains or directs the development of medicine in specific countries. Nor can we do this here other than briefly noting the influence of British on Canadian medicine (but, see 10).

Conceptual difficulties regarding the changing role of medicine involve the similarities and differences amongst medical dominance, professionalization and proletarianization. Freidson (11) has described dominance as consisting of control over the content of care, over clients, over other health occupations and over the context of care. But Freidson's early contention that medicine is dominant in the health division of labor failed to adequately explain the reasons for that dominance and to situate the concept of dominance within a broader theory capable of explaining change in the role of medicine. Freidson's latest claims that medicine is not declining in power (5, 6) are contradicted by his slide from the postulation of medical dominance to a defense of the more restricted notion of medical autonomy (this partly due to a confounding of these concepts in his earlier work). In fact, a close reading of Freidson's recent writings reveals an implicit admission of a decline of medical power.

While the professionalization literature has been attacked from all sides, Marxist writers on medicine have claimed that medicine could only be adequately analyzed by situating it within the larger social formation (12–18). Medicine was viewed as the intermediate rather than ultimate controller of health care events. More important were the logic of the capitalist system and the class struggle. One stream within Marxism was the assertion that recent changes in the United States had produced the proletarianization of medicine (4). This follows earlier Marxist analyses of occupational/class trends as exemplified in Braverman's *Monopoly Capital* (19). The claim is that twentieth-century medicine is beginning to suffer the same fate that had overtaken nineteenth-century crafts workers, a fate facing all or most (skilled) workers under capitalism.

It is not my task here to settle the conceptual issues involved in various theoretical approaches to changes in medicine. Rather, I want to use the concepts of medical dominance and proletarianization as orienting concepts with which to describe and analyze the historical development of medicine in Canada before commenting on the implications of the findings for the various contentions about continued or declining medical power. This analytical description is based on the assumption that medicine and health care in general are not separable from the socio-economic context in which they arose and are reproduced and changed and that national case studies can help to provide a base for later international comparisons.

## MEDICINE IN CANADA

In describing Canadian medicine it must be noted that Canada did not exist as a nation until 1867 and that Alberta and Saskatchewan, for example, only became provinces in 1905. And, because health is a provincial rather than a federal responsibility, there has been provincial variation within a broadly similar stream of development. Ontario is used as the major example.

The social history of Canadian medicine can be described in terms of three stages: a rise to dominance (to the end of World War I), the consolidation of that dominance (World War I to the 1960s), and since about 1962 (the year of the Saskatchewan doctor's strike), the beginnings of a decline in dominance (see 1).

## THE EMERGENCE OF MEDICAL DOMINANCE

The emergence of medical dominance in Canada took place between the early nineteenth century, when medicine lacked power and status, and the early twentieth century, by which time it largely controlled the emerging health means of production.

Two problems faced Canadian medicine in the nineteenth century: restricting or eliminating competition from the irregulars who had enough popular support to resist attempts to make their practice illegal, and convincing the "regulars" to actually become licensed themselves. The main divisions within medicine were between allopathic medicine and the homeopaths, Thompsonians or eclectics; between an elite group of urban physicians and the lower status doctors in the towns and in the countryside; and, in Lower Canada (Quebec), between anglophone and francophone doctors. Finally, there was conflict between the medical schools (which had an incentive to produce students) and practitioners (who wanted to avoid competition).

There were repeated attempts by the regulars to gain legislation in Upper and Lower Canada to license practitioners and suppress irregular healers. Licensing in Quebec dates from 1788. A Medical Board to license physicians had existed in Upper Canada since 1795 but enforcement of licensing was minimal. The public, legislative, and irregular opposition to medicine is indicated by the rejection by the Ontario Legislature around mid-century of numerous attempts by the profession to pass legislation which would establish a monopoly for the "regulars."

Even so, as Kett (20) has noted, medicine in Canada has never been as uncontrolled as it was in the United States in the mid-nineteenth century. Regulatory institutions in Canada have a more or less continuous history from the early nineteenth century on. In particular the number of medical schools in Canada were always limited by the number that could obtain university affiliation. There was never the proliferation of proprietary schools as in the United States (hence, never the same sharp decline in schools in the early 1900s).

After mid-century the major challenge to medicine came from the homeopaths and eclectics, who had spread to Canada from the United States and gained a considerable popular following. The "irregulars" were strong partly because they were often the only source of care, while homeopathy, with its much less drastic treatments than allopathy, recommended it to some influential citizens. A strong anti-monopoly sentiment was reinforced by orthodox medicine's lack of a curative advantage over other forms of healing.

While some doctors were socially prominent (the first president of the Canadian Medical Association later became Prime Minister) the status of the profession as a whole was dubious at best. Newspapers delighted in reporting the vituperative attacks by one doctor on another. Educated laypersons displayed their contempt for bleeding, blistering and purging, the main treatments of the time. The disjunction between personal and professional standing gave the impetus to a professionalizing elite to push for higher educational and practice standards, an aim which coincided with the goals of practitioners to reduce competition.

Competition was the major concern (21). The 1861 Ontario Census lists 974 physicians while by 1871 the total was 1574, an increase of 60 percent as compared to a population increase of only 16 percent (22). One doctor noted in *The Canada Lancet* in 1873 that he settled in a village of 400 in which the Justice of the Peace practiced medicine, a local dentist advertised himself as knowing eye and ear problems, and another member of the College advertised cures for many incurable diseases (23). Another doctor complained about midwives in a county already "flooded with trained practitioners." His competition got about 60 cases a year "which would amount in my hands to a very decent living for my small family" (23, p. 152).

The Ontario Legislature repeatedly rejected bills for a medical monopoly for the regulars. Then, the Legislature confounded orthodox medicine by authorizing a Board for Homeopaths in 1859 and one for eclectics in 1861. Finally, in response to one of many medical petitions, the politicians stunned the "regulars" by including both homeopaths and eclectics along with the orthodox practitioners in the Act establishing the College of Physicians and Surgeons (24). But, the embrace of regular medicine quickly proved fatal for the eclectics; they had disappeared by the 1880s and, though homeopathy still lingers on even in the 1980s, it has not been a serious threat to orthodox medicine for nearly a century.

By the middle of the 1870s there was no universal valid principle for therapeutics and: "Active interventionism thus gave way to an emphasis on restoring constitutional powers (often by the use of stimulants such as alcohol)" (25, p. 118) and by "the healing power of nature." The major advances in treatment came in the last third of the century with the revolutions in surgery made possible by the use of anesthetics and disinfectants and discovery of the germ theory.

Towards the turn of the century, the rise of medicine was aided by the development of public health, part of the broader Progressive Movement (the Social Gospel movement) (roughly 1890 to 1920). The Progressives (26) saw in the new industrial cities the antithesis of an idealized clean, healthy, rural environment they felt characterized their own past.

In the Public Health movement, "medical" science saw its first victories. It was the successful legacy of public health in reducing mortality and morbidity, rather than the results of ordinary medical practice, that medicine gave as evidence of its efficacy and of the power of the germ theory on which it was based. However, when public health advocates began to attack the inequities of capitalism as the source of illness the limits of a public health acceptable to the new industrial elite was reached (27). The public health movement was diverted towards education of the public rather than change in the social and physical environment (28), completely lost its dynamism and, in the 1920s, was superseded by curative medicine.

During the early part of the century the health care system was in transition from a home-based to the beginnings of hospital-based care. With its new scientific respectability medicine attained equal status in the hospital with administrators and philanthropic trustees. Simultaneously came the rise of health care occupations such as nursing to numerical predominance, and many types of auxiliary or para-medical occupations in the hospital, "born" under medical control (29).

The main roots of present day medicine were thus established in the nineteenth and early twentieth century. The first licensing acts, the first schools of medicine, the first associations, the first journals all came mainly in the second half of the nineteenth century. Medicine already controlled the content of medical practice. By the end of World War I it had also attained control over the burgeoning health means of production in the hospital and over other health occupations and clients. Self-care was attacked and a medical monopoly reinforced through control over patent and prescription medicines. Home-care texts reflected the increasing power of medicine. While early texts gave instruction on almost everything (including amputations described so that "any man, unless he is an idiot or an absolute fool, can perform this operation"; see 30, p. 25), by the early twentieth century these had become first-aid books only; anything else was referred to a doctor's care (31). Doctors had a monopoly over the provision of care even though there were still disputes with midwives (32), pharmacists, and non-allopathic healers such as homeopaths and chiropractors (33).

But, in a market economy, doctors were far from completely controlling the context of care. Within the profession there was concern over competition. Medicine was still opposed by those in fledgling municipal, provincial and federal bureaucracies and, most especially, by populist and working class organizations and politicians. Indications of opposition included vaccination riots, attacks on the medical monopoly by the Patrons of Industry (an agrarian populist movement, at times allied with labor) and other anti-monopoly groups, and rejection, by judges, newspapers, and legislatures, of medical attempts to eliminate competition.

These events occurred as Canada moved from being a British colony to an independent "Dominion" and as a purely subsistence economy was transformed into one characterized by production of a surplus and then of increasing industrialization. The British influence on early Canadian medicine was powerful because of the attraction of the British medical elite to aspiring Canadian physicians, because some colonial laws regarding medicine were applied in Canada, and because of the large number of "British" physicians in Canada. But the changes in the Canadian mode of production and in the class structure were also important. Both farmers and labor had anti-monopoly interests (although divided in other respects) and regularly attacked the professions in general and medicine in particular. In the 1920s agrarian parties did form a number of provincial governments and the Progressive (agrarian) party won the second largest number of seats in the federal parliament in 1921 (but refused to be the official opposition). Though populist movements had prevented medicine attaining a complete monopoly of care, agrarian/labor governments did not directly touch the work or status of physicians' which by the 1920s was entrenched and surrounded by the mystifying aura of medical "science." With the decline of subsistence farming, agrarian radicalism was increasingly confined to particular regions and was more and more replaced as an oppositional force by the urban working class.

After the turbulent years of World War I the post-war period was initiated by labor unrest, particularly in the West, and the Winnipeg General Strike of 1919. Petrified by the Bolshevik Revolution, the Canadian bourgeoisie suppressed dissent through suspending civil rights, intimidating unionists and strikers, jailings, beatings, and deportations (34–36). But efforts to unite discontented farmers and labor in an anti-capitalist crusade failed.

The medical elite had allied itself with the lingering colonial aristocracy (the Family Compact) and then with the rising (but quickly superseded) petite bourgeoisie. In tandem its justificatory ideology switched from an emphasis on classical learning to a focus on "science" (37, 38). As an organized occupation it never identified with the working class and always felt threatened by the labor movement although it had more ambivalent relationships with agrarian populism, some of whose sentiments it shared. But there were elements within medicine, particularly within the public health movement, which did agree with some of labor's anti-capitalist aims.

## CONSOLIDATION OF MEDICINE

The importance of associations in the rise and maintenance of medical power has often been stressed. The Canadian Medical Association (CMA) was founded in 1867 but by the 1920s was in a parlous state, threatened for Canadian members by more developed organizations in Britain and the United States. However, a suggestion to disband at the 1920 Annual Meetings was rejected and, after that, the association never looked back either in membership or in finances (much of its increasing affluence due to drug advertisements in its journal). By the 1930s the CMA (outside of Quebec, which developed its own associations loosely affiliated with those in English Canada) was a strong national voice and all provincial associations were divisions of the national group (though the Ontario Medical Association was frequently stronger than its parent) (39).

Despite medical power, medicine failed to completely suppress new unorthodox intruders such as chiropractic. Even though provincial commissions recommended their disappearance, in the 1920s the "drugless practitioners" obtained a foothold they have fought hard to make more secure ever since.

The social unrest of the post-war years and the relative prosperity of the 1920s, gave way to the Depression. Doctors, especially those in the hard-hit prairies, suffered a drastic loss of income. Medicine adopted a more open attitude to schemes to hire doctors on salary, and to plans which promised to pay at least some of the bills for the poor. Provincial governments in four provinces ceded to organized medicine the administration of plans to pay for medical care for indigents.

Various provincial commissions were set up to examine the issues of health services and health insurance. All of these came to nought, partly, but not completely, because of medical opposition (40). Medicine wanted health insurance but only their own form of health insurance on their own terms.

The medical elite made an increasingly sharp distinction between a national health service, which they saw as payment by salary and state ownership of health facilities, i.e., "State Medicine," and national health insurance. Totally opposed to the former the profession was not as completely against the latter, provided they retained control of payment and adminisration.

The 1930s and 1940s were also a time of social unrest. The unemployed marched on Ottawa only to be brutally halted by the police. Despite "camps" for the unemployed, desperate men marched and rioted in Vancouver and elsewhere. Protest political parties arose. The most notable was the Co-operative Commonwealth Federation (the CCF), an avowedly anti-capitalist working class party, which, however, received a great deal of support from prairie farmers. And, Social Credit, a populist party and one with, at least initially, an anti-monopoly capital theme (it later became highly conservative), contested the political terrain in some Western provinces. The 1930s and 1940s, not coincidentally, also brought moves towards the building of the welfare state in Canada (41–43). Doctors became more amenable to some form of health insurance, if only for their non-paying customers.

During the war years the reform rhetoric grew more prominent, especially during times of CCF strength, as in 1943. Of four federal by-elections in that year, one seat was won by the communists and two by the CCF. In the same month the CCF became the official opposition in Ontario winning 32 percent of the vote. In September of 1943 an opinion poll indicated that the CCF was the most popular party in the whole country with 29 percent followed by the Liberals and Progressive Conservatives, both at 28 percent. In 1944 the CCF attained power in Saskatchewan. The need to legitimate the war effort, fears of the CCF and a post-war Depression and fear of disorder, all contributed to the reform push by the Liberal party (44). Even the federal Conservative Party, in 1942, changed its name to "Progressive" Conservative.

The wartime pressure for reforms in health and health care continued. The Beveridge Report in Britain published in November 1942 provided a huge stimulus. Within Canada the Heagerty Report on Health Insurance was published in March 1943 (45) at the same time as the Report on Social Security in Canada (the Marsh Report) (46). There was movement on family allowances and on old age pensions. But, with the re-election of the Liberals in 1945, the beginnings of the Cold War, the post-war economic boom, the fading of the socialist "threat," and conservative governments in such provinces as Alberta (Social Credit), British Columbia (Social Credit), but most importantly, Ontario (Conservative) and Quebec (Union Nationale), the pressure for reform was undermined.

Although it had made some policy concessions because of the Depression, the medical profession survived the 1930s intact and influenced all subsequent developments in health care. During the war, government practically integrated its policy and planning with that of the profession. The recommendations of the federal governments' Heagerty Committee on Health Insurance directly reflected the aims of the CMA's "Committee of Seven." Military manpower planning was largely left to the profession. By the end of the war a medical official of the Department of Health could unabashedly state that: "we do our utmost to maintain at every turn the interests of the practitioners of Canada as well as organized medicine" (47, p. 285). Still, the federal and provincial governments were much more powerful after than before the war.

The war-time schemes for medical care insurance came to nought, foundering partly on federal-provincial wrangling, but the federal government did announce, in 1948, a series of grants for training personnel, health surveys and construction of hospitals as: "fundamental prerequisites to. . .health insurance" (48, p. 238). There were other developments. Doctor sponsored medical plans spread to a number of provinces leading to a decline in any previous medical enthusiasm for government health insurance, except for the poor.

Though health insurance had foundered, hospital insurance survived and was implemented by the CCF in Saskatchewan in 1947 with little opposition. Partly in response to the parlous financial condition of hospitals, hospital insurance, generally welcomed by medicine, was put in force across Canada in 1957.

## THE DECLINE OF MEDICINE?

The major battle for medicine came in Saskatchewan where a CCF government had been re-elected in 1960 on a platform which included a provincial medical care plan. The story of the war waged by doctors against medicare in Saskatchewan has been told elsewhere (49). Medical care insurance was implemented, but only after a twenty day strike by doctors accompanied by vicious attacks by medicine and anti-CCF forces on the government, and with significant government compromises.

Medicine in the 1960s and 1970s had two strategies in combatting the spread of government sponsored medical insurance outside of Saskatchewan. The first was to push the doctor-sponsored voluntary plans as an alternative to government-administered schemes. The second was to influence those provincial governments that were ideologically opposed to national health insurance to implement programs which conformed to the CMA's own aims. In Alberta, Ontario, and British Columbia, conservative provincial governments went along with profession designed plans. A draft health insurance plan in Ontario "incorporated the basic principles which the Ontario Division supports—the non-compulsory aspect, universal coverage by multiple carriers, and subsidy by Government for those individuals who require assistance for coverage" (50, p. 436).

But, the profession was faced with a Royal Commission on health care, set up at its own suggestion as an apparent tactic both to stall government health insurance on a national scale and to give medicine possible influence over government policy.

Despite strong medical representation, and briefs from dozens of medical organizations opposing universal health insurance, the Commission's Report in 1964 recommended a national health insurance plan (51) which, after many delays, was finally implemented in 1966 by a minority Liberal government propped up by the NDP (the CCF had combined with labor in 1961 to become the New Democratic Party). All provinces were part of the plan by 1971—they could hardly resist 50 percent funding by the federal government.

Some writers claim that health insurance, itself an indication of medical power in opposing "State Medicine," leaves the basic structure of health care untouched. But events in Canada show that while health insurance had little immediate impact on the structure of health care the consequences of health insurance are still reverberating in the health care system, greatly influencing the role of medicine.

Medical insurance, and its consequences for the public purse and the health of Canadians, prompted a huge number of provincial and federal studies of health "problems" from the early and sweeping Castonguay-Nepveu Commission in Quebec 1967–71, to the Ontario Committee on the Healing Arts 1970, and a large number of other provincial and federal studies [e.g., federally, the Task Force on the Costs of Health Services (1970), the Community Health Center Project (the Hastings Report (1972)) the Lalonde Report (1974) and many others]. All of these reports concerned the inter-relationships among health care personnel and the re-organization of health care services in the name of effectiveness and efficiency. Prominent in the reports were calls for a more integrated system of social and health services, community health centers, and the necessity of administering and "rationalizing" health care services. Implicit in most of the reports, and explicit in some, was the desire to reduce the overwhelming power of medicine to control health and health care.

But medicine still had the power to either completely prevent suggested reforms—for example, the Hastings Report which recommended community health centers, was shelved—or to negate these once implemented—for example, the medical profession in Quebec successfully by-passed a proposed system of government/lay health and social services centers, by setting up hundreds of doctor-controlled polyclinics (52, 53). Schemes for nurse-practitioners came to nought. However, doctors could not halt the organizational consequences of government concern with costs and the politicization of health care.

With government health insurance, medicine immediately lost its control over the terms of the provision of health insurance. And, the fee-for-service system, along with the use of computers and central payment, permitted complete documentation and surveillance of the work and income patterns of Canadian doctors (54, 55). Medicine also now had to negotiate its fees with increasingly cost-conscious provincial governments rather than set these unilaterally.

The documenting of practice patterns led to concern with those physicians billing unusually large numbers of procedures. In most provinces joint government-profession Medical Review Committees were set up to investigate over-servicing. In cases of abuse payment could be reduced or refused. But relatively few physicians were disciplined.

Faced with a relative decline in incomes from a 1971 high, doctors in the 1970s began to support their demands for fee increases with threats to "withhold services" or outright strikes. In Quebec, even before health insurance, specialists struck to preserve opting out and extra-billing. Significantly, they were not supported by the general practitioners. The strike failed. As the decades wore on withdrawal of services and strikes were no longer isolated events. On the government side came tough bargaining including the publishing of the incomes of all doctors (in British Columbia) (56).

A major aim of government was to control hospital costs, the most expensive portion of health care. Hospital budgets were given line by line scrutiny or hospitals were placed on strictly controlled global budgets. Pressure was exerted to intensify the work of hospital employees and to restrict the right of hospital workers (including, in some provinces, nurses) to strike. The strong pressure for the "rationalization" of hospital care resulted in a strengthening of hospital management, though still constrained by the parallel medical structure.

Wahn (57) provides a number of instances in which the drive for efficiency directly affected medical control in hospitals in all three of the areas mentioned by Larson (58), i.e., economic, organizational, and technical alienation. Wahn notes that although not many doctors were on salary they were being treated *as if* they were employees. And governments did apply pressure to institute salaried work in some instances—compelling some hospitals to put emergency room physicians on salary.

There were greater organizational controls. In one hospital budgetary constraints forced the hospital administration to divert neurosurgery cases to another hospital, in the face of violent opposition of the medical staff in neurosurgery, which ultimately admitted defeat. Similarly, studies of differential surgical rates provided ammunition for governments to control various surgical procedures. And, doctors faced competition for power in the hospital from militant nurses and technical workers.

On the labor process level, government had to approve any new facilities. The increased use of research and clinical trials, computer protocols and computer diagnosis and treatment also impinged on the day to day work of physicians in hospitals. The power of studies to influence what doctors do is being transmitted partially through doctors' own organizations both in hospitals and outside—"Doctors are becoming active participants in the processes that are taking away their autonomy and power" (57, p. 431).

Physician as well as hospital costs were a problem. At first governments concentrated on strict negotiations over fees with provincial medical associations. But, fees are not incomes.

Medical economists found that, regardless of fee levels, physicians tended to attain self-set income levels by manipulating utilization and mix of procedures (56). It was a common insight that each additional doctor generated high levels of costs in the system. Both the numbers and the (mal)distribution of physicians became salient issues. Though some provinces attracted physicians to underserved areas by offering financial inducements, Quebec simply refused to pay full fees to those moving into overserved areas. British Columbia attempted to control the issuance of all new government insurance billing numbers in the province and where they will be issued, thus effectively controlling all medical practices. Ontario, New Brunswick and other provinces are moving in the same direction.

In 1975 the profession had successfully persuaded the federal government to restrict the immigration of physicians. In the 1970s new medical schools opened and older ones expanded. But this expansion was short-lived. Burgeoning costs and lower government revenues turned physician "shortages" into "over-supply." As a consequence, in the late 1970s governments reduced the number of funded post-graduate training places and influenced universities and medical schools to reduce their student intake and to maintain general practitioner graduates at about 50 percent of the total. Government funding of universities and hospitals and control of immigration gave them great influence, if not complete control, over medical manpower. In 1992 a 10 percent reduction of entrants to Canadian medical schools was enacted by the co-ordinated policy of all provincial governments.

Finally, there were vast increases in government health care bureaucracies. The few physicians in government service soon were swamped with the new tide of "corporate rationalizers"—lay planners, accountants, and managers. Medicine, which had never completely controlled politicians but had had much greater influence in health care bureaucracies, lost the intimate association with officials it had previously had. As one Quebec doctor noted, from the time of health insurance on, doctors simply reacted to what emanated from government rather than being on the ground floor of planning from the beginning—even though this control varied by province (in Alberta there was close AMA-government co-operation).

Although health insurance brought a long-range decrease in power it was immediately preceded and accompanied by a rapid rise in income, reaching a high in 1971 at which time physicians' incomes relative to other self-employed professionals were 161:100. Doctors incomes rose so high they became something of an embarassment. But initial increases were followed by rapid declines in incomes between 1971 and 1974–76 and, thereafter, a period of slight relative increase (meanwhile the wages of the average Canadian have declined relative to inflation since 1981). But, fees (as opposed to incomes) declined after the implementation of medicare until 1983–84 (56)—incomes reflected increased utilization, something which provincial governments quickly came to try to control by limiting physician numbers and by capping total physician payments (56).

By the middle of the 1970s, although medicine had other concerns—abortion, foreign born versus Canadian medical graduates, control of the proliferating allied health occupations, and negotiations with provincial governments—the issues which dominated the era were extra-billing and user fees, issues with strong overtones of a fight for control over health care.

Extra-billing, charging patients more than government insurance would pay, was effectively banned in Quebec. In the other provinces, most commonly, physicians billed government and accepted this payment as their full fee. But, even in Ontario where less than 15 percent of doctors extra-billed some patients and only 5 percent of claims concerned extra-billing, there were problems. Extra-billing was concentrated in particular specialties, such as obstetrics and anesthesia, and, often, in particular localities.

A Liberal federal government asked Justice Emmett Hall, the Chairman of the original Royal Commission on Health Services, to study the situation. The profession went to extraordinary lengths to persuade Justice Hall that extra-billing and user fees were necessary and that the main problem in health care was underfunding. But Hall recommended that extra-billing should be forbidden (59).

The Hall Commission led directly to the Canada Health Act to ban extra-billing. The Act produced open and acrimonious debate between medicare supporters and the medical profession. Medicine along with conservative provinces faced a Health Care Coalition of hundreds of public groups and health occupations, largely organized by labor, (but aided by the federal government). The enactment of the Canada Health Act in 1984, in an election year, supported by all parties, was a bitter blow, yet another defeat for medicine and led directly to the doctors' strike in Ontario.

In Ontario, a Conservative government, in power for over forty years, had been replaced in 1985 by a minority Liberal government supported by the New

Democratic Party. The banning of extra-billing had been one of the conditions under which the NDP agreed to support the Liberal government. Bill 94 to ban extra-billing provoked the most vicious and public reaction from medicine since the Saskatchewan doctors' strike nearly twenty-five years earlier. In the summer of 1986 doctors stormed the legislative buildings, publicly castigated the government as Nazi's and/or communists, and eventually went on a twenty day strike in which they withdrew all but essential services (in some areas, even hospital emergency rooms were closed). But, even at its height less than 60 percent of doctors took part in the strike, many were against it or provided only lukewarm support, and it turned into a costly and complete failure. With public opinion firmly against the strike the hysterical reaction of the minority of right wing doctors and their supporters backfired. Physicians trickled back to work—extra-billing in Ontario, and in Canada, was at an end (60).

Though the power of medicine is indicated by the caution with which the government treated the strikers (in contrast, a few years earlier hospital workers and union leaders had been jailed because of an illegal strike) still the most powerful provincial association in Canada had been humiliated. Medicine's image was in tatters as a result of the wild behavior and the exaggerated rhetoric of some of its members.

Medicine was also facing challenges from other directions. Previously subordinate health occupations were struggling for independence and encroaching on medical territory. Nursing, at one time completely subordinate to medicine, now seeks to be "separate but equal" to medicine and to practice independently in the community. Nursing strongly and publicly opposed extra-billing and even suggested that all health workers be put on salary. Midwives are gaining recognition and were legalized in Ontario in 1992. Similarly, other healers, such as chiropractors, have been gaining in legitimacy (if at the expense of a narrowing of their scope of practice) despite medical opposition (33, 61). Even occupations such as physiotherapy, which medicine once used as a weapon against chiropractic, sought independence from its original sponsor. The burgeoning system of health occupations is increasingly out of medicine's direct control.

The efficacy of medicine and its right to determine the form under which medical care is delivered are being questioned, as is the emphasis on cure rather than prevention. The public now seeks to recover both birth (alternative birthing centers and home births) and death (the living will) from medical control. From the women's movements have come challenges to medical control over childbirth. Ex-psychiatric patients contest medical legal prerogatives; patients' rights groups challenge the adequacy of medical self-regulation. Though nowhere near as prevalent as in the United States, malpractice cases are increasing in number. In 1970 there were only 80 malpractice writs issued in Canada; in 1987 there were 915. In 1971 damages awarded to patients in malpractice cases were $276 thousand; in 1988 over $25 million was awarded to patients (62). And, in legal precedent, Canadian courts have, over the years, more and more moved to a patient rather than a doctor-centered view of what constitutes adequate "informed consent" regarding medical treatments. From the state, from other health occupations, from the public, and in law, medicine is faced with encroachment on its previous unchallenged domain—even its clinical methods are questioned.

And, internally, medicine is changing. There are more physicians than previously in administrative posts, in community health or public health, and in the medical educational complex. These often have quite different views than their confreres in practice. Though one of Freidson's (5, 6) arguments is that medical power has been preserved through physicians, controlling physicians, this assumes all physicians are alike and have similar interests. This view overemphasizes socialization as opposed to social structure as a determinant of physician behavior. There is an incipient split between general practitioners (who have formed 50 percent of the profession in Canada for many years) and specialists. The CMA and the College of Family Practice argue over who has the mandate to put forward medicine's political and economic views. General practitioners fight for more equitable fees relative to specialists. Medicine is also being rapidly "feminized." Females now form over 40 percent of medical school enrollments.

In Quebec, the medical associations are in all respects like trade unions with an annual dues check-off, a clear focus on the self-interests of the profession, and many of the rights and duties of a union. The provincial Colleges and associations are now clearly separate organizations with the former, though medically dominated, having lay representation and some duties to protect the public, and the latter, more clearly representing the economic and political interests of doctors, without the automatic claim to represent the public interest they once had.

All this while the political discourse was largely dominated by a mildly liberal Liberal party in an economy increasingly controlled from the United States. During the decades following health insurance, however, politics was characterized by a revival of neo-conservatism. By 1984, a Conservative Prime Minister, pro-business and pro-American, boasted to Margaret Thatcher that Canada had business governments from coast to coast. This did not last long as both Ontario and Quebec turned Liberal (and in 1993 the Liberals are far ahead in popular opinion polls). However, in the middle 1980s the NDP narrowly lost crucial provincial elections in Saskatchewan and British Columbia to neo-conservative parties. While big business became more American, unions shed their American ties.

Throughout Canada social services were being cut back, business was ideologically dominant, and there were attempts not only to roll-back wages, but to attack the very existence of unions. The internationalization of capital had made even indigenous Canadian capitalists use "international competition" in an attempt to undercut welfare state measures and the "social wage." These efforts were not entirely successful as the percentage of the labor force unionized remained nearly 40 percent, well above that in the United States (to some degree because of the high degree of unionization among white-collar state workers). Though the Conservatives successfully undercut the universalization of a number of social programs through taxing back "universal" benefits, they dared not touch others, such as medicare. The claim was no longer that welfare measures ameliorated capitalism. Business now said that social security measures destroyed initiative. Inequality was no longer excused but was declared a necessary part of capitalism. Throughout, organized medicine supported any measures that would weaken government control over health and health care.

## THE PROLETARIANIZATION OF MEDICINE?

Viewed in terms of medical dominance regarding the content of work, and control over clients, other occupations, and the context of care, there has been a definite decline in medical power in Canada. This has been most pronounced regarding the context of care, but has been evident in all areas. Even so, some Canadian observers contend that many reforms have been negated by medical power and that medicine's basic control over health and health care is largely untouched (see e.g., 44, 53, 63, 64). How to account for these differences? Partly it is a question of viewing the glass as half full or half empty. Certainly medicine is still powerful, it has successfully opposed many potential reforms; the point is that it is not as powerful as it once was. And, it is a mistake to view every frustrated reform as due solely to medical opposition. There are numerous health institutions with vested interests. For example, hospitals, and not only doctors, strenuously opposed the idea of community health centers. Medicine is not the only actor in the health care system. And, the rationalist schemes of academics or bureaucrats often have little support outside these groups.

State involvement, itself a product of pressure from the organized working class, has produced a decline in sweeping medical powers regarding the health care system, health policy, and regulations governing medicine, but these are partial and limited just as medical power has its limits. There has been an increasing control by others over the organization of health and health care and medical work itself is being "rationalized." The work of physicians is open to monitoring and manipulation.

There is a beginning of proletarianization. But it is a process which is far from advanced. And, in terms of class structure and the class struggle, how has medicine been proletarianized? It could be argued that the nineteenth century saw the rise of medicine as a self-governing occupation, whereas the late nineteenth and early twentieth century saw an increasing *de facto* medical control over an emerging health division of labor. That control has been recently decreasing. Was medicine first petite bourgeois, then bourgeois, and now somewhere in between? Medicine is certainly less class homogeneous than it once was and now seems the epitome of an occupation in a contradictory class location. Its interests are not those of labor, nor are they entirely coincident with those of a bourgeoisie intent on efficiency in the public sector and profit in the private sector.

But politically and ideologically medicine has not changed much. Organized medicine has become increasingly conservative, although this conservatism does not necessarily accurately represent the divergent views of its membership. The recent revival of conservative free-enterprise movements in Canada has made more "legitimate" the free-enterprise minority within medicine. But, medicine has always espoused petite bourgeois ideas. Organized medicine, if not all of its members, closely followed Cold War rhetoric in the post-war years. The medical leadership has always seemed more at home, and friendly, with Conservative rather than Liberal or NDP provincial and federal governments. The present medical push for partial privatization of health care, user fees, and "private funding" is congruent with the wishes of the more conservative governments in Canada, and there is continual pressure from the more affluent towards development of a more "private" form of medicine in which there would be a private upper tier for those who could afford it and a universal or public secondary tier. Those in contradictory class locations are influenced by external ideological and political forces. A decline in conservative forces generally (and, in 1992 no Conservative government in Canada can count on re-election) could reinforce the more liberal reform groups within medicine itself. The situation is fluid.

The beginnings of proletarianization are evident as are some of the expected consequences. Government as sole paymaster has produced strikes and walkouts. But medicine is not part of the labor movement and has no allies within it, reflecting the continuing predominance of private practice within the profession. This situation contrasts sharply with that of teachers and nurses whose militant unions are now at the forefront of labor struggles.

But medicine has far from given up the fight to push back control by the state. The recent "free-trade" agreement between the United States and Canada, arranged by the Conservative government, would clearly have a long-term impact in strengthening conservative forces within the country and weakening those forces which helped initiate and preserve medicare to data. Free-trade supporters openly speak of the agreement as ensuring that market forces will predominate in the Canadian political economy (65). The fight over free-trade has a definite class basis (66). A market emphasis would lead to a system of health care in Canada more like that of the United States. While a small group of ideologues within the profession would approve such a change, it is unlikely the majority of Canadian doctors would do so. The practice of "corporate medicine" is not attractive. Doctors are faced by equally unpleasant alternatives: becoming increasingly subordinated within a public system or becoming the employees of large corporations, the unattractive image from the United States.

Certainly, medicine has lost some of its control over the provision of health care. However, it is still the central health occupation and the outcome for medicine, and for other occupations, cannot be predicted from the idea of proletarianization as a slippery slope with no return once started. The fate of classes, and of occupations, like medicine, depends at least partially on the outcomes of struggles which by definition are not predetermined. And, in defending its privileges, and fighting against proletarianization, medicine, like other occupations, is also helping to reproduce proletarianization within the health division of labor.

A decline in dominance, yes. The beginnings of the proletarianization of medicine in Canada, a change in medicine's objective class position, if not its class relationships, yes. But medicine is still powerful; it has far from given up the struggle and the "ultimate" outcome for medicine and health care is still indeterminate and dependent on broader events in Canadian society.

*Acknowledgments*— This chapter was developed from a larger study of the rise and fall of medicine in Canada funded by S.S.R.R.C. Grant Number 410-85-0539, in manuscript form titled "Medicine—Nursing and Chiropractic in Canada: The Rise and Fall of a Profession," 1990. I owe much to discussions with C. Lesley Biggs and to her archival skills. I would particularly like to thank George Torrance for the use of materials he originally wrote on the rise of medicine and Joseph Kaufert for his collaboration on an earlier paper on the topic. Thanks also to Elaine Gort and Rick Edwards for their aid in this research.

## REFERENCES

1. Coburn, D., Torrance, G. M., and Kaufert, J. Medical dominance in Canada in historical perspective: The rise and fall of medicine? *Int. J. Health Serv.* 13(3): 407–432, 1983.
2. Haug, M. R. The deprofessionalization of everyone. *Sociol. Focus* 8: 197–213, 1975.
3. Haug, M. R. The erosion of professional authority: A cross-cultural inquiry in the case of the physician. *Milbank Mem. Fund Q.* 54: 83–106, 1976.
4. McKinlay, J. B., and Arches, J. Towards the proletarianization of physicians. *Int. J. Health Serv.* 5(2): 161–195, 1985.
5. Freidson, E. The changing nature of professional control. *Ann. Rev. Sociol.* 10: 1–20, 1984.
6. Freidson, E. *Professional Power: A Study of the Institutionalization of Formal Knowledge.* The University of Chicago Press, Chicago, 1986.
7. Larkin, G. *Occupational Monopoly and Modern Medicine.* Tavistock, London, 1983.
8. Starr, P. *The Social Transformation of American Medicine.* Basic Books, New York, 1982.
9. Willis, E. *Medical Dominance:The Division of Labour in Australian Health Care.* George Allen and Unwin, Sydney, 1983.
10. Johnson, T. The state and the professions: Peculiarities of the British. In *Social Class and the Division of Labour*, edited by A. Giddens and G. MacKenzie. Cambridge University Press, Cambridge, 1982.
11. Freidson, E. *Profession of Medicine.* Dodd, Mead and Co., New York, 1970.
12. Derber, C. *Professionals as Workers: Mental Labour in Advanced Capitalism.* G.K. Hall and Co., Boston, 1982.

13. Derber, C. Physicians and their sponsors: The new medical relations of production. In *Issues in the Political Economy of Health Care,* edited by J. B. McKinlay. Tavistock, New York, 1984.

14. McKinlay, J. B. (ed.). *Issues in the Political Economy of Health Care.* Tavistock, London, 1984.

15. Navarro, V. *Medicine Under Capitalism.* Prodist, New York, 1976.

16. Navarro, V. *Class Struggle, the State and Medicine: An Historical and Contemporary Analysis of the Medical Sector in Great Britain.* Martin Robertson, London, 1978.

17. Navarro, V. Radicalism, Marxism, and medicine. *Int. J. Health Serv.* 13: 179–202, 1983.

18. Waitzkin, H. *The Second Sickness: Contradictions of Capitalist Health Care.* The Free Press, New York, 1983.

19. Braverman, H. *Labour and Monopoly Capital.* Monthly Review Press, New York, 1974.

20. Kett, J. F. American and Canadian medical institutions, 1800-1870. In *Medicine in Canadian Society: Historical Perspectives,* edited by S. E. D. Shortt. McGill-Queen's University Press, Montreal, 1981.

21. Hamowy, R. *Canadian Medicine: A Study in Restricted Entry.* The Fraser Institute, Vancouver, 1984.

22. McGaughey, D. Professional militancy: The medical defence association vs. the college of physicians and surgeons of Ontario, 1891–1902. In *Health, Disease and Medicine: Essays in Canadian History,* edited by C. G. Roland. The Hannah Institute for the History of Medicine, Toronto, 1984.

23. *Canada Lancet,* 6, 1873–1874.

24. Gidney, R. D., and Millar, W. P. J. The origins of organized medicine in Ontario, 1850-1869. In *Health, Disease and Medicine: Essays in Canadian History,* edited by C. G. Roland. The Hannah Institute for the History of Medicine, Toronto, 1984.

25. Howell, C. D. Elite doctors and the development of scientific medicine. In *Health, Disease and Medicine: Essays in Canadian History,* edited by C. G. Roland. Hannah Institute for the History of Medicine, Toronto, 1984.

26. Allen, R. *The Social Passion: Religion and Social Reform in Canada, 1914-1928.* University of Toronto Press, Toronto, 1973.

27. Bator, P. A. Saving Lives on the Wholesale Plan: Public Health Reform in the City of Toronto, 1900 to 1930. Ph.D. dissertation, Department of History, University of Toronto, Toronto, 1979.

28. Biggs, C. L. The Movement from Home to Hospital Births, Ontario 1920-1940. M.Sc. Thesis, Department of Behavioural Science, University of Toronto, Toronto, 1984.

29. Torrance, G. Historical Introduction. In *Health and Canadian Society,* second edition, edited by D. Coburn et al. Fitzhenry and Whiteside, Toronto, 1987.

30. Risse, G. B., Numbers, R. L. and Leavitt, J. W. (eds.). *Medicine Without Doctors: Home Health Care in American History.* Science History Publications, 1977.

31. Vogel, M. J. and Rosenberg, C. E. (eds.). *The Therapeutic Revolution: Essays in the Social History of American Medicine.* University of Pennsylvania Press, Pittsburgh, 1979.

32. Biggs, C. L. The case of the missing midwives: A history of midwifery in Ontario from 1795-1900. *Ontario History* 75(1): 21–35, 1983.

33. Coburn, D., and Biggs, C. L. Limits to medical dominance: The case of chiropractic. *Soc. Sci. Med.* 22(10): 1035–1046, 1986.

34. Cruikshank, D., and Kealey, G. S. Strikes in Canada, 1891-1950. *Labour/Le Travail* 20: 85–145, 1987.

35. Palmer, B. D. *Working Class Experience: The Rise and Reconstitution of Canadian Labour, 1800-1980.* Butterworths, Toronto, 1983.
36. Robin, M. *Radical Politics and Canadian Labour 1880-1930.* Industrial Relations Centre, Queen's University, Kingston, 1968.
37. Edwards, R. K. Ideology and Canadian Medicine, 1880-1920. M.A. thesis, Department of Environmental Studies, York University, Toronto, 1986.
38. Shortt, S. E. D. Physicians, science, and status: Issues in the professionalization of Anglo-American medicine in the nineteenth century. *Med. Hist.* 27 (1): 51–68, 1983.
39. MacDermot, H. E. *One Hundred Years of Medicine in Canada:1867-1967.* McClelland and Stewart Ltd., Toronto, 1967.
40. Naylor, C. D. *Private Practice, Public Payment: Canadian Medicine and the Politics of Health Insurance, 1911-1966.* McGill-Queen's University Press, Montreal, 1986.
41. Guest, D. *The Emergence of Social Secruity in Canada.* University of British Columbia Press, Vancouver, 1980.
42. Moscovitch, A., and Albert, J. (eds.). *The Benevolent State: The Growth of Welfare in Canada.* Garamond Press, Toronto, 1987.
43. Palmer, B. D. *Solidarity: The Rise and Fall of an Opposition in British Columbia.* New Star Books, Vancouver, 1987.
44. Swartz, D. The politics of reform: Conflict and accomodation in Canadian health policy. In *The Canadian State: Political Economy and Political Power*, edited by L. Panitch. University of Toronto Press, Toronto, 1977.
45. Canada. *Health Insurance Report Special Committee on Social Security.* Advisory Committee on Health Insurance, J. J. Heagerty, 1943.
46. Canada. *Report on Social Security for Canada.* Prepared for the Advisory Committee on Reconstruction, House of Commons Special Committee on Social Security, L. C. Marsh, 1943.
47. McGinnis, J. P. D. From Health to Welfare: Federal Government Policies Regarding Standards of Public Health for Canadians. Ph.D.dissertation, Department of History, University of Alberta, Edmonton, 1980.
48. *Can. Med. Assoc. J.*, Supplement 1949, p. 238.
49. Badgley, R. F., and Wolfe, S. *Doctors' Strike.* Macmillan, Toronto, 1967.
50. *Can. Med. Assoc. J.* 89, September 7, 1963.
51. Hall, E. J. *Report of the Royal Commission on Health Services.* Queen's Printer, Ottawa, 1964.
52. Lesemann, F. *Services and Circuses: Community and the Welfare State.* Black Rose Books, Montreal, 1980.
53. Renaud, M. Reform or illusion: An analysis of the Quebec state intervention in health. In *Health and Canadian Society: Sociological Perspectives.* second edition, edited by D. Coburn et al. Fitzhenry and Whiteside, Toronto, 1987.
54. Charles, C. A. The medical profession and health insurance: An Ontario case study. *Soc. Sci. Med.* 10: 33–38, 1976.
55. Tuohy, C. J. Medical politics after medicare: The Ontario case. *Can. Public Policy* 2(2): 192–210, 1976.
56. Barer, M. L., Evans, R. G., and Labelle, R. J. Fee controls as cost controls: Tales from the frozen north. *Milbank Mem. Fund Q.* 66(1): 1–64, 1988.
57. Wahn, M. The decline of medical dominance in hospitals. In *Health and Canadian Society,* second edition, edited by D. Coburn et al. Fitzhenry and Whiteside, Toronto, 1987.
58. Larson, M. S. Proletarianization and educated labour. *Theory and Society.* 19: 131–175, 1980.

59. Hall, E. J. *Canada's National-Provincial Health Program for the 1980's: A Commitment for Renewal.* Report of Health Services Review '79, Saskatoon, Saskatchewan, 1980.
60. York, G. *The High Price of Health.* James Lorimer and Co., Toronto, 1987.
61. Baer, H. A. A comparative view of a heterodox health system: Chiropractic in America and Britain. *Med. Anthropol.* 8(3): 151–168, 1984.
62. Canadian Medical Protective Association Annual Reports.
63. Contandriopoulos, A.-P., Laurier, C., and Trottier, C.-H. Towards an improved work organization in the health care sector. In *Medicare at Maturity: Achievements, Lessons and Challenges,* edited by R. G. Evans and G. L. Stoddart. Banff Centre School of Management, Banff, Alberta, 1986.
64. Lomas, J., and Barer, M. L. And who shall represent the public interest? In *Medicare at Maturity: Achievements, Lessons and Challenges,* edited by R. G. Evans and G. L. Stoddart. Banff Centre School of Management, Banff, Alberta, 1986.
65. Segal, H. *The Globe and Mail,* Toronto, November 19, 1987, p. A7.
66. Laxer, J. *Leap of Faith: Free Trade and the Future of Canada.* Hurtig Publishers, Edmonton, 1986.

Reprinted with permission from The Milbank Quarterly, Volume 66, Supplement 2, Pages 92–116, 1988.

# Epilogue

## Vicente Navarro

The United States is the only major industrialized nation that does not have a National Health Program. In no other country are people refussed health care because they cannot pay for it. Access to health care in time of need is a privilege, not a right in the United States. Because of this unique situation thirty-seven million people in the United States do not have any form of health benefits coverage, either public or private; fifty million people have major problems with their coverage; and over two hundred million do not have comprehensive coverage, that is, if they need long-term care they are in deep trouble. The list of problems and human tragedies associated with this situation is endless. A very important question to ask is why this situation exists.

Limited health benefits coverage occurs in spite of the enormous funds that go into the health care sector; no other country spends so much. This is the heartbreaking paradox of U.S. health care: it is extremely expensive and dramatically insufficient. Again, we ask why the majority of Americans find themselves in this predicament.

Something is indeed profoundly wrong, and Americans know it. Poll after poll shows that Americans want major and profound changes in the health care sector. Health care has become the second most important issue for people, after jobs. People want a National Health Pregram funded and admisistered by the government. But in spite of its popularity, this wish is unlikely to be fulfilled by our government. Again, the question is why this situation continues to be reproduced without correction.

The deficiencies cited in these three question—the limited health benefits coverage of our people, the extremely expensive nature of our health care, and the inability and unwillingness of the political institutions to change the system of health care—are clearly related. They all are due to the enormous economic, political, and social power of corporate America. This volume and its accompanying volume (Part 1), plus the text, *Why the United States Does Not Have a National Health Program* in the same series, represent a powerful indictment of the power relations within and outside medicine that are responsibe for the current health care predicament of much of the the U.S. population.

These volumes show how the logic of the process of corporatization and the motor behind it, capital accumulation, is in direct conflict with the process of resolving and responding to people's needs. The search for profits and for higher and higher monetary benefits is increasingly in conflict with the realization of people's health. In no other country has the logic of capital accumulation in the health sector been more unrestrained than in the United States. And no other country faces so many unattended health care needs. The two situations are clearly interrelated. They are two side of the same coin.

The solution to this ineffecient and inhuman situation is to reverse this trend and to put human needs before greed. This reversal will not take place without enormous opposition from corporate America and its allies in the political institutions that govern our lives. It is because of the enormous power of those who oppose change that such change will not occur without a massive mobilization of the U.S. population to call for the realization of a basic human right: access to comprehensive health care in time of need; access without impediments, conditions, and discouraging constraints.

In this task academics can play a role. They can assist the emerging forces that are asking for change by providing them with the information they need to understand the causes of their problems and thus to resolve them. The contributors to these volumes have aimed at doing just that. These authors have contributed to the current debate on health policy, a debate that is still controlled by voices that reproduce too uncritically the discourse of the conventional wisdom that sustains our unjust system of health care. Equally important, the authors have provided information to those who want change, to help them to understand and change the current reality to ensure that health resources are allocated according to need rather than greed.

# Contributors

Howard S. Berliner is Associate Professor and Chair of the Health Services Management Program at the New School for Social Research. Previously he was Assistant Commissioner for Research, Policy, and Planning at the State of New Jersey Department of Health, and Associate Research Scientist at the Eisenhower Center for Conservation of Human Resources, Columbia University. He authored *A System of Scientific Medicine: Philanthropic Foundations in the Flexner Period* (Tavistock, 1985); *Strategic Factors in U.S. Health Care* (Westview, 1987); with Eli Ginzberg and Miriam Ostow, *Young People at Risk: Is Prevention Possible?* (Westview, 1988), and *Changing US Health Care: A Study of Four Metropolitan Areas* (Westview, 1992).

Robb K. Burlage is Professor and Director of the Joint Graduate Degree Program in Public Health and Urban Planning at Columbia University. His research interests have included the proprietarization of U.S. health care and the regionalization of community health services. He is author of *New York City's Municipal Hospitals* (Institute for Policy Studies, 1967), and coauthor of *The American Health Empire: Power, Profits Prestige* (Health PAC, 1988). He is founding director of the Community Policy Institute in Brooklyn, New York.

David Coburn is Professor in the Department of Behavioral Science in the University of Toronto. He received his B.A. in sociology from the University of Victoria, and his M.A. and Ph.D. from the University of Toronto. His major interests in the health field have been in the changing role of health occupations in Canada, work alienation, and patients rights. He authored *Medicine, Nursing and Chiropractic: The Rise and Fall of the Profession,* as well as papers on these three occupations in *Milbank Quarterly, International Journal of Health Services,* and *Social Science in Medicine.* He is co-editor of *Health and Canadian Society: Sociological Perspectives* (Fitzhenry and Whiteside, 1987), and co-editor of *Workers, Capital and the State In British Columbia: Selected Papers* (University of British Columbia Press, 1988).

Joe Feinglass is a Research Assistant Professor in the Division of General Internal Medicine, Northwestern University Medical School, and a Research Associate at the Center for Health Services and Policy Research at Northwestern University. He has taught history and political science and has an extensive background in labor and industrial relations. He is currently involved in research on patient outcomes, medical effectiveness, and variations in medical practice.

David U. Himmelstein is Associate Professor of Medicine at Harvard Medical School and chief of the Division of Social and Community Medicine at Cambridge Hospital, Cambridge, Massachusetts. He received his M.D. from Columbia University and completed internal medicine training at Highland Hospital in Oakland, California. He was founder of Physicians for a National Health Program, and he serves as the Co-Director of the Center for National Health Program Studies at the Cambridge Hospital/Harvard Medical School.

Sol Levine is Senior Scientist and Co-Director of the Joint Program in Society and Health, New England Medical Center and Harvard School of Public Health; and Professor of Health and Social Behavior and Professor of Health Policy and Management, Harvard University. Dr. Levine is studying factors affecting health-related quality of life and is developing a national and international research program in Society and Health. He was elected to the Institute of Medicine, National Academy of Sciences, and has also received the Leo G. Reeder Award from the American Sociological Association's Council of Medical Sociology. He co-edited and contributed to four editions of the *Handbook of Medical Sociology* (Prentice Hall, 1989). He edited *Social Stress* (Aldine Publishing Company, 1970) and *The Dying Patient* (with Norman A. Scotch), (Transaction Books, 1982) and *Epidemiology and Health Policy* (with Abraham Lilienfeld), (Tavistock Publications, 1987), and wrote *The Heart Patient Recovers* (Human Sciences Press, 1977), and *Life After a Heart Attack* (with Sydney H. Croog), (Human Sciences Press, 1982).

Nancy Milio is a Professor in the School of Public Health and in the School of Nursing at the University of North Carolina at Chapel Hill. She serves as consultant and analyst for the World Health Organization on health promotion, nutrition, and tobacco issues. Her teaching, research and publications center on policy development, implementation and evaluation; health policy and strategic analysis; community health-oriented information technology; and health promotion/education. She has worked with European and British Commonwealth institutions over the last two decades. Her recent books include *Promoting Health Through Public Policy* (F.A. Davis, 1981) and *Nutrition Policy for Food Rich Countries: A Strategic Analysis* (Johns Hopkins University Press, 1990).

Vicente Navarro is Professor of Health Policy, Sociology and Policy Studies at the Johns Hopkins University; founder and editor-in-chief of the *International Journal of Health Services;* and series editor of this Policy, Politics, Health and Medicine Series for Baywood Publishing Company, Inc. An advisor to several governments and international agencies as well as labor organizations, he has written extensively on the sociology and political economy of medical and social services. Dr. Navarro is the author of *Medicine Under Capitalism; Social Security and Medicine in the U.S.S.R.: A Marxist Critique*; and *Class Struggle, the State and Medicine: An Historical and Contemporary Analysis of the Medical Sector in Great Britain.* He is the editor of the collections, *Why the United States Does Not Have a National Health Program; Health and Medical Care in the U.S.: A Critical Analysis; Imperialism, Health and Medicine;* and (with D. Berman) *Health and Work Under Capitalism: An International Perspective,* all previous volumes in the Policy, Politics, Health and Medicine Series.

J. Warren Salmon is Professor and Head of the Department of Pharmacy Administration in the College of Pharmacy; and Professor of Health Resources Management in the School of Public Health at The University of Illinois at Chicago. He is the editor of the *"Special Section on the Corporatization of Medicine"* for the *International Journal of Health Services.* Professor Salmon's research interests have focused on urban health care delivery, comparative health care systems, alternative and complementary medicines, and selected health policy issues. Beside this volume, he edited *The Corporate Transformation of Health Care, Part I: Issues and Directions* (Baywood 1990); (with J. W. Todd) *The Corporatization of Health Care: A Two Day Symposium and Public Hearing* (Illinois Public Health Association, 1988); *Alternative Medicines: Popular and Policy Perspectives* (Tavistock/Methuen, 1984); and (with E. Goepel) *Community Participation and Empowerment Strategies in Health Promotion* (Zentrum fuer Interdisziplinare Forschung, 1990).

Victor W. Sidel, is Distinguished University Professor of Social Medicine at Montefiore Medical Center and Albert Einstein college of Medicine in the Bronx, New York. He is a past president of the New York City and American Public Health Associations, Physicians for Social Responsibility, and Physicians Forum, and is a member of the Board of Directors of the Physicians for a National Health Program. He has studied health services in a dozen countries, served as a consultant to the United Nations Children's Fund and the World Health Organization, and written and lectured extensively on health care problems and alternative health care systems.

John D. Stoeckle is Professor of Medicine at Harvard Medical School and Chief of Medical Clinics at the Massachusetts General Hospital in Boston. He has a long-term interest in the organization of care outside of the hospital, the doctor-patient relation, and social psychological factors in patients' seeking medical care and physicians' diagnostic and treatment decisions. He edited *Encounters Between Patients and Doctors* (MIT Press, 1987).

William D. White is Associate Professor in the Department of Economics at the University of Illinois at Chicago and Associate Director of the Institute of Government and Public Affairs at the University of Illinois. He received his B.A. from Haverford College and his Ph.D. from Harvard University. He has been a visiting fellow at Yale University, M.I.T. and the University of Chicago. His fields of interest are health economics and labor economics. He has written widely on issues in health care finance, the organization of markets for hospital services, the design of payment systems for health services, and professional regulation and credentially of health professionals, and the economic theory of agency. He is a member of the editorial board of the *Journal of Health Politics, Policy and Law.*

Steffie Woolhandler is an assistant professor of medicine at Harvard Medical School, an adjunct associate professor of public health at Boston University, and the Director of Inpatient Services at Cambridge Hospital, Cambridge, Massachusetts. She received her M.D. from Louisiana State University, New Orleans, and her M.P.H. from the University of California, Berkeley. She completed an internal medicine residency at Cambridge Hospital. Dr. Woolhandler was a founder of Physicians for a National Health Program, and she serves as the Co-Director of the Center for National Health Program Studies at the Cambridge Hospital/Harvard Medical School.

# Index